A Passion for F

A Passion for FOOD

Recipes from over
100 Top International
Chefs

Edited by Jean and
Christopher Conil

Foreword by
THE DUCHESS OF WESTMINSTER
In Aid of the National Children's Home

EQUATION

First published 1989

British Library Cataloguing in Publication Data

A passion for food
1. Food. Recipes
I. Conil, Jean II. Conil Christopher 641.5

ISBN 1-85336-081-3

Equation is an imprint of the
Thorsons Publishing Group Limited,
Wellingborough, Northamptonshire,
NN8 2RQ, England.

Typeset by Harper Phototypesetters Limited,
Northampton, England
Printed in Great Britain by
The Bath Press, Bath, Avon

1 3 5 7 9 10 8 6 4 2

Contents

Foreword by the Duchess of Westminster

I am delighted to have been asked to write the foreword to this very special cookery book. In my capacity as Patron of the National Children's Home (NCH) in the North-West it is special to me for many reasons, most importantly for the children and families you will be helping with the money raised from this book. It is full of delicious recipes from famous chefs which I am sure will excite and tempt you and your families.

There are many people to thank for the production of this book. First and foremost our thanks must go to Jean and Christopher Conil, the editors. This book cannot add to Jean's great fame as a chef but it does reveal in him a love for children and their welfare which surely magnifies his humanity. I also thank his son Christopher who has helped Jean so much in the compilation of the book. Their work for the whole of *haute cuisine* through the Cercle Epicurien Mondial (International Epicurean Circle) deserves the praise and thanks of all who love good cooking and wish to see its standards maintained and improved. I thank the publishers, Thorsons, for their generosity to NCH in agreeing to its publication and promoting its sales so vigorously. Also I thank all the chefs who have contributed their favourite dishes quite freely and added their star quality to this tremendous collection of recipes.

The money raised from this book will be used to help children in danger and families in need. With all the resources in the world it would be a slow job to win back the ground lost to deprivation and failure over the generations.

For the sake of NCH — thank you for buying this book. For the sake of the forgotten children, millions of them poor and cruelly disadvantaged in this brave new world of ours, please fight NCH's cause with us and help bring back hope into their lives.

The Duchess of Westminster

Introduction

We are proud to present to you this anthology of contributions from the kitchens of some great eating houses. Their recipes, in our opinion, truly reflect the modern culinary trend practised in restaurants and hotels of the highest repute.

By adding to them the profiles of their chefs, we are able to show you the development of their cuisine and the success they have achieved through sheer optimism and dedication to the art. Mobility and diversity are integral parts of our training, since good cookery includes the great repertoire of all countries. Taste and presentation play a crucial part in the acceptability of food in today's restaurants, irrespective of the style, be it modern, regional, ethnic, or *nouvelle cuisine*.

We have modified and adapted the recipes to suit the requirements of this book, but the ideas are based on the menus of the contributors listed. All French recipes were translated from the original abridged versions. We recommend the use of *only one set of measures* in a recipe; metric and imperial measures are not interchangeable. Conversion factors may vary in the recipes according to the conversion standards used by individual chefs.

Fish dominates many menus because it is a low-cholesterol food, but items such as frog's legs or snails appear because they are still popular in France. Nor could we omit foie gras, since it is so often used; frequently being presented in a creamy saffron sauce. We have also included a good sampling of mousses, soufflés, terrines, pâtés, salades tièdes (warm food items on lettuce) as starters, as well as the traditional range of couscous, cassoulets, and bouillabaisse. We have had to restrict the number of game recipes and other more complicated concoctions so often repeated in many of the regions we have reviewed in this book. French gourmets also enjoy beans in their salads and mutton or gosling stews, and many love to mop up gravies with their bread. But in general the emphasis is on dishes with a low fat content (despite all the cream and wine that appears in many of the recipes to add extra flavour).

We found it difficult to restrict luxury items, as eating in star restaurants is after all done for pleasure, but for the cost conscious we are able to offer a fair choice of popular cheaper menus.

We have tried to present a good cross-section of dishes to tempt every palate, from a basic French sausage recipe to Brioche aux moules (bun stuffed with mussels); Sweetbread with scampi on lettuce, or Sweetbread casserole with vegetables; Chicken cooked in sweet and sour sauce, as well as Chicken couscous; Blanquette océane (a medley of four fish in a cream sauce); and many exciting new sweets likely to appeal to children.

Whether you prefer to feed the family with a range of pasta or with foie gras in saffron sauce, you must agree with us that the modern dishes are appetizing — today we enjoy a popular cuisine. For all these splendid contributions we thank especially our eminent colleagues, friends, and associates of the Epicurean Circle and the World Master Chefs Society. We also thank Patrick Lyons and John Gray of the National Children's Home for their encouragement and guidance, and we are very obliged to Valerie Meboroh-Collinson, who typed this Anglo-French manuscript with great skill and enthusiasm. *Merci beaucoup*!

Jean and Christopher Conil

Antonio Arjol

Chef de Cuisine
The Little Dolphin
Eccles
Manchester M30 0DL
Tel: (061) 789 4489

Antonio Arjol learnt cookery at the Madrid Catering College. Francisco Fidalgo, the owner, gained his experience at the Ritz Hotel in Barcelona. Ably assisted by Mme Fidalgo they have succeeded in attracting a sophisticated clientele to a suburb of Manchester least likely to draw tourists.

It was during a television presentation that we had the opportunity to sample delicious hors d'oeuvre made up of baby artichokes, prawns in sweet and sour sauce, and a light pasta dish with mushrooms.

The main course was Vitello alla pomodoro. The veal tasted tender and the sauce fruity and cheesy. The Sabayon in sweet vermouth was prepared by the manager who enchanted us with the story of his gastronomic adventures in Spain.

Eccles is half an hour's drive from Manchester. The restaurant is located in the main road on a one-way traffic system. The dining-room with its arched alcoves creates a feeling of being back in sunny Spain.

Crêpe Royale

Thin pancakes filled with fillets of sole and prawns, topped with a thermidor sauce. Served as a starter

4 Portions

300 g (10 oz) lemon sole fillets, skinned
5 ml (1 tsp) English mustard powder and salt
15 ml (1 tbsp) flour
50 g (2 oz) butter
45 ml (3 tbsp) brandy
300ml (10 fl oz) double cream
50 g (2 oz) Parmesan cheese, grated
150 g (6 oz) prawns, cooked and peeled
4 thin pancakes

Thermidor sauce
15 ml (1 tbsp) butter
1 shallot, chopped
5 ml (1 tsp) flour
150 ml (5 fl oz) single cream
5 ml (1 tsp) made mustard
Parsley, chopped
Salt and pepper

Cut the sole fillets into small strips. Season with salt, and dust lightly with mustard powder and flour.

Heat the butter in a frying pan and fry the fish for 2 minutes until evenly cooked. Add the brandy to the pan and set it alight. Remove from heat until flames have died down then stir in the cream and half the Parmesan cheese and continue cooking for another minute. Finally mix in the prawns and adjust the seasoning.

Divide between the 4 pancakes, reserving part of the sauce. Roll the pancakes and place in a buttered ovenproof dish. Cover with remaining sauce and sprinkle with the Parmesan cheese. Place in a hot oven, 200°C, 400°F, gas mark 6, for 3–4 minutes until the cheese is lightly browned.

Thermidor sauce
Heat the butter and stir fry the shallot for 1 minute. Sprinkle in the flour and cook for ½ minute more. Stir in the cream and boil for 2 minutes. Season, dilute, and stir the mustard into the sauce until smooth and add parsley.

Vitello Alla Pomodoro

Tender slices of veal with chopped tomatoes, garlic, herbs and topped with Mozzarella cheese. Served as a main course

4 Portions

4 × 100g (4 oz) escalopes from ɔin loin or leg cut thin
Salt and pepper
Flour
5 ml (1 tsp) oil for frying
1 clove of garlic
30ml (1 fl oz) dry white wine
8 tomatoes, skinned and seeded
150 g (5 oz) Mozzarella cheese
Oregano
15 ml (1 tbsp) fresh chopped parsley

Beat the escalope thin with a bat or rolling pin.

Season the veal with salt and black pepper. Cut each escalope into 3 pieces for each person, then dust with flour. Heat oil and fry veal until lightly browned, and remove surplus fat. Place in an ovenproof dish.

Fry the crushed garlic gently for ½ minute. Add the wine and chopped tomatoes, and continue cooking for a further minute. Put the tomato mixture on top of the veal, and cover with thin slices of Mozzarella cheese. Sprinkle with oregano and parsley. Place in the oven at 180°C, 350°F, gas mark 4, until the cheese has melted.

David Bailey

Chief Executive Director
Travellers' Fare Ltd
Tournament House
Paddington Station
London W2 1HQ
Tel: 01-402 8822

David Bailey began his career in the catering department of the Royal Air Force, where so many of our eminent colleagues (chefs and managers) graduated. He has been the planning manager of the Transport Hotels since 1970. All these hotels are highly rated and the kitchens managed by top chefs of international fame. After a spell of management with leading catering companies such as Lyons, Fortes, the Rank Organization and Express Dairies, where he was immensely successful and respected by his staff, he organized the new catering set-up under the label of Travellers' Fare, the station catering division of British Rail, of which he is the Chairman and Managing Director. Talking food to David is like talking romance, as we debated the merits of a hot brioche and croissant for breakfast and the disappearing English breakfast of eggs and bacon and all the trimmings, he quickly told us that it was not dead yet. At Travellers' Fare, he said, 'we cook the complete eggs and bacon with tomatoes, mushrooms, and a mug of tea as the most popular item on our large menu of snacks, which are served all day long in the buffets of all main railway stations'.

Travellers' Fare is supported by 340 separate operations. All these supporting units supply coffee lounges, restaurants, taverns, cocktail bars, nightclubs, off-licences, station buffets, and snack counters. Mr Bailey controls 3000 staff.

Tian d'Agneau au Gâteau Barigoule

Best end of lamb, served on a pudding base of mixed vegetables with a wine sauce

4 portions

2 pairs of best ends of lamb, skinned and chined, with ribs

Gâteau Barigoule
(vegetable pudding)
225 g (8 oz) spinach, well washed and drained
225 g (8 oz) each of the following: courgette, aubergine, pumpkin, red pepper, and onion, all peeled and cut into ½-cm (¼-in) cubes.
90 ml (3 fl oz) oil and butter
3 whole eggs, beaten
90 ml (3 fl oz) red wine
Salt and pepper to taste
1 clove garlic, chopped

Sauce
4 shallots, chopped
50 g (2 oz) butter
150 ml (5 fl oz) St Emilion wine or other claret
50 g (2 oz) beef marrow
150 ml (5 fl oz) meat gravy
Seasoning

Garnish
4 medium-sized new potatoes, sliced thinly
1 or 2 sprigs of rosemary
100 g (4 oz) butter

Tie the best end of lamb with string. Season and roast for 30 minutes in a preheated oven at 200°C, 400°F, gas mark 6, keeping the meat pink and juicy. The meat should be placed on a trivet of bones with a bunch of rosemary for flavour.

Remove the joint and keep it in a flat dish. Discard fat. Add 300 ml (½ pint) water and boil for 20 minutes to obtain a gravy. Add the juice from the cooked meat to the gravy.

Gâteau Barigoule (vegetable pudding)
Scald the spinach in boiling water and remove within 10 seconds. Drain well and line 4 ramekin dishes or dariole moulds with the spinach leaves dried on a cloth. You can use raw spinach leaves for this. Be sure to grease the moulds.

In a sauté pan heat the oil and butter and stir-fry the diced vegetables for 5 minutes. Add 90 ml (3 fl oz) wine. Boil for 5 minutes more, then season to taste and remove the mixture.

In a bowl, blend 3 beaten eggs into the vegetables and fill the ramekin dishes with the vegetable and egg mixture. Bake on a tray half filled with hot water for 15 minutes until set like a baked custard.

Sauce
Boil the shallots for 10 minutes in the gravy with the red wine. Add the beef marrow and any remaining juice from the meat. Season to taste. Whisk 25 g (1 oz) of butter into the sauce (this is optional).

Garnish
Wash and pat dry the sliced potatoes with a cloth and deep fry for 3 minutes. Remove and drain well. Overlap the potato slices all around a large platter (such as a 30-cm/12-inch paella dish), cut the lamb between the ribs and arrange the 8 pieces evenly on the edge of the dish, turn out the egg and vegetable pudding mixture referred to as Gâteau Barigoule into the centre of the dish. Flash the dish in the oven and serve decorated with rosemary sprigs. Spoon a little of the sauce over the meat and serve the rest separately in a sauceboat.

André Barbier

Chef de Cuisine/Proprietor
L'Auberge Gourmande
Velars-sur-Ouche
Plombières-les-Dijon 21370
Burgundy
France
Tél: 80.33.62.51

M Barbier varies his menu according to market produce and seasonal changes. Our choice from his menu was the Jambon persillé, a sort of ham cooked in wine and served as a pâté in a luscious tarragon-flavoured jelly.

Burgundian dishes have made the grade all over the world, and Coq au vin, Beef à la bourguignonne, and Escargots in parsley butter are among the specialities which M Barbier, in his wisdom, has kept on as his culinary repertoire.

This lovely inn is located a few miles from Dijon, among the vineyards of the locality. Here we are in the centre of the finest Burgundy wines: Mâcon, Beaune, Pommard, and Puligny-Montrachet. It is also a region famous for its pickles, mustard, and vinegars.

Jambon persillé   Potted ham in white wine with tarragon

6 portions

1 knuckle of green gammon, net weight of meat 450 g (1 lb)
The meat should be boned and tied up with string as a joint, and soaked for 6 hours in cold water to desalt it
2 calves feet
1 small leek, cleaned and washed
1 large carrot
1 large onion
1 bouquet garni and 2 sticks of celery
1¼ litres (2¼ pints) water
½ bottle white wine (Mâcon blanc)
60 ml (4 tbsp) Orleans vinegar
Salt and black pepper
60 ml (4 tbsp) fresh parsley, chopped
25 g (1 oz) gelatine
1 bunch fresh tarragon

Place the knuckle of gammon and calves feet in a large pot with all the vegetables and water, and add bouquet garni. Boil gently for 1½ hours.

Remove the meat and vegetables. Discard the string and the rind, mince the meat, including the fat. Bone and dice the calves feet meat and add to the mixture. In another saucepan reheat the minced ham and calves feet meat with wine, and when it begins to boil dissolve the gelatine and simmer for 20 minutes. Season the liquor to taste, mostly using black pepper. Taste. Add the herbs and vinegar to the mixture at the last moment.

Stir well, cool and pot the mixture with the liquid. Chill and when set serve it like a pâté, cut into slices.

Jean Bardet

Chef de Cuisine/Proprietor
Jean Bardet Restaurant
57 Rue Groison
Tours 37100
France

Born in the Charentes, aged 48 and married with two children, Jean Bardet has become a missionary, a philosopher, and a mentor to many of our younger contributors who regard him with veneration and affection. Yet, apart from a spell at the Savoy in London, he admits to having worked as a chef–manager in many *bistros* (steak houses) until he decided that it was time to give himself to the more demanding task of *haute cuisine*. In 1979 he revised his culinary repertoire and went on a journey around the world; stopping in Tokyo, Hong Kong, Singapore, Jakarta, and Atlanta. He joined many reputable gastronomic clubs and culinary associations and worked very hard at creating his own style. The reward was endorsement as a master cuisinier, and the accolade of two stars in the *Michelin Guide* crowned his achievements, giving tangible proof of his talents and skills.

Among his many ideas about food, he advises the use of the flavour of a lavender seed inside the pulp of a ripe apricot. These flavours go together like wine and cheese. We are rather pleased to read his comments on the value of *fraîcheur* of fruits in savoury dishes such as mirabelle with smoked salmon, or adding garlic and some muscatel wine to pumpkin to produce a better soup. He recommends a garnish of aubergines for red mullet slightly flavoured with vinegar and basil herbs.

The sweet section includes mint sorbet as well as sorbets made from tea, mango, and jasmine flowers.

Jean Bardet has moved from Châteauroux, where he first ventured forth, to his present house in Tours, which is in the style of Napoléon III, in a three hectare park. Tours is the capital of Touraine and is crossed by the Loire and Cher rivers. The tourist is in a dreamland of cathedrals, museums, and castles of great antiquity.

Le Petit Ragoût fin d'Huitres sur une Mousse de Cresson   Oysters with watercress mousse

4 portions

24 green oysters, Marennes or
    Portuguese (6 per portion)
2 bunches of watercress (one for
    garnish and one for the
    mousse)
120 ml (4 fl oz) muscadet
2 shallots, chopped
Salt and coarsely ground black
    pepper
100 g (4 oz) butter

Mousse
2 eggs, beaten
120 ml (4 fl oz) double cream
Salt and pinch pepper and
    cayenne
100 g (4 oz) watercress purée
    (drained as much as possible)
100 g (4 oz) raw, minced white
    fish

Open the oysters and collect the juice in a bowl. Strain it through a cloth. Keep the oysters in a bowl until the garnish is ready.

Use only the leaves of the watercress.

Have ready a bowl with ice cubes and a saucepan filled with salted water.

Scald one bunch of watercress for 10 seconds and drain. Plunge into ice cubes to bring back the green colour. Drain again, squeeze, and pat dry on a cloth.

Liquidize the blanched watercress with the raw fish and eggs.

Place the watercress mixture in a bowl and blend in the double cream. Season with salt, pepper, and cayenne.

Grease four 5-cm-diameter moulds with soft butter. Fill them with mixture and place the moulds in a tray half filled with hot water. Poach in oven at 220°C, 410°F, gas mark 7, for 20/25 minutes. Keep warm and unmould like a cake on plates.

Now prepare the muscadet sauce
Boil the wine and shallots with the oyster juice for a good 8 minutes until reduced by a third. Now thicken the sauce by whisking in 100g (4 oz) of soft butter to obtain a perfect emulsion.

Heat the oysters for 10 seconds in the sauce, there is no need to cook them.

Pour the sauce onto 4 plates and arrange the mousse on the side. Decorate with fresh watercress leaves and peeled slices of lime or lemon.

Marc Bayon

Chef de Cuisine
Hôtel Sofitel
36 Boulevard Charles Livon
Marseille 13007
France
Tèl: 91.52.90.19

Marc Bayon learned his gastronomy at his parents' restaurant in Lyons where he also acquired further experience in some famous houses. He graduated to Head Chef at the Clos du Moulin and Coconas in Paris. This is owned by Claude Terrail of the Tour d'Argent, an old member of the Epicurean Circle. Marc Bayon now runs three restaurants in the same hotel.

The lavish menu of this southern hotel is loaded with fish scented with saffron and garlic, and light entrées epitomizing the meridional flavour of the Riviera at its best. The entrées were Sea bass cooked with sorrel, Ratatouille of courgettes and aubergines with red mullet, Foie gras presented inside a globe artichoke, and a Ragôut of lamb redolent of the beans and tomato sauce of the cassoulet of pre-war days. The hotel serves several hundred meals a day, and the kitchen with its brigade of 40 cooks is a busy food factory. The dish of the day was Terrine de morue en aioli (smoked cod in garlic).

The hotel is located 15 minutes from the famous Canebière (promenade) in the heart of the most famous sea port in France, nestling against the heights of the Pharo headland. The hotel proudly overlooks the sea and the majestic site of the Vieux Port, the finest view of Marseilles. The hotel is managed by M Jean Louis Chadel.

Tartare de Loup   Marinaded minced bass

4 portions

150 g (6 oz) sea bass, skinned and
    filleted (very fresh)
Juice and grated rinds of 2 limes
15 ml (1 tbsp) white spirit vinegar
25 g (1 oz) salt
25 g (1 oz) sugar
6 crushed black peppercorns
6 coriander seeds
75 ml (5 tbsp) olive oil
1 sprig of dill
125 g (5 oz) smoked salmon,
    thinly sliced.

Place the bass fillets in an earthenware dish. Sprinkle with oil, lime juice, vinegar, salt, sugar, coriander seeds, and peppercorns.

Marinade overnight in the refrigerator.

Next day mince the fish and mould it into 50 g (2 oz) egg-shaped dumplings. Wrap the dumplings with thin slices of smoked salmon. Serve on a plate with a sprig of dill and slices of lime.

Terrine de Morue en Aïoli   Smoked cod paste with garlic

4 portions

450 g (1 lb) smoked cod
    (or haddock), skinned and
    filleted
150 ml (5 fl oz) milk
1 carrot and medium onion, sliced
1 bouquet garni
2 crushed cloves of garlic
30 ml (2 tbsp) double cream
2 egg yolks
90 ml (3 fl oz) olive oil
Juice of ½ lemon
Seasoning to taste

Poach the cod in milk with carrot, onion, garlic and bouquet garni for 10 minutes. Cool in the same liquid.

Flake the fish free of skin and bones. Mince the fish and blend it in a bowl with cream and egg yolks. While stirring, pour in the oil in a thin thread, as if making mayonnaise, until the mixture is as thick as mashed potato. Season to taste. Add lemon juice and serve hot or cold with fried bread croûtons or on lettuce leaves, as a stuffing for large tomatoes.

Jacques Bedon

Chef de Cuisine/Proprietor
L'Aquitaine
Route de Toulouse
Cahors Lalbenque 46230
France
Tel: 65.21.00.53

Jacques and his wife Mireille run L'Aquitaine as a family hotel. They offer various set menus varying in price depending on whether you want to eat foie gras and truffles or the local mutton steak with beans. The menu conceals some delicious local specialities which, no doubt, Jacques Bedon would be glad to reveal.

We noted Soupe de poisson (Fish soup) with chilli sauce, Monkfish cooked in saffron, and the ubiquitous Wild duck with green peppercorns.

The hotel rooms are inexpensive, and for a family with children L'Aquitaine would be ideal for a holiday in the south.

Cahors, Figeac, and Gourdon are towns rich in old churches, medieval castles and the generous art of the Renaissance period.

In the autumn, when the copper leaves of the chestnut and oak trees blend with the red tiles of the dovecots, the splendid architecture stands out in mellow, bronzed relief.

With the subtle flavour of the truffle and mellow foie gras, you find the strong pungent sauces and soups reeking with garlic and saffron. At L'Aquitaine you will find the fare modern, yet now and then the old dishes creep back by popular demand.

Coq de Cahors   Chicken stuffed with foie gras

4 portions

1 kg (2 lb 2 oz) roasting chicken
   (oven ready)
1 truffle, sliced
150 g (5 oz) goose, duck, or
   chicken liver, cleaned and
   minced
1 egg, beaten
60 ml (4 tbsp) breadcrumbs
15 ml (1 tbsp) parsley, chopped
1 shallot, chopped
Salt and black pepper
50 g (2 oz) butter and oil
15 ml (1 tbsp) brandy
50 ml (2 fl oz) port wine

Between the skin and the breast of the chicken insert 4 slices of fresh raw truffle (tinned may do).

Chop the remaining piece of truffle and blend it with the minced liver and breadcrumbs. Mix this forcemeat in a bowl with a beaten egg, brandy, port wine, parsley, shallots, and seasoning.

Insert this forcemeat under the skin of the neck, and secure it with thread sewn into the skin. Brush the top of the chicken with the mixed butter and oil. Season inside and out. Roast in a moderately hot oven, 200°C, 400°F, gas mark 6, for 45–60 minutes, middle shelf.

Carve into portions and serve with a side plate of green salad or a dish of plain courgettes cooked for 2 minutes only.

No sauce is needed for this excellent dish, which tastes even better cold.

Antoine Benoit

Chef de Cuisine/Proprietor
Les Marissons
68 Rue de Marissons
Amiens 8000
France
Tel: 22.92.96.66

Antoine Benoit was trained in Belgium at the Catering College of Tournai. He gained experience at two sophisticated establishments: the Vivarois in Paris and the Château de Locguenole at Hennebont (listed in this book). When he was 25 years old he bought this modest restaurant in Amiens, where for the last 4 years he has been successful in attracting a faithful clientele.

The typical specialities of Amiens are mainly of Flemish character and the population tends to be very conservative in traditional dishes. Menouille, Pâté de canard, are still very much favoured here. We have included the classic Pot-au-feu (Boiled beef and vegetables) because it is the base of all good soups and sauces and could be used as a reference for other recipes in this book.

Antoine Benoit's menu features mainly river- and seafood products, but we agree with him that the Pot-au-feu in a big pot is a good contribution.

Fortunately, the clientele of this agricultural region are keen on wild ducks, partridges, rabbits, and good old-fashioned bacon dishes, as well as leek quiche known as Flamiche, and the famous desserts such as the home-made jams, tarts with fruits, Fruit egg flan and Pain d'épice, a sort of honey bread cake more subtle in flavour than the lean spicy gingerbread of Britain.

Pot-au-Feu   French beef hot-pot

6 portions

1 kg (2 lb 2 oz) lean beef
   (silverside, flank or shin)
1 marrow bone
1 small knuckle of ham
3 litres (5 pints) water
225 g (8 oz) carrots
225 g (8 oz) turnips
225 g (8 oz) small leeks
1 onion studded with 5 cloves
1 bouquet garni
20 g (¾ oz) salt
4 peppercorns, crushed

Bone the meat, and place it in a large 4-5-litre (8-pint) capacity stock pot with the bones. Leave to soak for 1 hour and then place on the stove and bring to the boil. Remove scum as it rises, and when clear add the onion and cook for 1½ hours. Add the vegetables, and bouquet garni next, and cook for another hour. Keep the liquid level by adding water and removing scum as it rises, also remove any fat floating on the surface. Add peppercorns.

Strain the broth and serve with a garnish of snippets of French bread and grated cheese. Alternatively, you may make a thicker soup by liquidizing the vegetables with the broth.

As a main dish, you can serve the boiled beef and knuckle of ham with cabbage, boiled potatoes, pickles and chutney; or use the broth to make a mustard sauce, simply by thickening it with a roux and adding made mustard, 5 ml (1 tsp) per pint.

The beef and knuckle can also be minced together and made into a tasty brawn. Dissolve 15 g (½ oz) gelatine to 250 ml (½ pint) stock broth and blend it into the meat. Set it in earthenware dishes.

Salt is added last to the broth at the ratio of 1 per cent or 10 g per litre ¹⁄₆ oz per pint). The broth is used for all meat sauces as a stock for other recipes in this book.

As a variation, add a dozen giblets or winglets of chicken or an old fowl. Make sure all fat is removed from the broth.

Clarification for consommé is done by blending together 450 g (1 lb) lean mince and 150 g (5 oz) each of carrot and celery with two egg whites. The cold stock is added to the mixture and reheated gently. The meat and vegetables are coagulated into a thick crust, thus clearing the broth and improving the flavour and clarity to a rich consommé.

Lilyanne Benoit

Chef de Cuisine/Proprietor
Le Soubise
Boîte Postale No. 3
Soubise 17780
Arcachon
France
Tel: 46.84.92.16

Lilyanne is a *cordon bleu* and hostess par excellence, who specializes in fish gastronomy. In a region dominated by a wealth of sea products, especially oysters and bass-like mullets, the fare is sumptuous, yet simple and reasonably priced.

Lilyanne learned her craft of country cooking from her grandmother. She has participated in more than 30 major fish fairs organized in many parts of the world, and is the recipient of the coveted Diploma of French Tourism as well as the medal of the Ministry of Agriculture and many other culinary awards.

The menu is a joy to read with all the great classics of fish cookery, beginning with delicious light soups and bisques, the mussels in white wine or in cream, and the oysters served by the dozen, plain or grilled.

The Arcachon region is a paradise for the naturalist. It has a bird island, oyster parks, a very complete aquarium and a fine observatory. Soubise is a small village 8.5 km (5¼ miles) from Rochefort in the Charentes Maritimes. The hotel restaurant Le Soubise is located centrally with its Spanish white walls, large curved windows, and terrace garden with sun canopies. The dining-room, with its fireplace and checked tablecloths, has a farm-like atmosphere which makes you feel at ease.

Blanquette Océane à 4 poissons   Medley of 4 fish in a cream sauce

4 portions

Stock

450 g (1 lb) mixed white fish
  bones and heads
1 litre (1¾ pints) (total) water and
  white wine in equal amounts
1 onion studded with 2 cloves
2 sticks of celery
150 g (6 oz) mushroom stalks
1 clove garlic, crushed
4 white peppercorns, crushed
2 anis seeds

Fish

150 g (6 oz) each of three firm
  fish: Bass, cod, halibut or John
  Dory, filleted, skinned and cut
  into small pieces weighing 50 g
  (2 oz) each

Garnish

50 g (2 oz) butter
150 g (6 oz) button mushrooms,
  washed, drained and sliced
150 g (6 oz) peeled prawns or
  shrimps (shells can be boiled
  with the stock)
Chervil, chopped

Thickening

2 egg yolks, 60 ml (4 tbsp) double
  cream, 3 ml (½ tsp) cornflour
  (mixed)
Salt, pepper and grated nutmeg

Boil the stock ingredients for 30 minutes and strain through a fine
conical strainer or muslin cloth.

Poach the fish for 5 minutes in the stock, remove and divide into 4
deep marmite earthenware soup pots.

Boil 600 ml (1 pint) of the stock and thicken it by gradually adding to
it the mixture of egg yolks, cream, and cornflour, creamed in a bowl.
Simmer the sauce for 4 minutes and season.

Garnish

Heat butter and stir-fry the mushrooms and peeled prawns or shrimps
for 3–4 minutes. Remove and divide into the serving soup pots.

Sprinkle chopped chervil in each serving. The remaining stock can be
used again for second helpings of this delicious soup.

Variation: Add 2 oysters per portion (poached 15 seconds).

Stanley Berwick

Executive Head Chef
London Marriott Hotel
Grosvenor Square
London W1
Tel: 01-493 1232

Born in Edinburgh and having worked at the Constitutional Club, Claridges and the Combe Grove Hotel, Stanley Berwick, Executive Head Chef of the London Marriott Hotel, has brought his old world background to bear upon new world cuisine.

Culinary architect of the Marriott's venture in Australian food and wine, 'A Taste of the New World', Stanley Berwick has already gained fame in the *Financial Times* and elsewhere for his work with 'A Taste of California' (still to be enjoyed in the Marriott's Diplomat Restaurant).

At 32, Stan is a veteran Marriott man — he has worked for the chain in Dhahran, Athens, and Jeddah — and has a reputation for innovation. He regularly experiments with dishes and uses different ingredients to enhance the quality of food served, whether in presentation or taste. His priority is, of course, to maintain the high standards of the hotel's cuisine and its reputation for serving attractive and unusual dishes.

The hotel is believed to be the only one in London to import US beef, which is considered by some to be tastier and more tender than Scottish beef. However, Scottish beef is always available if preferred.

The London Marriott Hotel opened in 1984. Stanley says: 'Establishing a new hotel and its cuisine takes time. After 2 years we are finding that guests and business people in for lunch and dinner are returning in increasing numbers — a sure sign that we are on the right track. Building a reputation is a lengthy process but we feel that we are already competing with hotels whose restaurants have been established and well respected for 25 years.'

The selection of specialities reads like an adventure trip to Oceania: Peppered sea scallops with mango, Swordfish with soya sauce, Blue fin tuna with saffron sauce, Warm goat cheese salad, Lightly broiled quail with wild rice, Flank steak Terriyaki with ginger and pineapple sauce, New York strip steak. You visit a corner of the United States of America at its best when you eat at the Marriott Hotel.

Behind the elegant Georgian stone façade on Grosvenor Square is concealed one of the most up-to-date, luxurious and truly exceptional hotels in London. The London Marriott has one of the largest pillar-free rooms in London, which is suitable for all kinds of functions.

Filet de Boeuf fumé coulis de Haricots noirs

Smoked beef tenderloin with pancetta chilli butter and black bean essence

6 portions

(Some ingredients in this recipe
need to be made in advance;
please read through before
starting out)

Marinade
3 ml (½ tsp) paprika
1.25 ml (¼ tsp) turmeric
30 ml (2 tbsp) brown sugar
3 ml (½ tsp) celery salt
5 ml (1 tsp) ground black pepper
5 ml (1 tsp) mustard seeds
3 ml (½ tsp) salt
450 ml (¾ pint) pineapple juice
450 ml (¾ pint) French dressing

Pancetta chilli butter
150 g (5 oz) pancetta (available
from most Italian food suppliers)
5 ml (1 tsp) yellow pepper,
   finely chopped
5 ml (1 tsp) red pepper,
   finely chopped
5 ml (1 tsp) green pepper,
   finely chopped
1.25 ml (¼ tsp) red chilli,
   finely chopped
5 ml (1 tsp) shallots,
   finely chopped
225 g (8 oz) unsalted butter
Freshly ground black pepper

Mix all the ingredients together well and store in a plastic container with a tightly sealed lid.

Finely dice the pancetta, and fry in a non-stick pan until crisp. Drain off and set aside. In the same pan, place all the chopped peppers and cook over a slow heat, taking care not to let the mixture burn. When soft, remove from heat and allow to cool.

Meanwhile, remove the butter from the fridge and place in a bowl. When the peppers and pancetta are cool, mix into the butter throroughly and season with the freshly ground black pepper. Salt should not be necessary.

Black bean sauce
50 g (2 oz) carrot, coarsely
    chopped
50g (2 oz) onion, coarsely
    chopped
50 g (2 oz) celery, coarsely
    chopped
1 clove of garlic, coarsely chopped
½ small red chilli (optional),
    coarsely chopped
75 g (3 oz) Parma ham trimmings,
    coarsely chopped
100 g (4 oz) dried black beans
    (available from wholefood
    stores) washed and soaked in
    cold water
600 ml (1 pint) rich beef stock
125 ml (¼ pint) red wine
15 g (½ oz) ground cumin
25 g (1 oz) vegetable oil

To finish the dish
1 kg (2 lb) best quality beef
    tenderloin (fillet)
850 ml (1½ pints) marinade
300 ml (½ pint) black bean sauce
25 g (1 oz) black beans
1 bunch fresh watercress

Heat the oil in a heavy pan and gently fry the carrot, onion, celery, chilli pepper and ham. Add 75 g (3 oz) of black beans, keep back 25 g (1 oz) to cook separately as a garnish. Cook for 5 minutes, stirring occasionally.

Add the wine and simmer until reduced to ¼ of its volume. Add the stock and continue to cook until the beans are tender. Test for seasoning, and add salt, freshly ground pepper and ground cumin. Liquidize the sauce and pass through a sieve to remove any husks or coarse pieces of ham. Correct the seasoning and reboil before use.

(This type of sauce freezes very well, and can be made in bulk for later use.)

Place the beef fillet into the marinade for 24 hours, turning occasionally. Remove from the marinade (which can be used again). The beef has to be cold smoked as it is, without any salting or washing. Some local butchers or fishmongers do this on the premises but, if not, they may know where this can be done. Smoking has to take place for 3 hours. If you prepare a whole fillet of beef, increase the smoking time to 6 hours. When you receive your smoked beef, keep it refrigerated for 24 hours longer.

Cut the beef into eight equal pieces and grill it until cooked to taste (grilling on the barbecue enhances the flavour of this dish). Place to one side and keep hot. Finish the sauce by reboiling and adding the whole beans. Place the meat on the centre of a warm plate. Put one rosette of butter onto each steak, cover with black bean sauce and garnish with watercress.

Serve with roasted new potatoes, and a Cabernet Sauvignon wine.

Hugh Bishop

Chef de Cuisine
Fleece Hotel
Market Place
Cirencester
Gloucestershire GL7 2NZ
Tel: (0285) 68507

Hugh Bishop graduated with Credits in the London City and Guild Certificates at Ealing College. He worked as a sous-chef in two of Britain's best restaurants, the Capital in London and the Gidleigh Park Hotel at Chagford, a famous stately home. He has recently been appointed head chef at the Fleece, and his manager, Andrew John Parffrey, who calls himself a frustrated cook, tells us that the fare has much improved since Hugh has taken charge of the kitchen.

The new menu of Hugh Bishop, includes Pressed salmon in dill as one of the starters and, as a main dish, Loin of lamb roasted with kidney and served with port wine sauce seemed to be a popular choice.

Poached pears served with a liqueur-flavoured sabayon is a perfect sweet to end this very light but good three-course lunch.

We also fancied a Cheese fondue with our beer in the Shepherds Bar, this little snack being available all day.

This hotel is part of the Resort Hotels group, which has a good reputation for food. The Fleece Hotel was originally a Georgian coaching inn and has been converted to a hotel with all modern conveniences. The old beams, log fires, and traditional fare are cheering.

Poire pochée au Sabayon de Sauterne   Poached pears in sabayon

4 portions

4 *ripe* Comice du Doyen pears, peeled, cored and halved

Sabayon
2 egg yolks
1 whole egg
50 g (2 oz) castor sugar
150 ml (5 fl oz) Sauternes wine, heated to boiling point
Juice of ½ lemon
30 ml (2 tbsp) pear liqueur or Kirsch

When ripe, this variety of pears is extremely juicy, soft and tasty. There is no need to cook them. Soak them in a pear liquor (1 small glass) or a hot syrup.

In a metal bowl place the egg yolks, whole egg and sugar. Whisk for 5 minutes over a pan of boiling water until the mixture begins to thicken, then gradually add the warm wine. Whisk all the time until the mixture thickens like a custard and also froths lightly like a mousse.

Finally add the lemon juice and liqueur.

The custard should be 4 times its original volume.

Place two halves of pears on each plate. Cover with the custard and glaze quickly under a preheated grill to obtain a thin skin slightly browned.

Serve immediately.

Anthony Blake

Chef de Cuisine
Lucknam Park
Colerne
Wiltshire SN14 8AZ
Tel: (0225) 742777

Anthony Blake was trained at South Warwickshire College, where he passed in all disciplines of catering with distinction. After the usual practical experience in reputable establishments, including the Manor House at Moretonhampstead and the Great Western Royal in London, he rose to sous-chef at the famed Castle Hotel at Taunton, under Mr Oakes (who is also listed in this book) and finally became head chef of the Eastwell Manor at Ashford. He now has a sophisticated repertoire of the finest modern cuisine.

The dishes on his menu reflect his creativity. Typical dishes include Terrine of quail wrapped in the finest Wiltshire bacon, Baby lamb with baby carrots and mange-tout, and Cherry millefeuille with apricot coulis, which is popular with both children and adults.

Lucknam Park, set in 280 acres of parkland, is owned by Mr C. Cole and managed by David White. After driving along a mile of road lined with beech trees, you are welcomed as if you were a duke. The dining-room is sumptuous and the hotel can house 36 guests in comfort and luxury.

Soupe rafraîchie au Stilton et aux Amandes

Chilled Stilton soup finished with an almond flavoured cream

6 portions

50 g (2 oz) butter
A few sticks celery, ⎫ Mirepoix,
½ onion ⎬ chopped
1 leek ⎭ finely
1 bayleaf
50 g (2 oz) flour
75 ml (3 fl oz) white wine
600 ml (1 pt) fresh chicken stock
Salt and pepper
50 g (2–3 oz) grated Stilton
50 ml (2 fl oz) cream to finish

Almond cream
100 ml (4 fl oz) cream, whipped
25 g (1 oz) ground almonds
Almond liqueur or essence

Heat butter and cook vegetables until soft but not browned, for 10–15 minutes. Season and add bayleaf and flour, cook gently for 5 minutes more. Add wine and stock.

Season with grated Stilton, salt, and pepper to taste and blend the cream. Boil for a further 5 minutes. Remove from heat and liquidize the soup until smooth. Check seasoning, and cool.

Chill soup in fridge or on ice until ready to serve.

Almond cream
Mix together the cream, almonds and almond liqueur and shape into small walnut-sized dumplings. Add these to the soup so that they float, allowing 2 per portion.

Note: Use only a small amount of Stilton as it has a strong flavour and the soup needs to be subtle, and to taste of chicken as well.

Erwin W. Bottner

Chef de Cuisine
The Londonderry Hotel
Park Lane
London WIY 8AP
Tel: 01-493 7292

Erwin Bottner has seen the sun of Africa and also that of Karachi. He was executive chef of Intercontinental Hotels in Pakistan and later of the Ramada Hotel in Abu Dhabi. In 1985 he went to North Africa to work at the Isle Metropole Hotel in Luxor, Egypt.

He told us of the days when he worked in Zaïre in the heart of Africa. We discussed the training of local staff in modern cuisine: he trained a complete kitchen brigade in Baghdad for the luxury Rashid Hotel. Erwin received his all-round training in the famous German spa of Wiesbaden.

In a large hotel organization, including several establishments, the chef is responsible for masterminding the menu, and ensuring the profitability and efficiency of his own department.

Looking at the menu, the Duck terrine appealed to us, and we knew that the cold buffet preparation was Erwin Bottner's forte. Pointing out other interesting items, he explained that the Filets de sole Ile de France was garnished with a claw of lobster and served with two sauces, one creamy and the other red for contrast and flavour. Another dish consisted of mushrooms and lined with Colchester oysters and served in a pool of lobster and saffron sauce.

The Londonderry Hotel occupies a historical site but had stagnated for many years before the new company took over and injected a style of luxury and comfort. Located opposite the Inn on the Park and next to the Hilton, it had to come into line with these two hotels. The general manager is Dirk Grote, a very good administrator.

Terrine de Canard à la Erwin Bottner   Duck terrine

12 portions

2 kg (4 lbs 4 oz) duck, not too fat,
  plus the liver (cleaned and the
  gall bladder removed)
90 ml (3 fl oz) white port or dry
  Madeira wine
30 ml (2 tbsp) Cognac
3 ml (½ tsp) mixed spices
225 g (½ lb) lean pork or sausage
  meat
1 egg
60 ml (4 tbsp) double cream
8 bacon rashers, streaky if
  possible and rindless, blanched
25 g (1 oz) fat
25 g (1 oz) breadcrumbs
25 g (1 oz) ground or sheet
  gelatine
1 carrot
1 onion, quartered
1 stick celery
1 bouquet garni
1 sprig of thyme
15 ml (1 tbsp) green peppercorns
  (use Madagascar in tin)
Salt to taste

Bone the duck. First remove the skin and put it aside with the bones,
when all the meat from legs and breasts has been removed.

Cut the breast meat into 1-cm (½-in) cubes (leave leg meat in pieces).

Place the meat in an earthenware dish and cover with brandy and port
wine with mixed spices and a little thyme. Leave to marinade for 24 hours.

On a tray, brown the bones and skin with carrot, onion, and celery in
a hot oven, 220°C, 425°F, gas mark 7, for 30 minutes. Transfer to a
pan, add 1 pint water, and boil for 1 hour to get a well-reduced gravy.
Strain it and when cold remove the fat.

Boil this gravy again for 2 minutes and dissolve the gelatine in it.
Simmer for 12 minutes, and strain again. If done properly this aspic
should be clear and of a light golden colour. Season to taste and set
aside.

Brush a 2-litre (3-pint) terrine (oblong if possible) with melted fat and
line the bottom and walls with blanched rashers of bacon. This is to
encase the duck meat mixture.

Mince the leg meat with the lean pork or sausage meat and the
cleaned liver of the duck.

Blend the mixture in a bowl with 1 beaten egg, the cream, and 15 ml
(1 tbsp) breadcrumbs.

Stir in the wine and liquid of the marinade in which the meat has
been macerated for 24 hours. When this is smoothly blended to a
dropping consistency (neither too soft nor too stiff) mix in the diced
meat from the breasts, add the green peppercorns and just enough salt
to make it palatable (about 3 ml (½ tsp)). Fill the terrine to the top and
cover with more rindless streaky bacon.

Bake in preheated oven at 200°C, 400°F, gas mark 6, middle shelf in
a tray half-filled with hot water. Cook for 1½ hours.

On removal from the oven tilt the terrine to pour the unwanted
melted fat into a bowl. This fat can be used elsewhere.

Use a piece of wood, which fits the top part of the inside of the
terrine, with a heavy weight on it to press the meat while it cools. Leave
under pressure in the refrigerator overnight. Next day, unmould the
block of cooked duck without breaking it and place it in another clean
mould.

Reheat the aspic made the day before, and pour it on to the meat,
letting this liquid soak well in. Chill the terrine overnight.

To serve, unmould and cut into thick slices. Place these over a bed of
lettuce or spinach leaves with a few green peppercorns sprinkled
around.

Campbell Bruce

Chef de Cuisine
Old Mansion House Hotel
Auchterhouse by Dundee
Tayside DD3 0QN
Scotland
Tel: (082626) 366/7/8

Campbell Bruce completed a 5-year apprenticeship at the Station Hotel in Perth and received his City and Guilds certificate with credit at the age of 26. He was promoted recently from sous-chef to head chef.

Scottish fare at its best is featured on the menu. Cullen Skink is simply a haddock soup with potatoes, but the rest of his specialities are pure Escoffier, reminding us that the 'auld alliance' is not dead yet! Beef Tournedos périgourdine, Lobster Thermidor and Veal escalope cordon bleu will be firm favourites for many years to come.

The three main specialities were the Mussel chowder with garlic croûtons and a dash of double cream; a Filet de Sole Lydia with multiple garnish of asparagus, prawns, and mushrooms in a delicious wine sauce; and the Angus beef fillet steak flavoured with a lemon and orange sauce. The dessert Brandy basket is a classical brandy-snap biscuit as brittle as glass but as sugary as honey. It is served with scoops of ice cream and coated with a butterscotch sauce.

The house and grounds, steeped in Scottish history, have been in the ownership of several noted families, namely the Ogilvies, Strathmores, and the Earls of Buchan. It has been skilfully renovated into a hotel by the present owners, Nigel and Eva Bell. Both are famed for the excellent service they provide by way of comfort, food and wines.

Auchterhouse village is 7 miles (11 km) from Dundee, set amid the rolling farmlands of Angus. Shooting and fishing can easily be organized by arrangement. The ski slopes at Glenshee are accessible by car. It is also a championship golf area.

Filet Mignon Vivigne   Angus beef fillet steak

4 portions

8 small steak fillets, 75 g (3 oz)
   each, trimmed, free from skin
   and fat
25 g (1 oz) butter
2 shallots, chopped
25 g (1 oz) demerara sugar
Zest and juice of 1 lemon and 2
   oranges
50 ml (2 fl oz) port wine
300 ml (½ pint) demi-glacé
   (brown sauce)
Seasoning

Boil zest of lemon and oranges in water for 5 minutes. Refresh and keep aside for garnish.

Slightly flatten out the medallions of beef and season.

Heat the butter, stir-fry the chopped shallots then fry the beef steaks. Cook gently for about 2–3 minutes each side, then remove meat from pan. Keep warm. Discard unwanted fat. In the same pan add sugar, lemon and orange juice, port wine and reduce by two-thirds.

Stir in the demi-glacé and reduce again until a thick consistency is reached, season, add the blanched zest and coat the steak.

Serve on 4 plates.

Note: Use a special rinder or zester knife to obtain thin lemon and orange peel strips.

Venison can be used instead of beef.

Panier de Nougat   Brandy basket

4 portions

50 g (2 oz) butter
50 g (2 oz) sugar
30 ml (2 tbsp) golden syrup
50 g (2 oz) plain flour
3 ml (½ tsp) ground ginger
3 ml (½ tsp) lemon juice
4 scoops vanilla ice cream

Butterscotch sauce
100 g (4 oz) butter
200 g (8 oz) demerara sugar
300 ml (½ pint) cream

Decoration
150 ml (5 fl oz) cream, whipped
Fresh fruit, such as berries,
   tangerines, etc.

Put butter, syrup and sugar into a pan and heat until melted.

Sift the flour and ginger together and add to the melted mixture with the lemon juice.

Drop heaped spoonfuls of the mixture on to a well-greased tray (well apart to allow for spreading out), then place in preheated oven at 200°C, 400°F, gas mark 6, for 5–6 minutes.

When cooked, leave to cool for about 1 minute then remove from the tray with a palate knife and place on to the base of a tea cup and mould into shape (while hot, before it hardens).

Leave until firm, then remove and allow to cool.

Butterscotch sauce
Slowly dissolve the sugar in the butter. Add cream and reduce until it coats the back of a spoon. Allow to cool.

Presentation
Place a brandy basket on each plate, place two scoops of vanilla ice cream into the basket and coat with butterscotch sauce.

Garnish the plate with whipped cream rosettes and fresh fruits.

Bruce Douglas Buchan

Chef de Cuisine
Fossebridge Inn
Fossebridge
Near Cheltenham
Gloucestershire GL54 3JS
Tel: (028572) 721

During his career Bruce Buchan has been fortunate enough to participate in gastronomic festivals with Jean Bordier, chef patron of the Michelin-starred restaurant, L'Aubergade at Pontchartrain, in France, and also with Jean Galega who cooked for General Franco and King Juan of Spain in Madrid, and many other no less famous chefs. After an apprenticeship at the Yew Tree Restaurant near Stafford, Bruce graduated to sous-chef at the Bear Hotel, Hungerford, under David Evans, then to chef de cuisine at the Fleece in Cirencester for 2 years. He became chef at the Fine Inns' flagship, the famous Bear Hotel in Hungerford, where he excelled himself with his own particular style of cookery.

Reading his menu is fascinating, as one can study the career of a great cook: Panache of Cornish lobster with spiced cabbage or Terrine of marinaded chicken with apple chutney for starters; or Petite marmite d'écrevisses et de volaille — a medley of crayfish and chicken; or Émincé de St Jacques au poivron doux — a ragout of scallops with leeks and peppers.

The whole tone of the menu is an embellishment of English fare, at its best where it remains genuine. Local deer, Devon salmon, Cornish crab, or hake — even the sticky Toffee pudding with caramel sauce has a touch of good Queen Bess about it.

The handsome ivy-covered inn standing in extensive grounds by the River Coln, with its spacious rooms and a splendid fifteenth-century bar with stone walls, oak beams and inglenooks, held us all spellbound.

The restaurant seating 60 has two Georgian rooms that overlook the Fossebridge Lake. The owners are Suzanne and Hugh Robert, and Andy Rork, a creative director of Saatchi and Saatchi, who also owns a château near Toulouse in Southern France.

This old-fashioned inn has stood on its present ground for more than 500 years — no doubt it will still be there in the year 2500.

Marmite d'Écrevisse et de Volaille   Crayfish and chicken in broth

6 portions

24 crayfish
100 g (4 oz) breast of chicken
    (maize fed)
2 carcases of chicken including
    necks, hearts, and kidneys
300 ml (½ pint) fresh cream
30 ml (2 tsp) cornflour mixed with
    60 ml (4 tbsp) single cream
1 small bunch chervil
100 g (4 oz) onion
125 g (5 oz) carrots
100 g (4 oz) celery
100 g (4 oz) leeks
Bouquet garni
Salt and freshly ground black
    pepper

Preparation
Remove the intestinal vein from the crayfish tails. Roughly cut the
chicken carcases. Dice the onion and 50 g (2 oz) each of the carrot,
celery, and leek. Cut the remaining carrot, leek and celery into strips
(julienne). Pick the chervil into small strips.

Cooking
Prepare the chicken stock using the carcases, the diced vegetables
(mirepoix) and the bouquet garni. Boil in 600 ml (1 pint) water for 1
hour.

When the stock is ready, strain and bring it back to the boil, add the
crayfish and cook for 1 minute only.

Remove the crayfish from the liquor. Separate the tails and return the
heads to the broth and simmer. After 10 minutes, strain the broth and
poach the chicken until just cooked (15 minutes).

Add the julienne of vegetables and cook for 30 seconds more.

Thicken the broth with the cornflour and finish with cream and
butter. Whisk into the sauce. Season to taste.

Shell the tails, cut the chicken into strips and reheat in the broth
gently.

Presentation
Serve on octagonal plates, with 20-cm (8-in) underplate and doily.
Sprinkle the dish with fresh chervil.

Note: The success of this dish depends upon each item being only
just cooked. The dish should not be flooded with too much broth.

Pierre Chevillard

Chef de Cuisine
Chewton Glen House
New Milton
Hampshire BH25 6Q5
Tel: (04252) 5341

Pierre Chevillard began his career at the Troisgros Restaurant in Roanne, France. He was promoted to head chef at Chewton Glen after he had served a long term under the previous chef, who left in 1986.

His menu is highly sophisticated, with a selection of exquisite items beautifully presented. We were impressed by the Salade de raie et homard, with a French dressing flavoured with curry and garnished with mango. Skate and lobster might seem strange partners, but on the plate they were pure harmony. The Beignets de crabe en filo is a sort of fritter draped in that thin Arab pastry which many chefs have used as a wrapping to fry good things. It is Oriental in concept but a very good idea as a light hot entrée. Aiguillette de canard aux groseilles is a dish of wild duck. Big enough for two portions, the breasts are cut in thin slivers and served pink with various fruit sauces.

New Milton is located between Lymington and Christchurch, with acres of land bordering the New Forest and the south coast.

Salade de Raie et Homard   Skate and lobster salad

4 portions

50 g (2 oz) mâche lettuce
(corn-lamb plant)
1 frisée lettuce
1 head of radicchio
4 blanched tomatoes, cut into
strips
450g (1 lb) French beans
1 large mango
1 cooked lobster about 600g
(1 lb 4 oz)
200 g (8 oz) skate fillets
125 g (5 oz) butter

Vinaigrette
5 shallots, chopped
200 ml (7 fl oz) vinegar
15 ml (1 tbsp) of curry powder
200 ml (7 fl oz) virgin olive oil
Salt and pepper

Remove the flesh of the lobster. Cut it into 16 escalopes and place them on a tray with 25 g (1 oz) of butter.

Cut the skate fillet into 16 escalopes and place them on a tray with 25 g (1 oz) of butter.

Wash the salad vegetables separately, and then cut them into pieces and mix together in a bowl. Cook the French beans for 5 minutes in salted water, plunge into cold water and cut into thin strips. Peel the mango and cut it into strips.

Place the skate in a hot oven 220°C, 425°F, gas mark 7, and let it cook for about 5 minutes. Then place the lobster in the oven to warm.

Vinaigrette
Sweat the shallots in a pan for 2 minutes. Add the curry powder and the vinegar, and let it reduce by half. Allow to cool, then add the oil and season to taste.

Season the salad with the vinaigrette, divide it into four and place in middle of the plates. Arrange the fish and lobster around the salad, 4 escalopes of each per plate. Sprinkle the strips of tomato, beans and mango on to the fish and serve.

Jeffrey Condliffe

Chef de Cuisine
Thatcher Hotel
Epsom Road
East Horsley
Surrey KT24 6TB
Tel: (04865) 4291

Jeffrey Condliffe studied at North Staffordshire Polytechnic. He was promoted to sous-chef at the Bear Hotel, Hungerford under David Evans and after a few years was transferred to Thatchers, part of the same hotel group — Fine Inns — the owners of 4 hotels. Jeffrey is now the head chef of this establishment under the management of Carol Richardson, herself of *cordon bleu* standard.

This hotel makes good use of local products with fresh vegetables, high grade meat and poultry, and a good assortment of English cheeses. In the menu the dishes are printed in English but somehow I felt that the Scallops mousse had something French about it, it tasted absolutely divine in its chervil butter sauce.

Liver has always been a favourite, especially calves' liver, the most tender of the large animal offals. It was prepared with an apple and spring onion garnish in a pool of saffron sauce.

The Summer pudding has always been a success everywhere we have seen it featured, because it is English — it represents the Garden of England. All the berries are buried in casings of thin slices of bread soaked by the mixture of juices and, as a manager remarked to me one day, 'It must be pressed and should not be jellied with gelatine — too many cooks use this shortcut'. We were glad to notice that Jeffrey Condliffe had respected the recipe to the letter. That is the mark of a good craftsman.

The hotel is set in 3 acres of land, part garden and part lawn. Many National Trust properties are located within the vicinity of Guildford, Leatherhead, and Weybridge, only 24 miles from London.

In this old half-timbered hotel, you can sleep in a four-poster bed and enjoy the amenities of a private heated swimming-pool, from May to September. With golf courses and racing at Ascot and Sandown, it has everything a guest could wish to enjoy on a perfect holiday.

Foie de Veau en Compote d'Oignon et de Pomme   Liver with apple and onion

4 portions

25 g (1 oz) butter and 15 ml
   (1 tbsp) oil
1 large onion, sliced
1 large apple, peeled, cored and
   sliced in triangular pieces
1 kg (2 lb 3 oz) calves liver,
   trimmed, sliced
30 ml (2 tbsp) flour seasoned with
   salt and pepper
50 g (2 oz) butter and 30 ml
   (2 tbsp) oil
75 ml (3 oz) white wine
125 ml (5 fl oz) veal stock
3 strands of saffron
50 g (2 oz) butter or cream
4 spring onions scalded for 30
   seconds in boiling water

Prepare the onion and apple mixture first.

Heat the butter and oil, sauté the onion until translucent for 2 minutes (slow heat), add the apple pieces and stir-fry for 3 minutes more. Remove and drain off the fat over a colander, keep warm.

Season the liver slices and coat them with the flour. Shake off surplus. Heat the oil and butter and pan fry the liver slices for 3 minutes; they should still be juicy and pink. Remove and keep warm.

In the same pan, remove surplus fat, add wine and veal stock and boil quickly for 3 minutes to reduce it by half. Season and stir in the cream or softened butter while whisking. Add the saffron, simmer for 1 minute and strain the sauce through a conical strainer.

Pour a pool of sauce on four plates. Arrange liver on each plate with the garnish of apple and sliced cooked onion.

Decorate with one blanched spring onion.

Mélange de Fruit Estival   Summer fruit and bread pudding

6 portions

8 slices of brown bread without
   the crust, 225 g (8 oz)
125g (5 oz) raspberries
50 g (2 oz) each of the following
   fruits: blueberries, redcurrants,
   blackcurrants and strawberries
   — total 225 g (8 oz)

Coulis sauce
100 g (4 oz) raspberries
50 g (2 oz) icing sugar
Juice of ½ lemon

Decoration
100 ml (4 fl oz) whipped cream
100g (4 oz) assorted currants

Line four individual metal pudding basins with cling-seal wrapper. Grease the inside with soft butter. Line each pudding basin with thinly sliced pieces of bread. A small round for the bottom and a large one for the top.

Clean all the fruits for the filling. Place in a bowl, add sugar and stir.

Fill each pudding basin with the fruit and juice. Cover the top with the last round of bread. Place a small saucer on top so that the bread is pressed down and soaks up some of the fruit juice. Seal wrap and refrigerate overnight.

To make the coulis, just liquidize the ingredients.

To serve, pour a pool of sauce on four plates. Turn out the puddings upside down on to each plate, discarding the seal wrapping (of course). Pour a little coulis over each pudding.

Pipe the cream over the sauce, around the pudding, for decoration.

Decorate the top of each pudding with a sprig of fresh redcurrants and blackberries or other berries.

Christopher Conil

Secretary, Cercle Epicurien
Mondial
Master Baker/Confectioner-
Patissier/Proprietor
Havengore House
Registered Residential Home for
the Elderly
27 Fairfield Road
Eastwood
Leigh-on-Sea
Essex SS9 5RZ
Tel: (0702) 529243

Aged 43, Christopher is a graduate of the National College of Bakery, Confectionery, and Catering. He has run three of his own establishments and a food factory with great success.

He now runs a residential home for elderly people, assisted by his wife Suzanne and an amiable staff.

Cornucopia of Fruits

An abundance of red berries flowing from a horn of plenty, biscuits with flaky crumbs in a pool of smooth sabayon

8 portions

Puff pastry
225 g (8 oz) strong breadmaking
flour
50 g (2 oz) butter
Pinch of salt
150 ml (¼ pint) cold water
A drop of lemon juice
225 g (8 oz) butter

Sabayon
4 egg yolks
150 g (5 oz) sugar
175 ml (6 fl oz) Advocaat liqueur

Fruits
175 g (6 oz) redcurrants
225 g (8 oz) strawberries
225 g (8 oz) stoned red cherries

Rub the butter into the flour and salt. Add the water and lemon juice, and make into a dough. Allow to rest for 30 minutes. Roll out to an oblong and spread the butter over ¾ of the dough. Fold and roll, twice, then rest the pastry. Repeat. The pastry is now ready for rolling into thin strips about 25 cm (10 in) long by 1 cm (½ in) wide. Dampen the surface. Using a metal horn mould and starting at the bottom, roll the strips around the horn, dip the tops in granulated sugar, place on baking sheets and bake for 15–20 minutes at 200°C, 400°F, gas mark 6, until crisp and golden. Remove the metal horns and allow the pastry to cool.

Sabayon
Cream the egg yolks and sugar and cook in a double saucepan until thick and creamy. Add the Advocaat.

To finish the dessert
Half fill the pastry horns with sabayon topped by a mixture of fruits. Pour the remainder of the sabayon on to plates. Place the horns in the centre and decorate plates with the surplus berries. A few sprigs of mint dotted here and there adds a finishing touch.

Tasha Soufflette

A light sponge turnover filled with redcurrants and raspberries embedded in a light vanilla cream floating on a raspberry coulis, with Viennese finger biscuits temptingly placed to dip into this creation

6–8 portions

Sponge
5 egg yolks
150 g (5 oz) caster sugar
5 egg whites
150 g (5 oz) caster sugar
300 g (10 oz) plain flour
2 drops vanilla essence

Cream filling
600 ml (1 pint) milk
5 egg yolks
50 g (2 oz) cornflour
100 g (4 oz) sugar
4 egg whites
90 g (3 oz) caster sugar
225 g (8 oz) raspberries
100 g (4 oz) redcurrants

Raspberry coulis
300 g (10 oz) raspberries
90 g (3 oz) sugar
90 ml (3 fl oz) red wine
15 ml (1 tbsp) lemon juice

Sponge
Using a whisk, mix the yolks and sugar to a smooth paste. In another bowl whisk the egg whites and sugar together to a stiff peak. Blend in the yolk mixture. Finally, fold in the flour and vanilla and clear. Using a piping bag (1-cm) and (½-in) tube, pipe 15-cm (6-in) round or oval discs of sponge on to baking sheets lined with silicone paper. Bake in a hot oven, 230°C, 450°F, gas mark 8, for 5–7 minutes until soft and golden. Do not overbake otherwise the sponge will be too crisp for folding. Remove from the paper and fold over a rolling pin to keep shape.

Filling
Boil the milk. Mix the yolks, cornflour, and sugar with a little of the milk to form a paste. Stir in the boiling milk and cook in a double saucepan until thick and creamy. Allow to cool. Whisk the egg whites and sugar to a peak. Fold this into the cool custard and continue to cook until the cream mixture thickens. Cool slightly.

Partially fill the sponge soufflettes with some of the fruit, and then fill remainder with the cream filling, covering the fruit. Decorate the top with berries. Glaze all over with gelatine, if preferred, or dust with icing sugar, and score the top with a red hot wire or knife for effect. Place soufflettes on a bed of raspberry coulis, which is the fruit, sugar, wine, and lemon juice boiled, puréed and poured on to the plates, awaiting the launch of Tasha Soufflette.

Jean Conil

Chef de Cuisine/Food
    Consultant/Lecturer/President,
    Cercle Epicurien Mondial/
President World Master Chefs
    Society
Principal, Academy of
    Gastronomy
282 Dollis Hill Lane
London NW2 6HH
Tel: 01-452 9679

Jean Conil has travelled all over the world learning the culinary style of many countries in depth. In the last 30 years Jean has seen the development and changes of culinary repertoire and the modification and improvements effected through the various ethnic influences which together have inspired *nouvelle cuisine*. New trends and attitudes in healthy eating have forced chefs to adapt their recipes and to create dishes of their own in an effort to meet the new requirements. As a consequence, Jean developed his vegetarian cuisine as a first step towards satisfying the need for better vegetable preparations. His *cuisine fraîcheur* took on a new lease of life in response to the demand for fresh fruits to garnish savoury meals.

Jean is now dedicated to the therapeutic properties of food and in his radio broadcasts has become the new food guru of the profession, preaching less reliance on convenience foods and more on natural products.

For his contribution Jean has formulated two vegetarian dishes which can be presented artistically and decorated with baby vegetables and coulis sauces — Terrine d'aubergines au cumin with its black skin used for colour and taste, and Polenta of sweet corn semolina, with a garnish of green, yellow and red peppers.

Terrine d'Aubergines au Cumin *Egg-plant pudding with cumin*

6 portions

50 ml (2 fl oz) butter and oil
   mixed together
2 medium aubergines
1 large onion, chopped
4 cloves of garlic, chopped
3 ml (½ tsp) cumin seeds, ground
Salt and pepper
4 eggs, beaten
15 ml (1 tbsp) sesame paste
15 ml (1 tbsp) tomato purée

Garnish
4 cherry tomatoes (red and
   yellow)

Peel the aubergines with a potato peeler to obtain ribbons of skin uniform in length and width.

Slice the aubergine, sprinkle with salt, and leave in a bowl for 30 minutes to remove bitter juice. Rinse off and drain well.

Heat the butter and oil in a sauté pan and sizzle the onion and garlic for 2 minutes until soft. Do not allow to brown. Remove the mixture from the pan and blend in a bowl with the beaten eggs.

Fry the aubergine for 3 minutes in the same fat, drain well and liquidize to a purée. Blend the purée with the onion mixture. Season to taste with the spices and tomato purée and mix in the sesame paste. Grease 6 ramekin dishes of 150 ml (5–6 fl oz) capacity.

Scald the aubergine ribbons for 30 seconds and line the greased ramekin dishes with the ribbons, coloured skin outwards, leaving two lengths to cover the top.

Fill the ramekins with the aubergine mixture.

Place the ramekin dishes in a deep tray half-filled with hot water and bake in a pre-heated oven at 200°C, 400°F, gas mark 6, for 40 minutes. Cool.

Turn out on to 4 plates, like small puddings, and decorate with red and yellow cherry tomatoes, cut in halves.

Polenta aux Poivrons Catalane

Sweet corn semolina puddings with mixed peppers. Corn semolina is available in 225 g (8 oz) packets and if you follow the instructions you will notice that it should be cooked for 5–8 minutes.

6 portions

225 g (8 oz) corn semolina
1 litre (1¾ pints) water
3 ml (½ tsp) salt
50 ml (2 fl oz) oil
2 egg yolks, beaten
100 g (4 oz) hard grated cheese
   (Cheddar, Gruyère, Edam, or
   Cantal)
A good pinch of freshly milled
   black pepper
30 ml (2 tbsp) oil for greasing
   moulds (tumbler or pyramid
   shapes)

Garnish
18 leaves of raw spinach, washed
   and drained
1 red, 1 green, and 1 yellow
   pepper, split, deseeded, with
   the inside membrane removed,
   and cut into very thin strips
100 g (4 oz) white mushrooms,
   washed, trimmed and sliced in
   strips

Dressing
30 ml (2 tbsp) sunflower oil
Juice of 1 orange
15 ml (1 tbsp) raspberry vinegar
Salt and pepper to taste
3 ml (½ tsp) made mustard
   (English)

Bring the water to the boil and sprinkle in the corn semolina. Cook for 5–8 minutes. Remove the pan from heat but while still hot stir in 50 ml (2 fl oz) oil and beaten eggs, and cheese to mixture. Beat until smooth and season.

Grease the moulds with oil and fill them with mixture. Cool.

Line each plate with 3 spinach leaves and turn each mould on to the plate, right in the centre. The spinach should form a triangle.

Mix the ingredients for the dressing in a bowl and toss the strips of mixed pepper and mushroom in it. Toss again and arrange on each plate all around the polenta pudding.

Serve cold.

With left-over polenta, shape mixture into small balls, roll in flour and shallow fry in oil for 1 minute until golden. Drain well and serve them as snacks; or as additional garnish, contrasting hot and cold polenta for appetite stimulation.

Terry Coyle

Deputy Service Manager
Intercity Services
Tournament House
Paddington Station
London W2 1HQ
Tel: 01-922 6690

Terry Coyle attended Slough College where he learned advanced cookery and catering, and at Kingston College where he studied for a management diploma. He then worked for many years for British Airways, as manager of their Flight Catering Centre, and later moved to Scandinavian Airline as special project manager at Heathrow.

Intercity meal services are provided on the following routes: Paddington to Penzance; Euston to Blackpool; St Pancras to Sheffield; and King's Cross to Newcastle. We have travelled on all these lines and have had splendid meals on every occasion.

Une Triade de Viandes à la Sauce Béarnaise

Three loins of assorted meats with egg and tarragon sauce

1 portion

3 × 100 g (4 oz) tender loins of lamb, beef and pork
50 ml (2 fl oz) mixture of oil and soft butter
Salt and pepper
30 ml (2 tbsp) Worcester sauce

Garnish
150 g (5 oz) French beans, headed, tailed, and cooked for 6 minutes

Sauce Béarnaise
25 g (1 oz) of shallots, chopped
6 crushed white peppercorns
3 tarragon leaves
45 ml (3 tbsp) water and 30 ml (2 tbsp) tarragon vinegar
3 egg yolks
150 ml (5 fl oz) melted butter

Garnish
15 ml (1 tbsp) mixed fresh herbs, chopped (parsley, chervil, and tarragon leaves)

Prepare the Béarnaise sauce first.

Heat the shallots with water, vinegar, and peppercorns until reduced by half, leaving 30 ml (2 tbsp) liquid. Away from heat, add egg yolks and whisk until the mixture becomes creamy (like a thin custard). This can be done by placing the saucepan in a tray half filled with boiling water. The sauce will thicken at coagulation temperature (76°C, 169°F). At this stage, add the butter bit by bit, as if making a mayonnaise, until the sauce is thick. Strain the sauce through a muslin cloth. Then add the tarragon leaves and keep at a tepid temperature (not hot, as it would curdle).

To cook the meat, sprinkle salt and pepper over the tender fillet steaks, and pour a few splashes of Worcester sauce over the 3 small pieces. Heat the butter and oil in a pan, and then quickly cook the meat for 4 minutes. Drain well and serve on plates with cooked French beans.

Serve the sauce separately. The meat can be grilled, but the heat must be adjusted to keep the juice of the meat from drying up.

Michael Croft

Chef de Cuisine
The Royal Crescent Hotel
Bath
Avon BA1 2LS
Tel: (0225) 319090

Michael gained a Credit after 3 years' training at the celebrated Westminster Hotel School. A gold medal at Olympia crowned his final examination as a chef. A succession of posts in gourmet establishments proved the finest finishing-grounds for this industrious cook. The Connaught Hotel in London, followed by a long spell at Graveyte Manor in West Sussex as a chef tournant (relief cook). His main achievement before his present position was to serve as sous-chef at the Ritz, where we first heard of him when we attended a special function.

Michael has held the post at the Royal Crescent's kitchen since 1984. The courses in his menu began with a Fish soup flavoured with basil and saffron. A Scallop terrine with oysters and spinach was our favourite starter, followed by Gâteau of wild rabbit with leek served with potato galette.

Michael recommends Wild pigeon Pithiviers and Lobster and crab salad with avocado and grapefruit as his other specialities.

The manager is Michael J. Cavilla and the hotel belongs to Norfolk Capital Hotels.

The Royal Crescent Hotel is an outstanding architectural masterpiece, one of several aristocratic houses which have been converted into luxury hotels. It is set within beautiful gardens and reminds you of the elegance of eighteenth-century Bath when gentry used to come for the waters (or the gossip).

Coquilles Saint Jacques Royal

Baby scallops and freshwater crayfish tails with a delicate essence of wild mushrooms scented with garden chives

1 portion

50 g (2 oz) unsalted butter
3 fresh baby scallops, sliced through the belly
4 or 5 tails of freshwater crayfish
50 g (2 oz) washed mixed wild mushrooms, garnish size
100 ml (4 fl oz) fish stock
Dash of vermouth
Fresh chives cut in 1-cm (½-in) lengths

Melt a knob of butter in a small sauteuse. When bubbling, throw in the lightly seasoned scallops, turn them over quickly in the butter and remove them. Do the same with the crayfish tails and add to the scallops. To the liquid now in the pan add the mixed wild mushrooms and cook for 2 or 3 minutes at a high heat. Remove the mushrooms and keep with the fish. Add a dash of vermouth to the juices in the pan as well as the fish stock and crayfish liquor and reduce this mixture down to 45–60 ml (3 or 4 tbsp); throw in the chives and add the fish and any juices. Reheat slowly and gradually mix in 75 g (6 tbsp) of butter.

Serve on a large plate at random, with no additional garnish.

James Currid

Chef de Cuisine
Old Waverley Hotel
43 Princes Street
Edinburgh EH2 2BY
Scotland
Tel: (031) 556-4648

This chef was a commis student at the British Hotel in Edinburgh and Turnberry in Ayrshire. He joined Scottish Highland Hotels in 1982 as a chef de partie for 2 years at the Old Waverley. He then was appointed head chef at the Sandygate House Hotel in Yorkshire. He returned to the Waverley as sous-chef and in 1987 was promoted to head chef.

When we asked him to provide us with typical Scottish recipes he sent us a starter of Melon bathed in Drambuie (whisky-flavoured liqueur) garnished with shelled prawns — a fine combination. The next course was Salmon dumplings shaped like quenelles served with scampi. That too was a dish perfected over the years. The sweet was a mousse flavoured with — yes, whisky again. This use of local products is what we have tried to encourage in all our epicurean promotions.

The manager of this hotel is Mr C. S. Hansen. The Old Waverley, occupies one of the finest positions on Princes Street.

Eventail de Melon aux Crevettes Charles Stuart   Fan of melon with prawns

4 portions

1 small ogen, peeled and
    quartered
4 large king prawns, boiled
    5 minutes and peeled, use tails
1 large king prawn, boiled
    5 minutes, peeled and chopped
Mint or watercress for garnish

Sauce
2 egg yolks
5 ml (1 tsp) Dijon or English
    mustard
5 ml (1 tsp) honey
Pinch salt
150 ml (5 fl oz) olive or peanut oil
15 ml (1 tbsp) coriander leaves,
    chopped and 2 mint leaves
    chopped
30 ml (2 tbsp) Drambuie liqueur
15 ml (1 tbsp) wine vinegar

Prepare a mayonnaise sauce as follows: In a bowl place egg yolks, mustard, salt, and pepper.

Pour the oil in a thin thread while beating with a whisk to emulsify the mixture, continue until all the oil is used. Flavour the sauce with Drambuie liqueur, honey, and vinegar. Finally blend in the chopped prawns and herbs.

Cut each quarter of melon and place on plates in a fan shape with one prawn tail between each slice.

Serve the sauce immediately.

Garnish the melon with mint leaves or watercress.

Quenelles de Saumon Mallaig Bay   Salmon dumplings garnished with scampi

4 portions

450 g (1 lb) filleted and skinned
  fresh salmon, minced
1 whole egg, beaten
50 g (2 oz) butter
150 ml (5 fl oz) white wine
Salt and pepper
1 sprig of dill
300 ml (½ pint) double cream
450 g (1 lb) scampi
Juice of 1 lemon
5 ml (1 tsp) parsley, chopped
5 ml (1 tsp) thin lemon rind
1 bunch watercress, trimmed, to
  garnish
8 slices of peeled cucumber

In a bowl blend the salmon purée with the beaten egg. Season to taste.
   Shape into quenelles using two spoons. Dip the spoons into hot water before using them to mould the quenelles and again to release the quenelles.
   Bring the white wine and dill to the boil in a sauté pan. Dip all the quenelles in this pan and let them poach for 5 minutes or so. Remove them with a slotted spoon. Keep warm.
   In another pan, heat the butter and gently cook the scampi for 2 minutes. Remove from the pan.
   Boil the wine until reduced by half and blend in the cream. Cook for 5 minutes, season to taste. Add lemon juice.
   On four plates pour a pool of sauce and garnish each plate with the salmon quenelles and the scampi (4 per portion). Decorate with watercress and cucumber and sprinkle with lemon rind thinly zested with a lemon rinder.

Crème d'Amande au Whisky   Almond cream Edinburgh fog

4 portions

600 ml (1 pint) double cream,
  whipped
50 g (2 oz) honey
50 g (2 oz) caster sugar
30 ml (2 tbsp) whisky
4 egg whites
Pinch salt
25 g (1 oz) dark chocolate, grated
100 g (4 oz) flaked almonds,
  toasted

Whip the cream until fluffy. In another bowl, whip the egg whites with a pinch of salt until stiff, then add the caster sugar a teaspoonful at a time until all is used, beating between each addition.
   Combine the whipped cream and honey and fold the meringue, without beating it, into the mixture. The whole operation must be lightly conducted. Finally flavour the cream with whisky.
   Spoon the mixture into tulip glasses. Decorate with flaked almonds and grated dark chocolate.

Stuart Currie

Chef de Cuisine
Alexandra Hotel
Oban
Argyll PA34 5AA
Scotland
Tel: 0631 62381

Stuart Currie trained at the Poachers Restaurant in Glasgow, and is rated as one of the best caterers in Scotland. He perfected his skill at the Central Hotel, also known for its cuisine, and has enjoyed the last 5 years having the run of the Alexandra's kitchen at Oban, where he constantly upgrades his own ideas on cooking fish.

Scotland is famed for its food not only because its cooks have access to good cheap products, but also because they have the knack of changing a simple haddock into a delicious delicacy.

When the fish is freshly caught and cooked the same day, there is no need for a fancy sauce to make it palatable. The mouthwatering list of items on the menu include haddock simply fried in butter, or in oil, with a coating of nuts and oatmeal and served with a garnish of banana fritters, fresh grapefruit segments, and green curly leaves with a yoghurt mustard sauce.

The Alexandra Hotel has an air of calm behind its summery frontage, as it stands overlooking the perpetual bustle of Oban's harbour. You can enjoy your meals watching the boats come in with their catch; and many smaller boats are available for daily sightseeing trips around the coast.

Oban, the undisputed capital of the West Highlands, is one of the most popular of holiday destinations in Scotland, with all the usual seaside amenities and safe bathing at Ganavan Sands.

To the north-east lies Glencoe, scene of the infamous massacre of the MacDonald clan by the Campbells, while to the west is the seaway to the green hills of the island of Kerrera, the mountains of Mull and the mystical history of Iona.

The general manager of the Alexandra Hotel is David Brown.

Eglefin d'Oban aux Bananes et Crevettes

4 portions

4 by 225 g (8 oz) haddock fillets
50 g (2 oz) brown flour with 1 tsp
    salt and mustard powder
1 beaten egg
60 ml (4 tbsp) milk
50 g (2 oz) mixture of oatmeal
    and crushed peanuts or
    hazelnuts
Oil for deep frying

Sauce
150 ml (5 fl oz) plain yoghurt
75 ml (3 fl oz) mustard
    mayonnaise
30 ml (2 tbsp) chives, snipped
50 g (2 oz) peeled boiled shrimps,
    chopped

Garnish
4 bananas, peeled and sliced and
    tossed in butter until soft
4 curly lettuce leaves
8 grapefruit segments
50 g (2 oz) red berries

Wash the fish and skin the fillets. Dry and dip into seasoned flour then into beaten eggs and lastly into the mixture of oats and nuts.

Heat the oil and deep fry the fish fillets when ready to serve them. Cook for 7 minutes and drain well.

Combine the ingredients of the sauce and pour a pool of sauce on to 4 plates. Arrange a leaf of curly lettuce or chicory and over each leaf place a few berries. On top of each fish fillet place a spoonful of cooked sliced banana and grapefruit segments.

Eric Deblonde

Chef de Cuisine
Inn on the Park
Hamilton Place
Park Lane
London WIA IAZ
Tel: 01-499 0888

Eric Deblonde served his apprenticeship at the famous Hôtel de Dieppe in Rouen with M Gueret, Maître Cuisinier de France, an officer of the Circle, who taught him the celebrated specialities of Rouen in Normandy.

M Gueret first sent him to London's Inn on the Park in 1973, where he took up the position of chef de partie saucier. This was his first experience in a foreign country. In 1976 he became sous-chef and was promoted head chef in 1986.

One of the features in the hors-d'oeuvre section which attracted our attention was not the usual foie gras and lobsters, but a salad made up of shin of veal (knuckle of veal) with onions and orange. The Wild mushroom soup too was imaginative. A Marmite de sole with aniseed and vegetables in the fish section and the Filet de veau with spinach and artichokes show good taste and care for patrons anxious to have their calories monitored as well as lowering their cholesterol and sodium intake. A special 600-calories luncheon can be devised with care to allow a gourmet this kind of diet.

The Inn on the Park, though, is one of the most luxurious hotels in the group, which is hardly surprising when you consider that it is run by Ramon Pajares, a graduate of the Hotel Institute of Madrid. Mr Pajares was voted hotelier of the year in the early 1980s, and is one of the patrons of the Epicurean Circle.

The hotel is situated between Park Lane and Piccadilly with a fine view of Hyde Park. It has its own secluded garden and two superb restaurants. A top-flight menu features mainly French cuisine. It has 228 bedrooms and 26 suites, 2 bars, and function rooms for special occasions.

Darne de Saumon au Xérès

Wild salmon steak served with deep fried salmon dumplings, butter sauce and shallots, sherry vinegar

4 portions

Wild salmon has a distinctive saline flavour of the sea as opposed to the blander taste of farmed fish.

Fish dumplings
150 g (5 oz) raw minced salmon
1 egg white
Salt and pepper
5 ml (1 tsp) chopped dill
Oil for deep frying

Yeast batter
100 ml (5 fl oz) flat beer
75 g (3 oz) flour
10 g (½ oz) baker's yeast
Pinch salt

Salmon steaks
4 × 75 g (3 oz) salmon fillets cut in neat pieces, seasoned to taste

Sauce
1 shallot, chopped
45 ml (3 tbsp) sherry vinegar
15 ml (1 tbsp) unsalted butter in 150 ml (5 fl oz) double cream
Pepper

Garnish
4 wedges of lemon
Curly lettuce
Sliced cucumber
Sprig of dill

Fish dumplings
In a bowl blend the raw minced salmon with the egg white and chopped dill. Season to taste. Divide into 8 balls, roll in seasoned flour like dumplings.

Yeast batter
Mix the flour and beer, crumble the yeast in it and let it ferment for 20 minutes.

To cook dumplings
Heat oil in a pan. Dip the dumplings in batter and deep fry for a minute. Drain well and keep hot.

Salmon steaks
Heat butter in a pan, quickly sauté the salmon steaks for 2 minutes. Remove and keep hot. Remove butter from the pan.

Sauce
Boil vinegar and shallots for 2 minutes. Whisk in butter and cream. Season to taste.

Garnish
To serve. Place one steak on 2 dumplings on each of 4 plates with a pool of sauce. Decorate with curly lettuce, sliced cucumber and lemon wedge.

Claude Deligne

Chef de Cuisine
Taillevent
75 Rue Lamennais
Paris 75008
France
Tel: 45.63.39.94.

Claude Deligne has maintained the three-star rating of this major restaurant, which is owned by the son of the founder, Jean-Claude Vrinat, an officer of the Circle. The name Taillevent was a nickname for Guillaume Tirel, who wrote the first cookery book in the fourteenth century and was chief cook to Charles VII at the time of Jeanne d'Arc.

The reputation of this restaurant comes not from the title of the place but from the hard work put in by the Vrinat family in making it that elegant rendezvous of epicures.

You may choose Lobster and asparagus as a starter on a thin pastry, or indulge in a Loin of venison in port wine sauce, or have an Ice cream bombe shaped like a turban, or a Salamis of duck, as Taillevent would have prepared it, in green grape juice or acid wine.

In the dining-room the comfortable chairs, the draperies, the silver trolley, create an atmosphere of elegance and luxury. It is relaxed and informal, and yet there is that feeling of old times when kings were honoured as saints and the gentlemen were all knights in shining armour.

Terrine de Brochet Taillevent   Pike terrine

8 portions

Choux paste
300 ml (½ pint) milk
150 g (5 oz) butter
200 g (7 oz) flour
4 egg yolks
Salt and pepper

Filling
50 g (2 oz) butter
225 g (8 oz) pike fillets, skinned
    and minced raw
2 egg whites
300 ml (½ pint) double cream
225 g (8 oz) sliced mushrooms
    (soaked in the juice of a lemon
    for 12 minutes)
15 ml (1 tbsp) parsley or coriander
    leaves, coarsely chopped

Green sauce
45 ml (3 tbsp) oil
15 ml (1 tbsp) cider vinegar
1 shallot, chopped
15 ml (1 tbsp) cream
15 ml (1 tbsp) parsley and 2 of
    spinach, mint and watercress
    leaves
Rind of a small lemon
Salt and pepper
5 ml (1 tsp) Dijon mustard
    (optional)

Garnish
A few leaves of lettuce or
    radicchio
Lemon slices

First make the choux paste like a sauce. Heat the butter in a pan with the milk until melted. Add the flour and mix well until the dough is firm and can be lifted in one mass. Cool and blend in the egg yolks to make it into a soft paste. Season.

In a mixing bowl blend the raw fish with the egg whites and the choux paste. Finally add the cream and seasoning.

Oil an oblong mould of 1 litre (1¾ pints) capacity and fill it with half of the mixture.

Arrange slices of raw mushroom over and sprinkle with parsley. Then add the remaining fish paste and top with layers of mushrooms. Cover with greased foil and bake in a preheated oven at 170°C, 325°F, gas mark 3, for 1¼ hours. Cool or serve hot.

Sauce
Just liquidize the ingredients like an emulsified vinaigrette.

To serve
Cut into slices and place on plates. Arrange a little sauce on the side and add a few lettuce leaves and lemon slices.

Annie Desvigne

Chef de Cuisine and Proprietor
La Tour du Roy
02140 Vervins
Near Amiens
France
Tel: 23.98.00.11

Winner of countless awards for good food, Annie Desvigne is as much at ease with the marinading of wild boar meat as she is preparing other, less complicated, dishes.

Perusing her large menu is like reading a cookery book and not knowing which fine food to select. There are various table d'hôte menus on offer at different prices, all with many tempting entrées, such as Lobster in cream sauce and sherry, Duckling with sour cherries, and Wild boar meat cooked in wine, the great speciality of the château.

The dessert menu included our favourite Marquise au chocolat, not a mousse, not a pudding, but something very tasty like manna from heaven. Ile flottante aux framboises was a familiar dessert of Jean Conil's childhood.

Claude Desvigne, her husband, looks after the cellar and the wines, some of which are as old as this fabulous château.

La Tour du Roy is located in historic Picardy, city of Vervins, where Henry IV was acknowledged King of France.

The hotel is perched on the highest part of the city, overlooking its ramparts. Vervins is only a few miles from St-Quentin and Amiens, and is an ideal spot for honeymooners and gourmets.

Ile flottante aux Framboises   Meringue island with raspberry sauce

4 portions

25 g (1 tbsp) soft butter, to grease
   4 individual metal moulds
5 egg whites
Pinch salt
250 g (10 oz) granulated sugar

Sauce
225 g (8 oz) fresh or frozen
   raspberries
Juice of ½ lemon
5 ml (1 tsp) cornflour and 60 ml
   (4 tbsp) water

Decoration
225 g (8 oz) fresh or frozen
   raspberries

Beat the egg whites with a pinch of salt until firm, and then gradually add the sugar, 5 ml (1 tsp) at a time, beating between each addition of sugar until the meringue is stiff each time.

Lightly butter the moulds and sprinkle flour inside. Shake off the surplus and then fill the moulds with the meringue, packed tightly.

Place all the moulds on to a tray half filled with water and bake at 200°C, 400°F, gas mark 6, middle shelf for 20 minutes like a soufflé. Meanwhile make the raspberry sauce.

Boil 225 g (8 oz) raspberries with the lemon juice for 2 minutes, and then pass the purée through a nylon sieve. Reheat to boiling point and thicken with cornflour and water mixed in a bowl. (Optional) Boil for 3 minutes more to achieve a smooth consistency.

Pour a pool of sauce on to 4 plates and arrange the meringue turned out on the plate. Ladle more sauce over the floating island and serve with fresh raspberries as garnish.

Marquise au Chocolat   Chocolate mousse

8 portions

225 g (8 oz) grated dark chocolate
14 g (½ oz) cocoa powder
150 g (5 oz) double cream
150 g (5 oz) icing sugar
5 egg yolks
5 egg whites
15 ml (1 tbsp) rum

Melt the chocolate and cocoa powder in a bowl placed in a saucepan of hot water. Stir until melted but do not overheat.

Blend the sugar and egg yolks in another bowl and gradually add the melted chocolate.

In another clean bowl whip the egg whites with a pinch of salt until they peak but are not dry and fold into the chocolate mixture with the double cream.

Pour the mixture into individual ramekin dishes of 150 ml (5 fl oz) capacity and let the mixture set overnight in the refrigerator.

Note: The mixture can be flavoured with rum or Grand Marnier liqueur.

Sylvain Duparc

Chef de Cuisine
Carlton Hôtel
58 Boulevard Croisette
Cannes 64000
France
Tél: 93.68.91.68

Sylvain Duparc was apprenticed in Annecy and in Evian. He moved to the famed Pavillon Henry IV in Paris to gain more Parisian experience, and then returned to the Riviera to work at the Martinez next to the Carlton, where he has been head chef since 1986.

The large menu of the Carlton is not entirely different from the bill of fare of other hotels of less prestige, and we read items seen elsewhere: caviar, foie gras, oysters, lobsters and a range of salades tièdes as starters. We noted a Ravioli with lobster aux herbes fraîches and a Consommé of shellfish which is now featured in all luxurious restaurants. A bass was cooked with thyme instead of fennel with vermouth wine, and was served with a garnish of scallops. In the meat course, Saddle of lamb with basil herb stuffing was in evidence, and the dessert menu had all the usual sorbets, and gratiné de fruits which are now the norm. The recipe of Turbot in cider butter does not reveal the Provençal touch, and we thought that garlic and saffron were getting too boring elsewhere. We approve of the light touch of this master chef.

The Carlton Inter-Continental Hotel in Cannes has for half a century been a temple of gastronomy, epitomizing the very best in food and wine. Located on the Croisette, the promenade fringed with palm trees, it attracts the international élite who make up the clientele of the Hermitage at le Touquet and the Savoy in London.

Suprême de Turbot au Beurre de Cidre   Poached turbot in cider butter

4 portions

2 Cox's apples, peeled, cored and
  cut into wedges
50 ml (2 fl oz) dry cider
30 ml (2 tbsp) Calvados
  (apple-jack)
225 g (8 oz) butter
Juice of ½ lemon
4 fillets of turbot, skinned, 150 g
  (5 oz) each
500 g (1 lb 2 oz) spinach
Grated nutmeg

Cook the apples in 50 ml (2 fl oz) of dry cider for at least 5 minutes. Flavour with 15 ml (1 tbsp) Calvados, and then whisk 100 g (4 oz) soft butter into the mixture. Finally add the juice of half a lemon as well as salt and pepper.

Place the fish fillets in a sauté pan and cook in 50 g (2 oz) of butter on both sides. Season to taste and cook for 8 minutes under a lid, turning the fish after 4 minutes.

Wash, blanch and drain the spinach. Squeeze it dry then reheat in 50 g (2 oz) butter with salt, pepper and grated nutmeg.

Divide the mixture of hot, seasoned spinach between 4 plates and on it place the fillets of turbot and cider butter, decorating with either a few slices of apple or wedges of apple slightly cooked in butter.

The best wine to drink with this dish is a Rosé de Provence, or you can drink a dry cider.

Jean-Pierre Emonet

Chef de Cuisine/Proprietor
Les Charmilles
Saint-Cyr-sur-Loire 37540
France
Tel: 47.54.02.01

Jean-Pierre Emonet takes pride in training his commis to a high standard, and to his credit three of his best assistant cooks won Diplomas with distinction at the Lycée in Dinard.

As we read through his table d'hôte and à la carte menus we noted Éffeuillé de raie au Xérès (Skate in sherry vinegar), which took our fancy. There were also Terrine de langoustines, Andouillette de saumon et sandre (a sort of fish sausage), and Noisette de lièvre, which is certainly less messy than old-fashioned jugged hare.

Reading the wine list was like shopping at some of the great vineyard houses. There were over 19 different Vouvrays, many of priceless vintage, as well as a good selection of inexpensive wines. The whole selection was made up of local Loire wines, an amazing thing for such a small place. There were also ten Montlouis, four Sancerre and four Pouilly-Fumé, all of different vintage, and as they aged the price seemed to go up. There were also Chinon Rouges and many other wines.

This is a family restaurant with no pretentious furnishing — just plain tables and surroundings, decorated with pictures and plates. So there were no distractions to hinder the serious eater. In the summer, eating meals on the terrace overlooking the river adds to the charm of Les Charmilles.

Effeuillé de Raie au Xérès   Skate cooked in sherry vinegar

2 portions

2 × 150 g (5 oz) pieces of skate
   wing, black skin removed
1 medium onion, sliced
1 bouquet garni
300 ml (½ pint) water
45 ml (3 tbsp) sherry vinegar
45 ml (3 tbsp) oil
2 × 3-cm (1¼-in) squares of baked
   puffed pastry

Garnish
2 endives (chicory), sliced
2 apples, cored and sliced, but not
   peeled

Wash the skate in plenty of water. Place in a tray with water, vinegar, onion, bouquet garni and seasoning. Poach for 12 minutes, remove the fish and reserve the stock.

To serve, place slices of chicory leaves on 2 plates with thin unpeeled slices of green apples. Flake the fish, place on top and drizzle with a little of the stock and oil mixed together. Arrange 2 squares of baked puffed pastry on top.

Martyn D. Emsen

Vice-President, Cercle Epicurien
Mondial — The World Master
Chefs Society
Company Group Executive Chef
The Britannia Hotel
Portland Street
Manchester M1 3LA
Tel: (061) 228-2288

Martyn Emsen had a formal college background and brief spells abroad before settling down to his first head-chef post at the Chequers Hotel in Newbury. Then he moved to the Gifford at Worcester, after which he was appointed head chef at the Britannia, progressing to executive chef when the hotel opened their French restaurant. He is now the company group executive chef in charge of the Adelphi in Liverpool, Britannia in Manchester as well as the Ringway and the Disbury. All these hotels have various dining-room outlets, such as Italian pasta restaurants, French restaurants, and American discotheques, as well as function rooms of all sizes.

We were fascinated to hear the poetry of the culinary language; Ventaille de canard de Barbarie aux coulis de morilles for Free-range duck and wild mushroom sauce; Goutte d'or de lièvre et lapereaux aux quenelles de girolles for Jugged hare and wild rabbit stew; Carousel de volaille de hautes forêts en mosaic d'été for a medley of feathered game and poultry meat cut in strips stir-fried, flamed in rum and served with peppers.

The hotel amenities include health clubs, dancing facilities, conference facilities, and banqueting rooms. The total experience is for people with sophisticated tastes and a flair for good, wholesome and varied food, plus the opportunities to flex one's muscles. All the hotels under the culinary guidance of Martyn Emsen offer just that and much more.

Filet de Boeuf Britannia Fillet of beef with horseradish and shallots

4 portions

50 g (2 oz) butter
50 g (2 oz) oil
700 g (1 lb 8 oz) fillet of beef,
   skinned and trimmed
Salt and pepper
12 shallots, peeled and blanched
1 chopped medium carrot
1 chopped small onion
1 chopped small celery stick
40 g (1½ oz) fresh horseradish
   root, peeled and shredded
45 ml (3 tbsp) brandy
500 ml (16 fl oz) beef stock
175 ml (6 fl oz) single cream
Parsley sprigs to garnish

Heat the butter. Seal the beef in a hot pan, season and transfer to a hot oven. Roast at 220°C, 425°F, gas mark 7, for 15 minutes.

Heat oil. Sauté the shallots, carrot, onion, celery and horseradish until browned. Drain off the surplus fat and stir in the brandy. Flame, add the stock and reduce by about two-thirds. Strain into a clean pan and add the cream. Reduce until thick, correct the seasoning and keep warm.

Remove the beef from the oven and slice into 4 portions. Spoon the sauce on to 4 plates and place the meat on the sauce.

Garnish with sprigs of parsley.

Serve with onion, sauté potatoes, and purée of minted carrot.

Horseradish Sauce with soured cream and Russet apples

50 g (2 oz) pickled grated
   horseradish
1 large, slightly tart apple
90 ml (3 fl oz) soured cream
1 pinch salt
15–30 ml (1–2 tbsp) white meat
   stock

Wash, peel and grate the apple and blend with the soured cream and meat stock.

Add a little salt, and then mix in the horseradish and chill until required.

It will keep for 4–5 days in the refrigerator in a screw top jar.

David Evans

Chairman, World Master Chefs
    Society
Chef de Cuisine/Executive Chef
Mirabelle
56 Curzon Street
London W1Y 7PF
Tel: 01-499 4636

David Evans is a gold medallist and trophy winner in every discipline of advanced cookery. He learned his craft at various places after completing his training at North Staffordshire College. He has worked abroad, spending short seasons in Alsace, Burgundy, Normandy, Provence, Bordeaux, Spain, and Switzerland.

David creates dishes which reflect his international training and one of his previous positions was at The Bear, Hungerford, as chef-manager, where his reputation soared. He has recently been appointed to the Mirabelle, one of London's top restaurants.

Brochette de Langoustines à la vinaigrette rouge   Kebab of prawns

4 portions

Sole mousse
450 g (1 lb) Dover sole fillet
450 ml (16 fl oz) double cream
3 whole eggs
2 egg yolks
50 g (2 oz) soft butter
Salt, pepper and nutmeg

Red wine vinaigrette
180 g (6 oz) red onions, chopped
350 g (12 oz) tomatoes, skinned,
    seeded and cubed
25 g (1 oz) chopped parsley
25 g (1 oz) chives, snipped
100 ml (4 fl oz) first pressing
    walnut oil
100 ml (4 fl oz) red wine
45 ml (1½ fl oz) red wine vinegar
Salt and freshly ground black
    pepper

Langoustines (Dublin Bay prawns
    or scampi)
24 large langoustines
100 g (4 oz) white breadcrumbs
100 ml (4 fl oz) clarified butter

Mince the sole fillet and pass through a fine sieve. Place this mix in a bowl over iced water. Add the salt. Gradually add the cream, beating vigorously. Add the eggs, yolks, and butter, and season with the pepper and nutmeg. Allow this to rest.

Peel the langoustine tails, and insert 4 tails on to a bamboo skewer.

Pipe the sole mousse on to the langoustines in a zig-zag fashion.

Dip this mousse into white breadcrumbs and repeat procedure on the other side.

Place the red onions, red wine, and the red wine vinegar into a saucepan. Bring to boil and simmer for 10 minutes. Allow to cool. Add the walnut oil, whisking constantly, and add tomatoes, parsley and chives. Season to taste.

Heat the clarified butter in a teflon-coated frying pan. Cook the brochettes of langoustine and sole mousse until golden brown on both sides.

Presentation
Place the brochettes on to a 20-cm (10-in) plate and put a spoonful of the cold vinaigrette on both sides of the brochettes. Serve immediately.

Gratin de Pamplemousse rosé et Sorbet de Fruit de la passion — Grapefruit and passion fruit sorbet

4 portions

Passion fruit sorbet
450 ml (16 fl oz) water
180 g (7 oz) granulated sugar
6 passion fruit (pulp only)
75 ml (3 fl oz) dry white wine
15 ml (1 tbsp) Cognac
2 egg whites, beaten to a stiff
    meringue

Tulips of 'langue de chat'
100 g (4 oz) butter
100 g (4 oz) caster sugar
75 g (3 oz) egg white
120 g (4½ oz) flour
Vanilla essence

Gratin
6 egg yolks
50 g (2 oz) icing sugar
60 ml (2 fl oz) double cream

Garnish
4 pink seedless grapefruit

Scoop out the pulp of the passion fruit into a mixing bowl with the sugar, water, and wine. Transfer it to a pan and boil the mixture for 10 minutes to produce a syrup. Cool it. Add 2 well-beaten egg whites to the mixture and flavour with Cognac.

Line two ice-cube trays with cling film and fill them with the mixture. Freeze until set like snow (3 hours).

Tulip of 'langue de chat' mixture
Cream the butter and sugar to a smooth consistency and gradually add the egg whites. Lastly blend in sifted flour and vanilla essence.

Place the mixture in a piping bag fitted with a plain 6-mm (¼-in) tube and pipe circles of mixture 10 cm (4 in) in diameter on to a greased and floured baking tin.

Bake for 5 minutes at 200°C, 400°F, gas mark 6, until the mixture is golden. (The circles will widen on baking.)

Oil a small pudding basin turned upside down and place the hot rounds over it to shape them like cups (or tulips). On cooling the biscuits will harden and retain the shape of the basin.

Gratin sauce
In a bowl, mix the egg yolks, icing sugar, and double cream.

Presentation
Arrange segments of grapefruits on 4 plates in a floral pattern.

Cover with gratin sauce and brown under the grill.

Finally, place a scoop of passion fruit sorbet inside each tulip casting. Arrange each one on the grapefruit mixture.

Robert Favre

Chef de Cuisine/Proprietor
La Diligence et Taverne du
    Postillon
St-Julien-en-Genevois 74160
France
Tel: 50.49.07.55

Robert Favre learned his craft from his father in the family hotel restaurant at Cruseilles. He gained further experience in Paris at La Côte d'Azur and Le Centre, two restaurants under the same ownership. During his military service, he was the chef to Admiral Cochet. After his discharge he returned to the profession to work in Switzerland, at La Taverne St Jean and later The Bearn, where he gained a Michelin star. He bought his father's restaurant in 1960, and in 10 years of hard work established La Diligence at St Julien as one of the most outstanding inns in Savoy. In 1974 it was awarded a Michelin star for cookery.

From the menu we selected Le turbot aux algues dans sa carapace de sel, Fish baked in a salt paste used like clay to encapsulate the seaweed aroma. There were other dishes of equal merit, for example Bassine d'écrevisses. His Pigeonneau, a tame pigeon, tastes so much better than the wild variety. The inn is situated in a cheese-making region, and his menus reflect the local specialities in general.

La Diligence was originally a posthouse inn, and it has been converted into a luxurious restaurant by the Favre family. It is run like a tavern or brasserie, with two dining-rooms — one underground. It is located about 9 km (5 miles) from Geneva. The atmosphere is alpine and romantic. Here the rivers and lakes abound with fish, and the mountains are an ideal setting for hunting game. It is a paradise for people who love winter sports.

Turbot aux Algues   Turbot baked in a salt clay dough

6 portions

2 kg (4 lb 4 oz) turbot

Clay dough of salt and flour
700 g (1 lb 8 oz) coarse cooking
   salt
1 kg (2 lb 2 oz) strong bread flour
300 ml (½ pint) water

Stuffing
225 g (8 oz) cheap white fish
   (whiting or lingue) filleted and
   skinned
1 egg
150 ml (5 fl oz) double cream
50 g (2 oz) peeled prawns (the
   shells can be used in the stock)
15 ml (1 tbsp) chives, snipped
   with scissors
Salt and pepper

Sauce
6 crayfish
50 g (2 oz) butter
100 g (4 oz) all together of the
   vegetable flavouring, including
   1 stick celery, 1 small carrot,
   1 medium onion and 1 leek, all
   cut in fine cubes or chopped
15 ml (1 tbsp) tomato purée
1 pinch saffron powder
Salt and pepper
90 ml (3 fl oz) double cream
300 ml (½ pint) water and 300 ml
   (½ pint) white wine to produce
   1 pint stock

Clay dough pastry
The purpose of this paste is to make a clay casing which will hold all the flavour of the fish and prevent the aromatic fragrance from escaping.

Place the flour and salt in a bowl and rub together. Stir in the water to make a stiff but pliable dough. Knead a little and shape into a ball. It must not be too soft or it will be difficult to handle. Keep it covered while preparing the fish and stuffing.

Stock
Fillet the turbot to obtain 4 fillets.

Boil the bones and head in water and wine, with 1 sliced onion and the prawn shells for 30 minutes. Strain. This stock will be used for the sauce later.

Stuffing
Mince the whiting and place mixture in a bowl. Blend in egg and cream. Season and add the peeled prawns and snipped chives. This is the stuffing for the fish.

Preparation
Season the fish fillets with salt and pepper.

Place 2 very large sheets of aluminium foil on the table (big enough to wrap the fish, no more). Brush top sheet with oil. Arrange 2 fish fillets side by side in original shape of the turbot. Spread the stuffing over each fillet. Sandwich the mixture with the 2 other fillets so that you have the turbot now reconstituted to its original shape. Squeeze a little lemon juice on top and brush the top fillets with melted butter. Wrap the fish in the greased foil overlapping the whole contents. Shape it to imitate the turbot.

Now roll the clay salt dough, dusting a board with flour, to a thickness of 1 cm (½ in) so that it will completely encase the foil parcel. Wrap the fish with this paste. Make sure there are no holes or broken cracks in the paste. Use it as if it were clay.

In a flat roasting tray place 4 handfuls of seaweed alginates, the kind found on rocky beaches, or kelp which is dried and can be slightly rehydrated. Arrange it as a bed. Place the turbot on top of the seaweed.

Bake in a preheated oven at 200°C, 400°F, gas mark 6, for 35–40 minutes.

Meanwhile prepare the sauce.

Flavouring

1 kg (2 lb 2 oz) ordinary fresh
  seaweed (otherwise use 150 g
  (5 oz) dry kelp)

Garnish

225 g (8 oz) samphire, fresh if
  possible

Sauce

Heat 45 ml (3 tbsp) of oil and pan-fry the 6 crayfish until they turn red,
about 4 minutes, and remove. Shell the tails to remove the flesh.
Replace the shells in the pan and add the mixture of chopped
vegetables. Stir-fry and then add tomato purée and saffron, and stir in
the fish stock. Boil this sauce for 25 minutes and strain. Reboil while
stirring in the cream and reduce the mixture by half. Season to taste.
Add the flesh of the crayfish tails, cut into small pieces.

Presentation

If you can get samphire, which looks like a green fern plant, boil it for
30 seconds and refresh in cold water to keep the colour as green as
beans. Drain well and use as a garnish or decoration. To serve, present
the turbot parcel on a dish to the guest. Crack open the solid baked clay
and remove the foil wrapping delicately. Remove and cut the fish into 6
portions. Pour a pool of sauce onto 6 plates and place a piece of the
stuffed fish on top. Decorate with a sprig of samphire.

Potée Savoyarde   Chicken and bacon hot-pot

6–8 portions

1 small cabbage, cut in two with
  stalk and core removed
2 carrots, sliced
1 head of celery, cleaned and split
1 onion studded with 4 cloves
1 bouquet garni
2 cloves garlic, crushed
1 medium fowl, ready trussed
  with fat removed
450 g (1 lb) garlic sausage
1 green gammon knuckle
1 kg (2 lb 2 oz) new potatoes

Garnish

450 g (1 lb) peeled chestnuts
3 cumin seeds
Salt and pepper

Bring 3 litres (5 pints) of water to the boil. Blanch the cabbage for
2 minutes and remove. Blanch the green gammon for 5 minutes and
remove. Refresh the cabbage and drain well so that it stays green.
Discard all the boiling water.

Now half fill a large pot with cold water, and then add the chicken,
garlic, bouquet garni and the knuckle. Boil for 1½ hours, remove the
chicken and then add carrots, celery and onion. Cook for a further
20 minutes. Carve the fowl into 8 pieces. In a metal casserole arrange
the cabbage, celery, carrots and chestnuts with the chicken pieces and
the lean meat from the knuckle of gammon.

Strain the stock and degrease it. Add some to the casserole to cover
all the ingredients. Check seasoning and braise or simmer gently for
35 minutes. Garnish with the cooked sliced garlic sausage, and serve the
boiled new potatoes separately with this good old family dish.

Note: The broth is served as a soup.

Kevin Francksen

Chef de Cuisine
Middlethorpe Hall
Bishopthorpe Road
York YO2 1QP
Tel: (0904) 641241

Kevin Francksen has succeeded Aidan McCormack as head chef at Middlethorpe Hall. Aidan and Kevin worked as partners from 1984 when the Middlethorpe Hall opened as an hotel.

Kevin was trained at Basingstoke College of Arts and was at the Viking at York for two years prior to moving to Middlethorpe Hall.

In studying the menu we were delighted to discover our favourite pâté made of rabbit with a garnish of pears. Other well-known starters incuded Ravioli of lobsters (at twice the price of Rabbit pâté), and a Cornucopia of smoked salmon filled with artichoke mousse. We also noted Guinea-fowl salad as a starter.

On the fish course the Roulade of salmon and sole with a shellfish sauce, although not new, is very trendy, but we still prefer the Cassoulet of shellfish served with noodles. Would a few fresh beans be better as a garnish? The main courses were all classical dishes, Roast best end of lamb, Fillet of beef; but we like the title of 'Cannon of veal'. A cannon (the military kind) must refer to the shape of the boneless veal cutlet which suggests a cannon, a term often used for lamb and mentioned in many a French bill of fare. There was a vegetarian dish of Gâteau of root vegetables.

As for the sweets, they were all *nouvelle cuisine*; we would prefer to see some old-fasioned puddings in addition to sorbets and liqueur soufflés. We were glad to see an apple tart with honey and mango sauce.

Middlethorpe is managed by Malcolm Broadbent and is owned by Historical House Hotels.

The Hall is a William III country house overlooking the York racecourses. Built in 1699 for the Barlow family, it was later the home of the famous diarist, Lady Mary Wortley Montagu.

Its decoration, antiques, and fine pictures are consistent with the period of the house, and evoke an atmosphere of comfort and well-being. The garden, the small lake and fine trees give a feel of arcadian splendour.

The county is renowned for the beauty of the dales, the open glory of the Yorkshire moors, its coastal scenery, and castles, churches, and historical houses.

Pâté de Lapin aux Poires Rabbit pâté with pears

10 portions

600 g (1 lb 5 oz) raw lean rabbit
  meat, minced
450 g (1 lb) lean sausage meat,
  pork and beef if preferred
100 g (4 oz) lean cooked ham, cut
  in 4-mm (¼-in) cubes
200 g (8 oz) fat bacon
75 ml (3 fl oz) Cognac, calvados
  (apple-jack), whisky, or gin
1 small sprig of thyme
1 egg, beaten
3 bay leaves
Salt and pepper
6 rindless rashers of green bacon,
  parboiled, drained, and dried

Garnish
5 ripe Comice pears

Line the earthenware terrine with slices of fat bacon. In a bowl, combine the minced rabbit and sausage meat, stir in the Cognac or other spirit, season with salt, pepper and spices. Sprinkle in a little thyme and add the diced ham and one beaten egg to bind the mixture.

Place a layer of the mixture in the terrine and a layer of the blanched strips of bacon and repeat until the mixture is all used. Cover with strips of fat bacon.

Cover with bay leaves and greased foil, place in a tray half filled with water and bake in preheated oven at 200°C, 400°F, gas mark 6, middle shelf, for 1½ hours.

Chill the pâté and serve with half a cooked ripe pear per portion and a pickled cucumber or gherkins or pears pickled in vinegar.

Note: You can also use strips of raw rabbit to alternate with the minced mixture for better presentation.

Christine Fréchet

Chef de Cuisine/Proprietor
La Chaumette
17 Rue Racine
Le Havre 76600
Normandie
France
Tel: 35.43.66.80

Christine Fréchet learnt her profession from her husband, and successfully ran their small restaurant, which had been previously in debt, and made it pay. *Les péchés gourmands du Havre* (sins of le Havre), as she calls her specialities, are indeed delicious, light, and mouthwatering. Brioches de moules, Raie au soja, Oeufs à la gelée de poivrons rouges, and Bavarois de fromage blanc au coulis de framboises, make up a deliciously balanced meal. Although one would expect the local cider to be the beverage, her menu features Château de la Begude, a cheap, fruity wine produced in a small vineyard a few kilometres from Aix-en-Provence.

The restaurant/bistro itself is not luxurious, but it is beautifully clean, truly gastronomic, and dietetic.

Brioches aux Moules Havraise   Mussels in a brioche bun

4 portions

4 brioches
50 g (2 oz) butter
2 shallots, chopped
5 ml (1 tsp) tomato purée
1 litre (1¾ pint) fresh mussels,
    cleaned and washed
150 ml (5 fl oz) dry white wine
Bouquet garni
1 bunch of parsley, chopped
Salt and pepper
1.25 ml (¼ tsp) curry powder
60 ml (4 tbsp) single cream

Scoop out the 4 brioches to produce cavities. Keep the tops.

Heat butter in a saucepan and stir-fry the shallots for just 30 seconds. Add the tomato purée, mussels, wine, bouquet garni, and half the parsley. Boil for 5 minutes. Strain the liquid through a muslin cloth. Shell the mussels and keep them hot in a bowl.

Reboil the strained sauce to reduce it by half. Season with salt, pepper and curry powder. Blend in the cream.

Reheat the mussels in this sauce.

Fill the hot brioches with mussels. Replace the tops.

To serve, pour a pool of the sauce on 4 plates and place the filled brioches in the middle. Decorate with coarsely chopped parsley.

Raie au Soja   Poached skate with bean sprouts

4 portions

4 skate wings, ready skinned,
   about 200 g (6 oz) portion
30 ml (2 tbsp) cider vinegar
60 ml (4 tbsp) soya sauce
60 ml (4 tbsp) tomato purée
Juice of 1 lemon and 2 slices per
   portion of another lemon
2 shallots, chopped
450 g (1 lb) or 1 punnet of bean
   sprouts
1 bouquet garni
Salt and peppercorns
30 ml (2 tbsp) pickled capers

Place the cleaned skate wings in a sauté pan. Cover with water and cider vinegar. Add salt and crushed peppercorns. Poach for 10 minutes. Drain and keep warm.

In a bowl, blend soya sauce and tomato purée. Add chopped shallots, lemon juice, salt and pepper. This will be the sauce. Clean, wash, and drain the bean sprouts. You can either stir-fry them in a little butter for 30 seconds or use them raw in a salad with the dressing.

To serve, place a piece of the skate on each plate, drizzle the sauce over and sprinkle with a few capers and chopped parsley. Garnish with bean sprouts. Serve the sauce separately with slices of lemon.

Fromage Christine Fréchet au Coulis de Framboise   Cream cheese with raspberry sauce

4 portions

5 sheets of gelatine or 15 g (½ oz)
   powdered gelatine
50 ml (2 fl oz) hot milk
225 g (8 oz) fromage blanc
   (40% fat content)
30 ml (2 tbsp) double cream
50 g (2 oz) caster sugar
3 drops of vanilla essence
225 g (8 oz) fresh or frozen
   raspberries
2 egg whites
Juice of 1 lemon
Oil for greasing basins
Almond biscuits or macaroons

Whip the egg whites with a pinch of salt to help the coagulation into a firm meringue.

Dissolve the gelatine in the hot milk and cool. Stir the cold dissolved gelatine into the fromage blanc and cream. Fold the whipped meringue delicately into the mixture.

Oil 4 individual pudding basins (use almond oil or a bland oil) and fill them with this cheese bavarois.

Allow to set in the refrigerator for 2 hours.

Next prepare the raspberry purée as follows: Boil the sugar and 100 ml of water. Add the raspberries and juice of ½ lemon to keep it red (acid does that). Pass the purée and liquid through a nylon sieve.

To serve, pour the raspberry purée on to 4 plates, unmould the cheese bavarois and arrange over the sauce. Serve with almond biscuits or macaroons.

Solange Gardillou

Chef de Cuisine/Co-Proprietor
Hostellerie
Moulin du Roc
Champagne-de-Belair 24530
France
Tel: 53.54.80.36

The imaginative regional cuisine of super *cordon bleu* Solange Gardillou has earned her two Michelin stars. Trout with ceps, Duck with sorrel, Foie gras poêlé aux endives, Les pâtes fraîches aux truffes, and Morue fraîche au pied de cochon. In the meat section we find Boeuf aux truffes carré d'agneau à la crème d'ail and Pintade aux graines de moutarde, and guess what — Le pied de cochon farci aux truffes, as if a pig's trotter deserves such a rich accompaniment. Her Walnut cake with chocolate sauce is just a dream dessert.

This enchanting and most romantic seventeenth-century walnut mill has been converted by Solange and her husband Lucien into one of the most popular and peaceful abodes of the region. The cosy but elegant dining-room is decorated with antiques and bric-à-brac from the old mill. There are two terraces for outdoor dining and lounging, and a swimming pool too. The inn is about 5.5 km (3½ miles) from Brantôme. An exciting place and not too expensive, we urge you to try it for a vacation.

Les Filets de Truite saumonée fourrés aux cèpes   Salmon trout fillets stuffed with ceps

4 portions

25 g (1 oz) butter or oil
4 salmon trout, about 225 g (8 oz) each
225 g (8 oz) ceps, cleaned and chopped
50 g (2 oz) rillettes d'oie (goose meat pâté)
1 clove garlic, crushed
1 bunch parsley
1 bunch chives
Salt and pepper
25 g (1 oz) butter
4 aluminium foil sheets in which to wrap the trout
1 lemon

Fillet the trout neatly. Season each fillet with salt and pepper.

Wash, drain, and dry the parsley leaves and chop coarsely. Clean the ceps and snip the chives with scissors.

Heat the butter or oil in a sauté pan and stir-fry the ceps, garlic, and minced, cooked goose pâté (rillettes). Blend in the coarsely chopped parsley and chives. Cool the mixture after 3 minutes of cooking.

Spread the filling on each fish fillet and sandwich it with another fillet.

Grease a piece of foil with oil and wrap each stuffed fillet. Bake or steam for 8 minutes.

Froth a little butter in a pan for 30 seconds and pour it on to a hot plate and then place a stuffed fillet on it. Sprinkle with chopped parsley and lemon juice.

Jean Paul Gérin

Proprietor/Délégué National, and
Vice-President, Cercle Epicurien
    Mondial
Le Château de Collonges
Ruffieux 73310
Chindrieux
France
Tel: 79.54.27.38

Jean Paul Gerin has done wonders with the château. From the tiled main hallway with supporting classical columns, stairs lead up to bedrooms or spiral down to the old castle kitchens with rough stone walls. A blazing log fire welcomes you to the dining-room. Tables are laid with beautiful glass and cutlery, and colourful cloths and flowers, touches which will whet your appetite for the home-baked bread, fresh garden vegetables, and local specialities prepared by young Yves Robert, who was recently promoted from sous-chef to head of the kitchen at a relatively early age for such an important position. Yves was a student at Quimper and Granville College and has worked in several smaller restaurants before taking charge of the château's gastronomy.

The menu is in keeping with the local Savoyarde specialities, herbal soups consist of dandelion, chervil, nettle, sorrel, chard leaves, chives — anything green will find its way into the pot. *Agneletti* is another word for a sort of ravioli filled with lamb meat, *ravioule* is a patois word for a potato fritter. A *pormonaise* is simply a local sausage flavoured with fresh vegetables such as chard leaves, cabbage, and leeks, which flavour the meat in such a delicious way that they are worth eating on their own as an entrée. *Caion* is a patois word for pork. *Féra* is a fish of the trout family found in the lakes. It is said that Charlemagne liked it roasted on a spit. It is now baked or barbecued.

Filet de Boeuf à la Collonges Beef fillet with truffles

6 portions

1 kg (2 lb 2 oz) fillet of beef,
    skinned and trimmed
1 truffle, sliced
150 g (5 oz) pig's caul or rashers of
    bacon
Salt and pepper
6 artichoke bottoms (you can use
    tinned)
1 shallot, chopped
30 ml (2 tbsp) tomato purée
150 ml (5 fl oz) water and white
    wine
24 stoned green olives
Strips of lard

Stud the fillet of beef with strips of lard. Insert slivers of garlic and truffle into slits made with a small knife.

Wrap the fillet with pig's caul or rashers of bacon.

Season and roast for 25 minutes at 200°C, 400°F, gas mark 6.

Meanwhile, cook the artichoke bottoms in water and wine with shallots and tomato purée for 20 minutes. Season.

Slice the beef and serve on 6 plates with the artichoke garnish seasoned to taste.

Scald the olives and divide them among the 6 plates as an additional garnish.

Marie-Pierre Gicquiaux

Chef de Cuisine/Co-proprietor
  with Patrick Gicquiaux
Le Château de Léauville
Landujan 35360
France
Tel: 99.07.21.14

Marie-Pierre is the *cordon bleu* chef ruling the kitchen and keeping an eye on the accounts, while husband Patrick manages the château and the large estate. Keen to create a centre for leisure and pleasure, they have built a business out of a dilapidated castle and, after three years of toil and tears, have made it into a paradise for guests. 'The guests are our friends', they say, 'and our château, their home'.

The menu offers interesting local dishes such as Pot-au-feu-de-faisan (an old pheasant is used instead of the domestic fowl). The Terrine de gibier was as good as the Pâté-terrine from the local charcutier, and the Charlotte aux poires with a butterscotch sauce was a dream.

The château has the romantic appeal of a George Sand novel. The establishment is located 30 km (19 miles) from Rennes, outside the town of Landujan. It has a swimming pool and tennis court, with a golf course nearby. Léauville is set amidst greenery and woodlands and features an attractive rose garden which blooms till late November.

Oie de Léauville   Goose casserole flavoured with candied lemon

6 portions

3 kg (7 lb) goose
3 whole lemons
1 bouquet garni
75 g (3 oz) sugar
90 ml (6 tbsp) gin
Salt and pepper

Place the bouquet garni and water to a depth of 5 cm (2 in) in a pressure cooker and bring it to boiling point.

Cut the goose into 8 pieces, removing surplus fat. Place pieces in the pressure cooker and cook for 1 hour 15 minutes under pressure.

Peel the lemons with a zester or potato peeler to remove the thin skins without the pith. Remove the pips and pith completely, using only pulp and rinds. Cut into strips.

Preheat the oven at 180°C, 350°F, gas mark 4, and roast the goose after it has been steamed. The idea is to get it crisp and golden, so cook it for 25 minutes until golden brown. Season it at this stage.

Now candy the lemon. Dissolve the sugar in 45 ml (3 tbsp) water and heat until it caramelizes. Add the rind of lemon, pulp and cook like jam for 5 minutes. Remove from heat and leave mixture in the same saucepan.

Remove the goose. Remove the fat from the roasting tray but collect the meat juice, which you add to the caramelized lemon strips. Boil this gravy, adding a little water if necessary. Season it and pour gravy over the goose portions.

Garnish with new potatoes and serve a side plate of green salad as an accompaniment.

The two processes of cooking, part-steaming and part-roasting, ensure the elimination of surplus fat from the goose.

Paul R. Gilmore

General Manager/Executive Chef
de Cuisine
Swinfen Hall Hotel
Swinfen
Near Lichfield
Staffordshire WS14 9RS
Tel: (0543) 481494

Paul Gilmore was trained at Staffordshire College and gained his basic experience under David Evans at the Yew Tree Restaurant in Stratford-upon-Avon. He was appointed head chef at the Copper Inn in Pangbourne, and for many years thrilled the clientele with a very sophisticated cuisine based on common sense and much artistic licence. He had a spell of 3 years as a lecturer at Clarendon College in Nottingham, which gave him an insight into the teaching of cookery.

The menu offers Scallops in saffron sauce and a veal dish with unusual vegetables, namely baby beets and turnips all cut and served in small side dishes; also Chilled melon with smoked salmon, Salad of Cornish mussels and avocado with tomatoes, Game sausages with wild mushrooms, and Gingered carrot soup. Being traditional, he insists on continuing to serve the finest Aberdeen beef in red wine sauce as well as a vegetarian dish of Woodland mushrooms on a peppercorn custard. Three of his specialities show the artist, namely Langoustines royal (Mousse of king prawns), Ris de veau (Sweetbread with wild berries), and Noisette d'agneau (Lamb loin with Meursault wine).

The sweet section is equally well planned: Rhubarbe brûlée flavoured with saffron is most unusual and a Hot caramelized apple baked on pastry has that touch of delicate flavour which reminds us of the famous Tart of Mademoiselle Tatin (whoever she was), and the Corbeille of fruit recipe is included as his contribution.

The prices of the meals are quite reasonable and we wish Paul continued success in his new venture.

The hotel boasts magnificent rooms, including 19 luxury bedrooms and a 65-seat restaurant with an enchanting ambience.

The hotel is located only a few miles from Lichfield, the town of the family residence of the Queen's cousin, Lady Anson, who is one of our patrons. Lichfield, birthplace of Dr Johnson, lies amidst green fields and has a beautiful cathedral and a wealth of historical lore.

Corbeille de Fruit d'Automne   Autumnal fruit almond basket

4 portions

Almond pastry (based on 'langue de chat' mixture)
100 g (4 oz) plain flour
100 g (4 oz) sifted icing sugar
100 g (4 oz) butter
3 large egg whites
25 g (1 oz) nibbed almonds
2 drops orange essence or blossom

Filling
1 ripe, top-quality Comice or William's Bon Chrétien pear, cored, peeled, and sliced
100 g (4 oz) each of raspberries, stoned cherries, and wild strawberries, all cleaned and trimmed ready for use
15 g (½ oz) icing sugar

Pineapple sauce
2 slices of fresh pineapple
100 ml (4 fl oz) pineapple juice
100 ml (4 fl oz) yoghurt
2 strands of saffron

To make the almond baskets
In a bowl, cream the flour, sugar, butter and egg whites with a pinch of salt to a soft consistency. Add the almonds. Place 4 flan rings on a greased tray and into each one pour and evenly spread the mixture. Bake in a preheated oven for 8 minutes at 180°C, 350°F, gas mark 4, until golden. While the pastry is still hot divide it into 4 and place over 4 inverted pudding moulds so that the pastry takes on the shape of a basket. Leave to cool until hard.

Boil the pineapple pieces and juice for 5 minutes and liquidize, adding the saffron while still hot. Blend in the yoghurt and lemon juice and liquidize again or pass through a sieve. Cool the sauce and pour on to 4 plates.

Dust the baskets with icing sugar and place carefully on 4 plates, filling each, with a medley of fruits, and settling each basket into the pool of pineapple sauce. As a summer alternative to pineapple, raspberry, or strawberry sauce could be used.

Jany and Pierre Gleize

Chef-Proprietors
La Bonne Etape
Château-Arnoux 04160
Chemin du Lac
France
Tel: 92.64.00.09

Pierre was a patissier who, on a bike trip a long time ago, met the daughter of a hotelier. They married and lived happily ever after. He became a chef patron par excellence and now, with his son Jany, works in the kitchen of their restaurant. They use the produce from their garden, and Provençal herbs are the most aromatic additives to food you can possibly have. Take, for example, Mountain lamb roasted with rosemary, or the Local goat cheese on curly lettuce leaves. Pierre Gleize offers seven table-d'hôte menus, some featuring feathered game, with a break for a Pear liqueur sorbet to cool the mouth between each savoury course. Typically Provençal is his Terrine of scallops and sea urchins. On offer are Wild boar pâté, Caviar of red mullet roe, known as *poutargue*, and Fillet of beef flavoured with fresh vanilla and flamed in white rum. This Inn on the Hill (another name for the restaurant) has become a Garden of Eden for epicures for miles around.

The Bonne Etape, is an authentic eighteenth-century posthouse located in a setting of sweet-smelling hills and hundred-year-old olive trees, pines and cypresses. It is located on the Napoleon road half-way to Grenoble and the Riviera. From the top of the mountain the view is breathtaking. The guests can also enjoy the swimming pool on the terrace, where meals are served.

Terrine d'Oursins aux Coquilles Saint Jacques   Sea urchin and scallop terrine

6 portions

450 g (1 lb) white fish (sea or
    river) filleted, skinned and
    minced
2 egg whites
300 ml (10 fl oz) double cream
Salt and pepper
8 sea urchins, red coral of the
    flesh only
8 scallops, white meat and coral
    only, cut in slices if large,
    washed and dried
4 sprigs of basil, chopped

Sauce
45 ml (3 tbsp) olive oil
Juice and thinly grated rind of
    1 lemon
1 shallot
2 sprigs of basil
15 ml (1 tbsp) parsley or chervil
5 ml (1 tsp) sweet mustard
15 ml (1 tbsp) yoghurt or soft
    cream cheese

Garnish
Segments of lime and oranges
1 red pepper

Place the minced raw fish in a bowl over a basin filled with ice cubes. Blend in the egg whites and then the double cream. Season with 5 ml (1 tsp) of salt and a good pinch of white pepper.

Oil an oblong mould, and line it with cling film and vine leaves, bottom and sides. Place in it a layer of fish mousse and rows of scallop, urchin coral, and basil. Repeat. The final topping is minced fish. Smooth with a palette knife. Cover with oiled vine leaves.

Place a sheet of foil on top, and place the dish on a tray of water.

Bake in preheated oven at 200°C, 400°F, gas mark 6, for 40 minutes. Remove and cool. Then chill the terrine.

Sauce
Liquidize all the listed ingredients of the sauce at the last moment.

To serve, slice the terrine to a finger's thickness. Place on plates with the sauce and segments of orange and lime. A thin julienne of red peppers can be sprinkled over the orange or the terrine of fish for colour contrast.

Richard Green

Chef de Cuisine
The Bear Hotel
Charman Street
Hungerford
Berkshire
Tel: (0488) 82512

Richard Green learnt part of his craft in Alsace under Marc Decker, the owner of L'Homme Sauvage and, more recently, came second in the British best chef competition.

On perusing the menu, we were impressed by the variety of the food as well as the quality of service and high standard of this hotel under the eye of Miguel Aries who previously managed the Algeciras and the Campamento in Cadiz.

We recommend the Salmon with a pike mousseline and saffron sauce and the Best end of lamb cooked with herbs and served with a mustard sauce.

The hotel has been an inn since the thirteenth century. Each year it holds three week-long gastronomic festivals, during which a master chef presents his own specialities.

Carré d'Agneau à la Moutarde aux Herbes Rack of lamb with mustard and herbs

4 portions

2 best ends of lamb, trimmed, chined and skinned in one piece

Coating
30 ml (2 tbsp) made English mustard
15 ml (1 tbsp) mixed fresh and chopped herbs: basil, mint, tarragon, thyme, parsley and chopped chives
150 g (5 oz) brown breadcrumbs
60 ml (2 fl oz) butter and oil mixed
Salt and black pepper

Mint sauce
8 mint leaves
15 ml (1 tbsp) brown sugar
75 ml (3 fl oz) sherry vinegar
15 ml (1 tbsp) Crème de Menthe

Sprinkle seasoning over each rack of lamb.

In a bowl, mix beaten egg and mustard with salt and black pepper. Dip the fat part of the loin in this egg mixture, and coat with breadcrumbs, blended with herbs.

Place the 2 racks on a roasting tray and butter over the crumb-coated part.

Roast in a preheated oven at 200°C, 400°F, gas mark 6, and cook for 30 minutes, basting with butter from time to time over the roasted part. When cooked, the lamb is carved into cutlets, with 1 rib per cutlet, and served with courgettes or French beans.

Mint sauce
Liquidize all the sauce ingredients in heated vinegar.
Serve cold with the hot lamb.

Robert Grindle

Chef de Cuisine
Sunlaw House Hotel
Kelso
Borders TD5 8JZ
Scotland
Tel: (05735) 331

Robert Grindle was born in Normanton in Yorkshire. He attended Telford College in Edinburgh and gained further experience in many country houses of good reputation, including Nivington House in Cliesh, the Green Park in Pitlochry, Pollathie House Hotel in Stanley, Montgreenan Mansion House in Ayrshire, and the Duke of Roxburghe Hotel at Kelso.

Scotland is known for the quality of its Aberdeen Angus beef, its rivers teeming with salmon and trout, and its seaports with fish which are processed by the best methods: from freezing to canning and smoking.

Robert Grindle prefers traditional cooking to *nouvelle cuisine* although he presents the classical dishes of Scotland with imagination. The venison is now bred commercially and is very popular.

Looking at his menu, we noted grouse, the finest game bird in gastronomy, to be roasted pinkish for 17 minutes and served with bread sauce and gravy on a crust of bread. We were impressed by a haddock mousse, a change from smoked salmon, which is itself simply served, thinly sliced and wrapped round the haddock mousse.

The ducal castle is known for its romantic architecture, especially its crenellated walls. It is the home of our chief patron, The Duke of Roxburghe. The manager of the Hotel is David J. Corkill, one of the officers of the Circle.

Fishing and shooting are two outdoor activities enjoyed by visiting royalty such as the Duke of York, who is a frequent visitor. The Sunlaw Hotel's guests are always privileged visitors of the castle.

The spectacular Berwickshire coast offers everything from sailing to skin diving. Sunlaw is the perfect location for touring the Borders. Seven famous stately houses, including Abbotsford, the home of Sir Walter Scott, are within an hour's drive.

Escalope de Tweed à l'Oseille   Salmon with sorrel sauce

4 portions

1 600 g (1 lb 4 oz) fillet of salmon,
   skinned
150 g (5 oz) sorrel leaves,
   trimmed and washed
1 shallot, chopped
150 ml (5 fl oz) fish stock made
   with bones and water
75 ml (3 fl oz) vermouth
75 ml (3 fl oz) double cream
Salt and pepper

Garnish
Cherry tomatoes
Cucumber
Salmon caviar

Place a 600 g (1 lb 4 oz) salmon fillet between two sheets of oiled paper or polythene and flatten it gently with a wooden mallet into a thinner piece. Cut into four portions.

Boil the stock with vermouth and shallot for 15 minutes. Add the sorrel, and cook for 30 seconds, then whisk the cream into the mixture to emulsify it. Season to taste.

Heat 30 ml (2 tbsp) oil in a pan and pan-fry the salmon for 30 seconds. Pour a pool of sauce on to 4 plates and arrange a salmon piece in the centre of each. Decorate with cherry tomatoes, cucumber cut in boat shapes and filled with salmon caviar.

Duo de Cailles Kelso   Quails with chestnut dressing, Drambuie and kumquats

2 portions

2 plump quails, boned completely
75 g (3 oz) butter and oil

Forcemeat
50 g (2 oz) minced veal
50 g (2 oz) cooked chestnuts
1 egg
30 ml (2 tbsp) whisky
Salt and pepper
A pinch of mace
150 ml (5 fl oz) game stock made
   from the bones

Garnish
2 small toasts trimmed and cut to
   the size of the quails
2 kumquats
4 marrons glacés
60 ml (4 tbsp) Drambuie liqueur

Combine the ingredients of the forcemeat into a paste and season. Stuff the two quails with the forcemeat. Season the birds. Heat butter and oil and pan-fry the quails for 5 minutes to brown them all round. Remove from the pan and place in a small casserole dish. Add whisky and Drambuie and game stock. Cover with a lid. Roast in a preheated oven at 220°C, 425°F, gas mark 7, for 10–15 minutes. Remove the birds and keep warm. Boil the liquid in a small saucepan to reduce it by half. Season to taste. Strain.

Pour gravy on to 4 plates. Arrange each quail on a croûton of bread and garnish with kumquats, cut in half, and whole marrons glacés.

Michel Guérard

Chef de Cuisine
Les Prés d'Eugénie
Eugénie-les-Bains
Landes 40320
France
Tél: 58.51.19.01

A memorable moment in Michel Guérard's life came when his wife told him that he was too fat. From that moment he began to devise slimming diets, and consequently published the recipes as his outstanding *Cuisine Minceur*. His genius was revealed by the simplicity of the fare and its artistic presentation. He then went the opposite way with his next book, *Cuisine Gourmande*, which revealed him as the grand master of cuisine he has now become.

When you read a menu of his it is like enjoying a poem by Victor Hugo. It has rhythm, depth of thinking, and the power to make the gourmet's mouth water. He describes goose liver simply as Hachis of goose with truffles. He also mixes crayfish and frog's legs with *herbes fraîches*. His lobster is roasted and smoked on an open fire. Our favourite is the rabbit dish cooked in St Emilion. As for desserts, his Light pancake filled with passion fruit with a raspberry coulis has been served up by cooks the world over. But his Dessert du Roi takes our silver trophy. It is a hot soufflé with granite (a sort of sorbet) and a light cream custard.

Eugénie-les-Bains is a spa which attracts people from all over the world, and many come especially to eat at Les Prés d'Eugénie, where you have to book long in advance. It is a splendid establishment which has won him international fame.

L'Oeuf de Michel Guérard Creamed eggs with caviar

6 portions

6 eggs
25 g (1 oz) butter
15 ml (1 tbsp) chives, chopped
15 ml (1 tbsp) double cream
  (or yoghurt)
15 ml (1 tbsp) Beluga caviar
1 lemon, cut in wedges
Toasted fingers of bread (soldiers),
  Italian stick biscuits, celery
  sticks or other *crudités*
Salt and pepper

Slice the tops of 6 eggs with a fine, saw-edged knife, cutting the shell about 1 cm (½ in) above its widest part. Empty the contents into a bowl. Wash the shells and their 'hats' in hot water and put them on a cloth to dry.

Beat the eggs lightly. Heat the butter in a pan and scramble the eggs for a few minutes to a creamy consistency on moderate heat.

Season the mixture, and blend in the chopped chives and cream (or yoghurt, for low fat content).

Place the empty eggshells in eggcups and fill two-thirds of each shell with the egg mixture. Top up with real Beluga caviar. Replace the 'hats' and serve with wedges of lemon, fingers of toasted bread, Italian stick biscuits as thin as pencils, sticks of celery, or other *crudités*.

Michel recommends using other roes if caviar is too expensive, such as lump roe, cod roe, or salmon roe. If you wish, you could also use smoked salmon or chopped tomato pulp.

Philippe Guérin

Chef de Cuisine/Proprietor
Auberge de l'Ile
37220 L'Ile-Bouchard
France
Tel: 47.58.51.07

Philippe Guérin's name has been famous for a long while, even as far away as America. He was trained at the Collège Albert Bayet in Tours. He practised fish cookery at the famous fish restaurant Prunier-Traktir in Paris and then he worked in the USA and Canada, where he became well known for his fish specialities.

In 1978 he bought the Inn of the Ile-Bouchard, and has not looked back since. In his new career as a restaurateur he has blossomed and harvested many awards.

We selected from his comprehensive menu a Goat cheese in pastry to eat with a glass of the local Loire wine. The fish, which will always win the day, was monkfish, the monster angler fish with its huge head and tail yet with a flesh that has the delicacy of a scampi. Médaillons de lotte with a leek purée sauce was just right, and the two recipes collected are neatly formulated for anyone to prepare at home.

The restaurant is an old house on an island in the middle of a river. It has a terrace overlooking the river, and in the summer meals are served there. The dining-room is plainly furnished, but huge silver platters serve as under-dishes for the plated food. Philippe Guérin is affable and efficient and his manner betrays the kind-hearted cook with the gentle touch.

Sainte-Maure en Croûte   Goat cheese in pastry

4 portions

450 g (1 lb) puff pastry
1 large egg, beaten
300 g (11 oz) goat cheese

Garnish
Assorted wild lettuce and
    dandelion leaves

Roll the pastry 4 mm (¼ in) thick and with a cutter make 4 rounds 8 cm (3¼ in) in diameter and 4 rounds 9 cm (3½ in) in diameter for the toppings.

Cut the oblong goat cheese into thick slices 75 g (3 oz) each. Place the bottom rounds on a greased baking tray, and on each pastry base place a piece of the cheese. Brush the edges with beaten egg and cover the cheese with another layer of pastry. Mark cross lines with the prongs of a fork on top and brush the top with beaten egg again. Rest for 30 minutes and bake in a preheated oven at 200°C, 400°F, gas mark 6, for 20 minutes. Serve piping hot, on 4 plates over the green salad leaves.

Médaillons de Lotte à la Fondue de Poireaux   Monkfish with leek purée

4 portions

4 large leeks (use white part only)
150 ml (5 fl oz) white wine
1 kg (2 lb 2 oz) monkfish fillets,
    trimmed and sliced across the
    tail in small pieces 8 mm
    (½ in) thick
50 ml (2 fl oz) double cream
100 g (4 oz) butter
4 medium tomatoes, skinned,
    seeded and cut in wedges
450 g (1 lb) spinach, ribs removed
2 cherry tomatoes, skinned,
    halved and seeded (yellow
    kind)
Salt and pepper

Mince 3 of the leeks. Wash, and drain and keep aside in a bowl.
    Slice 1 leek. Wash, drain and keep in another bowl.
    Wash and drain the spinach. Boil for 1 minute. Drain well, squeeze
the moisture out and keep in reserve in another bowl.
    Bring the wine and minced leek to the boil and cook for 1 minute.
Season to taste, strain the minced leek and keep in a bowl. Use the
liquor to poach the fish for 1 minute only. Then remove it with a slotted
spoon.
    Finish the sauce by boiling the liquor with the minced leek again for
3 minutes. Add the cream and reduce by half. Season.
    In a pan, heat butter 25 g (2 tbsp) and cook the tomatoes for
30 seconds. Remove skins.
    Boil the sliced leek for 3 minutes in water and then drain.
    Reheat the spinach in 40 g (3 tbsp) butter for 3 minutes. Season to
taste.
    Now all the ingredients have been cooked separately.
    Arrange a pool of the leek sauce on 4 plates. In the centre, place a
heap of the sliced leek, and around it some spinach in a ring-like
presentation alternating with skinned raw tomatoes.

Michael Guillaumou

Chef de Cuisine
Hôtel le Mas d'Huston
Résidence du Golf
St-Cyprien-Plage 66750
France
Tèl: 68.21.01.71

Michael Guillaumou is a pupil of Michel Guérard, and his style of presentation has helped him to embellish the regional fish specialities of Languedoc.

His menu offers the whole range of seafood that one would expect from an establishment located on the Mediterranean and includes Red mullet, Monkfish roasted with garlic, Ratatouille of aubergines, Grilled sardines, and even Paella of shellfish and the luxury items of Foie de canard, wild duck and other game when in season. We favour his Râble de lièvre in wine.

The golf course is the main attraction in this part of the newly developed estate, which was launched in 1968. The hotel director is Patrice Socquet.

Filets de Maquereaux Bayaldi   Mackerel with aubergines and tomatoes

4 portions

Anchovy sauce
4 anchovy fillets (canned)
60 ml (4 tbsp) single cream
1 clove garlic
60 ml (4 tbsp) oil from anchovies
50g (2 oz) butter

Main ingredients
4 large mackerel fillets
4 large tomatoes, skinned, deseeded and sliced
2 aubergines, sliced with skin
2 courgettes, sliced slantwise with skin
4 basil leaves
Salt and pepper
60 ml (4 tbsp) oil

Garnish
Slices of lemon
Sprigs of basil and parsley

Anchovy sauce
Liquidize the ingredients wth the butter. Keep the mixture in a cup to be used at the last minute.

Wash the mackerel in water with a little vinegar and salt to remove all traces of blood. It will bleach the flesh too. Drain and pat dry. Brush on a little oil, and grill for 5 minutes.

Oil a shallow dish and place the mackerel fillets in it. Cover with tomatoes and courgettes.

Wash the aubergines in hot water to remove their bitter taste, and place them on top of the courgettes, overlapping neatly.

Pour the anchovy sauce over the aubergines and cover the dish with foil (well greased). Bake for 20–25 minutes in a medium oven at 180°C, 350°F, gas mark 4.

Decorate the dish with sliced, peeled lemon and sprigs of basil and parsley.

Râble de Lièvre au Vin   Saddle of hare in wine

2 portions

The whole saddle (loin part) of a
    large hare
150 ml (5 fl oz) red wine
1 carrot, cut in small cubes
1 onion, chopped
1 bouquet garni
4 juniper berries
4 crushed peppercorns
2 shallots, chopped
10 ml (2 tsp) wine vinegar
100 ml (4 fl oz) cream
5 ml (1 tsp) made mustard
Oil or butter

Skin the saddle and leave it on the bone. Soak it in the wine with carrot, onion and bouquet garni to marinade overnight.
   Remove and wipe dry.
   Boil the marinade until reduced by half.
   Roast the saddle for 15 minutes. Baste with oil or butter.
   Heat 30 ml (2 tbsp) oil and sauté the shallots for 1 minute, add vinegar and reduced wine marinade. Boil for 5 minutes more and strain. Reheat, and add cream and seasoning.
   Slice the meat from the saddle to produce about 3 thin slivers per portion. Pour a pool of sauce on 2 plates and arrange the meat neatly fanwise. Decorate with a sprig of watercress or crisp potatoes.

Terrine de Foie de Canard au Maury   Duck liver pâté with wine and Armagnac

8 portions

1 kg 200 g (3 lb) duck livers,
    cleaned and free from gall
20 ml (4 tsp) salt
1.25 ml (½ tsp) black pepper
1.25 ml (½ tsp) mixed spices
5 ml (1 tsp) sugar
50 ml (2 fl oz) Maury wine or
    sweet sherry
25 ml (2 tbsp) Armagnac spirit

Clean the liver carefully. Wash well and drain, then season and place in a container with all the other ingredients to absorb the flavour overnight.
   Next day, place all the ingredients in a greased oblong terrine. Cover with well-greased foil, place the terrine in a deep dish half filled with water. Bake at 150°C, 300°F, gas mark 2, for 40 minutes.
   Cool completely and refrigerate overnight.
   Note: The raw liver can be soaked in milk with a pinch of saltpetre before use; this will make it slightly pink like ham.

Paul Hart

Chef de Cuisine
Britannia Hotel
Portland Street
Manchester M1 3LA
Tel: (061) 228 2288

Paul spent a four years' apprenticeship with the Embassy Hotels. His first kitchen was at the Bellingham Hotel at Wigan and then Robert's Restaurant in the same town, where he learned Italian cuisine as well.

His father was a baker and his mother worked in a pastry shop, from where he got his inspiration to become a chef — undoubtedly inspired by the smell of hot bread.

Typical dishes on the menu include Joints of prime Scotch beef, Leg of pork with apple and cranberries, and classic Beef Wellington 'en croûte.'

He also has a Sole coated with brandy as one of the lighter entrées, and a vegetarian entrée of leeks, lentils and split peas rippled with cream.

The Britannia is located in the heart of busy Manchester and the business is thriving. My impression when we were staying at this Victorian-style hotel was of an old music hall.

Sole Britannia Fillets of sole poached in wine with grapes

2 portions

4 sole fillets, 100 g (4 oz) each
60 ml (4 tbsp) caviar
150 ml (5 fl oz) water and white
  wine mixed
225 g (8 oz) fish bones
2 shallots, chopped
1 bouquet garni
75 g (3 oz) seedless grapes
Salt and pepper
Juice of ½ lemon
Lettuce leaves for garnish

Flatten the fillets of sole lightly to break fibres. Spread a little caviar (sturgeon or salmon) on each side. Roll up from the filleted side. Tie up each fillet with string, or fix with a skewer.

Boil the water and wine with fish bones, shallots, and bouquet garni for 25 minutes. Strain the liquor into a small sauté pan and season. Poach the fish for 12 minutes. Scald the grapes for 20 seconds or leave raw. Serve the fish on lettuce leaves with grapes, plain and simple. Season to taste. Squeeze the juice of the lemon over the fish.

If you wish, the stock can be thickened with a little cream and the resulting sauce served separately.

Tranche de Boeuf au Vin rouge

Topside of beef, pot braised, with smoked bacon, field mushrooms, and red wine

4 portions

675 g (1 lb 8 oz) topside of beef (tied)
1 large onion, diced
2 large carrots, diced
150 g (6 oz) lean smoked back bacon, diced
100 g (4 oz) field mushrooms, sliced
150 ml (6 fl oz) red wine
Salt and freshly milled black pepper
Flour and water paste
600 ml (1 pt) beef stock

Place the meat on the vegetables and bacon. Moisten with red wine, cover with beef stock, and season. Seal the lid of your pot with flour and water paste. Cook in a low oven for 3 hours at 170°C, 325°F, gas mark 3.

Serve with braised cabbage and freshly made buttered noodles.

Pierre Hiély

Chef de Cuisine/Proprietor
Hiély
5 Rue de la République
Avignon 84000
France
Tel: 90.86.17.07

Hiély Restaurant has been famous for many years. Hiély's menus have changed to conform to current trends. His Soupe de coquillage with fennel is no longer Bouillabaisse. His pastry filling of oysters and scallops with Belgian endives has nothing local about it, but his Cassolette de corail d'oursins (sea urchins) was featured before in a different way. Even so we recognize the classic Provençal dishes he presents.

The Pieds et paquets Provençale, made up of sheep's tripe and trotters, is a regional dish, but in general we see the best ingredients presented more appetizingly on plates, for example Breast of chicken with cabbage and goose liver, Guinea-fowl with fruit, Saddle of rabbit with pepper sauce. These are old dishes looking the better for this revamped presentation. Hiély is the best eating place in Avignon.

The name Avignon means 'dominator of the river'. This is the region where the popes had their castles for many years in the fourteenth century and the Pope's Palace is worth a visit, as is the famous Bridge of St Bénézet.

Feuilleté d' Huitres de Bouzigues et St Jacques aux Endives
Oysters and scallops with chicory

4 portions

225 g (8 oz) puff pastry
Flour for dusting
4 oysters
4 large scallops
2 shallots, chopped
150 ml (5 fl oz) dry white wine
75 ml (2½ fl oz) double cream
Juice of ½ lemon
Salt and pepper
25 ml (1 fl oz) oil and butter
2 witloof chicories (Belgian
   endives), sliced across

Roll the pastry on a pastry board dusted with flour, and cut 4 triangles, 5 mm (¼ in) thick with 8-cm (3-in) sides. Place on a greased tray and bake in preheated oven at 200°C, 400°F, gas mark 6, for 15–20 minutes. Remove from the oven. This pastry will be used as a topping. It can be cut in different shapes: oval, round or square.

Open the oysters and scallops. Reserve the juice of the oysters in a bowl. Clean the scallops. Discard the beard and use only white meat and red coral. Cut the scallops in slices laterally.

Boil the shallots with the wine for 3 minutes. Poach the scallops for 2 minutes and the oysters for 30 seconds. Scoop out with a slotted spoon and keep warm on a plate while finishing the sauce.

Blend the cream into the sauce and boil for 2 minutes. Season and add half the lemon juice. Heat the oil and butter and stir-fry the chicory slices for 5 minutes. Keep them slightly crispy if possible. Season and add a little lemon juice.

Add the oyster juice to the sauce and on 4 plates place a row of the chicory slices, then the scallops and oysters, and then pour the sauce over. Top with the piece of pastry, placed on one side.

Note: A pastry casing can also be used, and the ingredients placed inside as a filling, as for a vol-au-vent.

Baba Hine

Chef de Cuisine/Proprietor
Corse Lawn House Hotel
Corse Lawn
Gloucestershire GL19 4LZ
Tel: (045278) 531

Baba Hine is a *cordon bleu* with a plus. She belongs to the famous Hine Cognac family, and one would think that the food would reek of spirit, from Bisque to Crêpes flambées, but to our surprise the fare was more simple and truly delicious.

However, the venison dish she cooked had been soaked in port wine, and the light Brochette de fruits served as a dessert could have been flavoured with Grand Marnier. Baba uses the vegetables from her garden.

Her contribution is based on snails in garlic butter, except she substituted stuffed Queen scallops.

Corse Lawn House Hotel is an elegant Queen Anne listed building set back from the village. It is fronted by an unusual ornamental pond and surrounded by 4 acres of gardens and fields. The hotel is located close to the Cotswolds, Malvern Hills, and the Forest of Dean, 20 minutes from Gloucester, Cheltenham, and Worcester.

Petites Coquilles Baba Hine Queen scallops with parsley butter

4 portions

48 fresh Queen scallops (allow 12 small scallops per portion) they are the small variety known as *petoncles* in French

Filling
100 g (4 oz) soft butter
25 g (1 oz) white breadcrumbs
2 cloves garlic, chopped
30 ml (2 tbsp) parsley, chopped
30 ml (2 tbsp) Gruyère cheese, grated
Salt and pepper

Open the scallops by sliding a small sharp knife between the top and bottom of shells. Cut through the muscle holding the flat shell in place. Remove the flesh from the concave part of the shell. Discard the fringe round it and use only the white part (noix) and the orange coral. Wash them in cold water to remove all traces of sand, and drain. Allow 3 small pieces per shell, using the concave shell as a container. Wash this part of the shell and discard the flat shells. (To produce 4 filled shells per portion.)

When the dish is required, simply fill each deep shell with 3 pieces of scallop and place it in a tray with coarse salt, or use snail dishes which have a hollow cavity to prevent the shell from tilting the filling out.

Filling
In a bowl, cream all the filling ingredients together. Place 5 ml (1 tsp) of the mixture on top of the flesh of each filled shell, and spread the butter over with a palate knife to cover the scallop meat completely. Sprinkle breadcrumbs on top. Then bake in a very hot oven at 220°C, 425°F, gas mark 7, for 5 minutes, as you do with snails cooked in this manner.

Note: Large scallops are called King scallops.

Colin Hingston

Chef de Cuisine
Thornbury Castle
Thornbury
Bristol
Avon BS12 1HH
Tel: (0454) 418511

Rhodesian-born Colin Hingston is the talented and imaginative chef who presides over the kitchen at Thornbury Castle.

Colin began his culinary career in Shropshire, where he developed his skills in various restaurants in that area. He joined the 'Castle' as sous-chef 8 years ago and has been promoted to his present position.

In studying the intriguing menu of this well-known establishment we were impressed by the wealth and quality of dishes offered. They all have a very grand and polished style, which is still characteristically British. Simplicity and good taste seem to be the hallmarks of this bill of fare. From the Mousse of Cornish crab to the Stuffed breast of chicken in Pernod, and including a vegetarian dish of Aubergines, wild mushrooms and pistachio nuts, all the items have that grand look of classicism. We were also tempted by the sweets — from a good old-fashioned Lemon syllabub (cream flavoured with lemon and wine) to the Hot butterscotch pudding and Honey saffron tart.

The Castle is owned by an American, Maurice C. R. Taylor and managed by J. Strong, both keen on maintaining their styles and welcoming important guests, like the Duke of Roxburghe. Thornbury Castle lies on the northern edge of the small country town of Thornbury, 5 miles (8 km) from the Severn Bridge and the junctions of the M4 and M5 motorways.

In 1510 it was owned by the ill-fated 3rd Duke of Buckingham, but he fell into disgrace and was executed by Henry VIII who appropriated it as a royal residence for 33 years. Today, Thornbury Castle still stands, surrounded by its vineyard gardens and high walls. The restaurant has two dining-rooms, which are baronial in style, with panelled walls, heraldic shields and large open fires.

Filet de Lotte à l'Aneth et Gingembre   Fillet of monkfish sautéd with dill and ginger

1 portion

50 ml (2 fl oz) clarified butter for
   frying
180 g (6 oz) monfish in thin slices
50 ml (2 fl oz) dry Martini
1 stem ginger preserved in syrup,
   thinly sliced
25 ml (1 fl oz) Crabbies Ginger
   Wine
100 ml (4 fl oz) double cream
salt and pepper
Chopped dill

Heat the butter in a heavy pan. Fry the fish, turning it over, then add
the dry vermouth and ginger. Cook quickly for 5 minutes, stirring from
time to time. Add the cream and seasoning. Simmer for 5 minutes.
   If there is too much sauce (monkfish can give out a lot of liquid),
remove the fish and boil the sauce down to a syrupy consistency.
   Serve with chopped dill.

Carré d'Agneau aux Amandes   Roast rack of lamb with mint and almond crust

4 portions

100 g (4 oz) fresh white
   breadcrumbs
15 g (½ oz) mint leaves, finely
   chopped
15 g (½ oz) small onion, finely
   chopped and sweated in butter
2 best ends of lamb total weight
   2 kg (4 lb 6 oz) (ask your
   butcher to French trim them)
50 g (2 oz) roughly chopped
   toasted almonds
Dijon mustard
100 ml (4 fl oz) red wine
300 ml (½ pint) strong brown
   lamb stock
25 g (1 oz) butter
Salt and pepper

For the crust: mix the breadcrumbs, mint, onion, and almonds together,
and season well with salt and pepper.
   Season the lamb. Heat a roasting tin. Seal the lamb quickly in the hot
pan on both sides. Roast for 10–12 minutes in a moderately hot oven,
200°C, 400°F, gas mark 6, until just pink. Remove the lamb and pour
off any fat that is in the pan. Deglaze with the red wine, add the stock,
and reduce by half. While the gravy is reducing, thinly paint the lamb
with Dijon mustard. Press the crust firmly on to the lamb, and brown
under a hot grill. Remove the gravy from the heat, and add a knob of
butter. Stir into the gravy, strain and serve.

Hugues Houard

Chef de Cuisine
Aux Armes de Champagne
L'Epine 51460
France
Tel: 26.68.10.43

The imagination and craftsmanship of Chef Houard is hard to define when one considers that a man who uses champagne in cooking has an obvious edge over our colleagues. His modesty does him credit, for the food he produces speaks for itself. Ably assisted by a brigade of seven, he offers a striking menu.

At the top of his menu is a glass of champagne for aperitif with a dash of ratafia liqueur for flavour. Not a drop of the bubbly is used in the starters, which include Raw marinaded salmon, Terrine of goose liver, and Rabbit terrine pâté.

In the hot entrées the liver is flavoured with the Bouzy wine. There is also Fricassee of lobster in Chinon wine and Fillet of turbot served with a soufflé of sea urchin. The Fillet of beef is served with port wine, but the Breast of hen pheasant is gloriously scented and simmered in good old champagne, which M Houard, in his gentle mood, decided to sweeten with honey. In this extraordinary menu we fancied a soufflé for dessert flavoured with lavender flowers. We never thought one could use such flavour in food. But it works.

This well-run hotel of modest appearance is located close to the old Gothic church. The building with red tiles could have been someone's house with its garden in front. The directors are M and Mme Denise Jean-Paul Pérardel, both perfect hosts and friendly people. The hotel is a traditional stopping-place for those who want to have a champagne meal and visit the great vineyards of Epernay.

Soufflé à la Fleur de Lavande Lavender-flavoured sweet soufflé

6 portions

8 lavender flowers, macerated in
    45 ml (3 tbsp) white grappa
    spirit for 30 minutes then
    strained to obtain the liquid
    flavouring agent
Flowers of 2 lavender sprigs
50 g (2 oz) soft butter
12 egg whites
1 pinch salt
150 g (5 oz) granulated sugar
5 egg yolks
100 g (4 oz) cooked pear purée
6 sponge biscuits
30 ml (2 tbsp) icing sugar (kept in
    dusting tin)

Apricot sauce
90 ml (6 tbsp) apricot jam or 5
    fresh or tinned apricots in
    syrup liquidized to a coulis

First butter the inside of 6 ramekin soufflé dishes (not melted). Sprinkle 30 ml (2 tbsp) granulated sugar on the inside and shake off surplus by inverting each mould. Make sure the sugar sticks to the walls of the moulds.

In a clean grease-free mixing bowl, place the egg whites (making sure that no specks of egg yolks go in). Add a pinch of salt and whip with a balloon whisk until stiff.

Add 150 g (5 oz) of granulated sugar, 1 tbsp at a time, beating between each addition until the meringue is stiff again. If you use an electric mixer the sugar can be added faster.

Fold the egg yolks and pear purée into this meringue, gradually and carefully mixing the meringue with a folding action.

Place a small broken biscuit in the bottom of each ramekin dish and soak it with the lavender spirit. Sprinkle with a few lavender petals as well. Fill the moulds to the brim with the mixture. Level off with a palette knife and make criss-cross marks with the prong of a fork.

Now, to help the soufflé rise straight without cracking, insert your thumb around the edges to detach the soufflé mixture a little from the walls of the moulds.

Place the moulds in a tray and bake in a preheated oven at 220°C, 425°F, gas mark 7, for 10–12 minutes. On removing from the oven, dust the top with icing sugar and serve the apricot coulis or jam sauce separately.

Iain Mackay Jack

Chef de Cuisine
The Park Hotel
Park Place
Cardiff CF1 3UD
Wales
Tel: (0222) 383471

Iain, a graduate of the City and Guilds in advanced cookery, has also served a full apprenticeship at the famous IOI restaurant in Glasgow, where many of our Scottish colleagues have learnt their gastronomic skills. In 1974 he worked for the Portpatrick Hotel, part of the Mount Charlotte Hotel group, and for the last 16 years has been employed at the Park Hotel in Cardiff.

Park Hotel's lavish menu does its job well, for it whets your appetite for a really good meal. Among the starters are the Platter of exotic fresh fruits with Malibu (coconut and rum liqueur).

The Terrine of crab and smoked salmon is a favourite in Wales, as is the Crab soup, for fish are plentiful. 'Surf and Turf' is a sort of medley of fillet of beef with large prawns and Maigret of duck with ginger and peach sauce has trendy appeal.

In Wales, both fish and the lamb are featured as part of the traditional cuisine. A recipe for Welsh salmon in foil as a starter and one for a loin of lamb are given to represent Park Hotel's worthy contribution to Welsh cuisine.

The Park Hotel has that warm atmosphere special to hotels rich in tradition. It is a conference centre of growing importance and provides banquets for up to 300 people in the White Hall Suite. The manager of this splendid hotel is Mr Hugh F. Hillary. The hotel is only 5 miles (8 km) from the M4 and 12 miles (19 km) from the airport.

Away from the city centre, but easily accessible, are Llandaff Cathedral and the Welsh Folk Museum at St Fagans. Cardiff is a tourist centre worth visiting, a door through which you can easily pass to reach the smooth green slopes of the Brecon Beacons — some over 2000 ft (600 m) high, and the cliffs and beaches of the Glamorgan Heritage Coast.

Aiguillette de Saumon à l'Aneth   Fillets of sewin (Welsh for small salmon) baked in foil

2 portions

2 skinned fillets of salmon 150 g
    (5 oz) each
25 g (1 oz) each of carrot, celery
    and spring onions, finely
    shredded or cut in strips
2 ferns of dill
50 g (2 oz) butter

Wine stock
150 g (5 oz) fish bones
1 small onion, sliced
150 ml (5 fl oz) white wine
1 bouquet garni
15 ml (1 tbsp) of kelp
    (dry seaweed)

Boil the stock ingredients for 30 minutes until reduced to 60 ml
(4 tbsp). Strain well.

Place the fish fillets on two pieces of foil. Top each fish with shredded
vegetables and fern of dill and 30 ml (2 tbsp) of reduced wine stock and
a little knob of butter.

Season to taste. Close the foil like a parcel and bake in a preheated
oven at 200°C, 400°F, gas mark 6, for 15 minutes. Serve from the
parcel with fresh salad of peeled cucumber and chopped mint with
yoghurt dressing (optional).

Longe d'Agneau Caerphilly   Loin of lamb stuffed with sweetbread and Welsh cheese

2 portions

1 boned loin of lamb 1 kg
    (2 lb 4 oz) weight
1 sweetbread

Stuffing
50 g (2 oz) Caerphilly cheese,
    crumbled
6 wild mint leaves
Salt and pepper
50 g (2 oz) honey
2 cloves of garlic, crushed
50 g (2 oz) chopped hazelnuts

Lay the boned loin of lamb on a board. Make sure to remove most of
the fat. Flatten it with a rolling pin. Season to taste.

Poach sweetbread for 8 minutes in water. Remove from heat. Refresh
in cold water. Drain and pat dry. Cut off skin and outside membrane
and cut the sweetbread into thin slices. Arrange the sweetbread slices
over the loin of lamb with the belly flap well spread. Sprinkle with
grated cheese and top with a few mint leaves. Roll the loin and tie it
with string.

Heat the honey and brush it on to the outside of the loin. Roll the
loin in garlic and crushed hazelnuts. Roast in a preheated oven at
200°C, 400°F, gas mark 6, for 18–20 minutes. Make sure to keep the
lean meat pinkish as most gourmets like it juicy.

Slice and place on two plates with French beans, asparagus tips or
with freshly boiled samphire (boil for 30 seconds only) — this seaweed
plant is very tender like asparagus. No gravy is required with this dish.

Note: The most widely known Welsh cheeses are Caerphilly Tiefi,
Tiefi herb, and Ponet Canet (a sort of goat cheese); all these excellent
cheeses are served with Welsh oatcakes or biscuits.

Claude Jaillant

Chef de Cuisine/Proprietor
Restaurant 'Le Mesnil'
2 Rue Pasteur
Le Mesnil-sur-Oger 51190
France
Tel: 26.57.95.57

Claude Jaillant was a student of the Hotel School of Rheims where he qualified in the fully comprehensive course of catering. He then went to gain more experience elsewhere, in such places as La Haute Mère Dieu at Châlons-sur-Marne, the exclusive Hôtel Roy René at Aix-en-Provence, the Château d'As at Baume-les-Dames and the Ferme de Saint-Simenon at Honfleur. In 1980 he started his own restaurant at Le Mesnil, under the same name. A 40-seater with sober décor but with generous fare. He stores 7000 bottles of wine in a cool cellar 7 metres (23 ft) deep. The wine is kept at 12°C in a chalk-lined vault.

The food reveals both the craftsmen and businessman, with 4 good simple table-d'hôte menus.

There are Snails cooked in champagne, Hot lobster terrine, Hot oysters, Duck stewed in wine, Beef champenoise and lovely desserts such as Charlotte Germaine, Sorbet in Champagne Sabayon aux fruits rouges. These are up-to-date menus which show that Claude Jaillant is in line with his contemporaries. This dedicated epicurean has given us two recipes: Monkfish in tomato coulis and Brill fillet in watercress sauce.

The restaurant is located in the heart of the Côte de Blancs, in a town in the middle of the Champagne region close to Epernay, Rheims and Châlons-sur-Marne.

The charm of this wine region is that you can visit the cellars of the big champagne houses and sample the bubbly.

Lotte rôtie au Coulis de Tomate   Monkfish in tomato coulis

4 portions

75 ml (3 fl oz) oil
2 cloves garlic, chopped

4 × 100 g (4 oz) monkfish fillets,
    or one large piece (tail part)

Tomato coulis
100 g (4 oz) butter
4 large tomatoes, skinned,
    seeded, and chopped
Salt and pepper

8 basil leaves

Heat 90 ml (6 tbsp) oil in a sauté pan and fry the garlic for 10 seconds.
    Pour this flavoured oil over the fish fillets on a roasting tray. Roast in preheated oven 225°C, 425°F, gas mark 7, for 12 minutes.
    Remove and keep hot. Cut into 4 portions if using 1 large piece. Cook the coulis ingredients until thick as jam. Season to taste.
    Pour a pool of this coulis on to 4 plates and arrange slices of monkfish over. Decorate with basil leaves.
    Variation: Serve sliced mushrooms cooked in butter for 30 seconds and blended into the tomato sauce.

Filet de Barbue Cressonière   Brill fillet in watercress sauce

4 portions

50 g (2 oz) butter
50 g (2 oz) sliced white
    mushrooms
4 brill fillets, 150 g (5 oz) each
150 ml (5 fl oz) white Macon wine
    or Champagne
1 bunch watercress, trimmed,
    minus stalks, leaves only,
    chopped
75 ml (3 fl oz) single cream
2 egg yolks
Salt, pepper and paprika
25 g (1 oz) peeled shrimps
150 g (5 oz) cucumber

Butter an ovenproof earthenware gratin dish. Sprinkle the sliced mushrooms all over the bottom and place the wine and 4 brill fillets on top, season to taste. Cover with greased paper. Bake for 10 minutes at 225°C, 425°F, gas mark 7. Keep hot.

Sauce
Drain the liquor into a saucepan, and boil it until it is reduced by half. Add the watercress leaves and boil for 30 seconds. Mix cream and egg yolks in a bowl and gradually add this to the sauce while stirring it to effect a liaison of a custard consistency. Season to taste. Simmer for 4 minutes.
    Heat the shrimps in the sauce for 20 seconds and pour this sauce on to 4 plates, arranging the fish fillets and the mushrooms over. Decorate with thin slices of raw cucumber. Dusk paprika pepper over the cucumber.

Martin James

Chef de Cuisine
Bodysgallen Hall Hotel
Llandudno
Gwynedd LL30 1RS
Wales
Tel: (0492) 84466

Martin began at Munich's best hotel, the Bayerischer, prior to a short spell at the Dorchester, then it was south to Bournemouth at the Carlton, where he began to reap the harvest of this sound training. The manager of the Bodysgallen Hall Hotel is Jonathan Thomson.

We like the idea of Sorbet and melon as a starter, or Hot Welsh shrimp salad, or Smoked breast of duck with Cumberland sauce.

The Loin of Welsh lamb with onion marmalade was something we were looking for as a local speciality. The Lemon sole with crab sauce reflects other specialities of this great country where one of our patrons, the Marquess of Anglesey, is representing our Epicurean Circle.

We were grateful to Kevin Pearson, the deputy manager, for introducing us to the splendour of this Welsh temple. Standing in its own grounds to the south of Llandudno and with spectacular views of Snowdonia, Bodysgallen Hall Hotel provides a warm hospitality to all visitors. This seventeenth-century house was restored and furnished in luxurious style, and outside the knot garden of box hedges filled with scented herbs, a rockery with a cascade, and the walled rose garden are fit to receive, if not the Prince of Wales, certainly all our epicurean princes.

Tartelette de Crabe Bodysgallen   Hot Anglesey crab and laver bread tartlet

4 portions

450 g (1 lb) short pastry
700 g (1 lb 8 oz) Anglesey crab
225 g (8 oz) Welsh laver bread
   (see the following recipe)
4 eggs
600 ml (1 pint) milk
2 shallots, chopped
1 bunch chives, chopped
5 ml (1 tsp) crushed coriander
   seeds
Salt and ground black pepper

Roll the pastry out thinly and line 4 individual greased tartlet moulds.

Boil the crab for 10 minutes, then crack the shell and remove all the meat. Combine the yellow meat with the white meat.

Whisk the eggs with the milk, chopped shallots, chives and coriander seeds then add the crabmeat.

Fill the tartlet moulds and put in a moderate oven, 180°C, 350°F, gas mark 4, for 20 minutes. Unmould and serve on a mixed lettuce leaf salad with a vinaigrette dressing, and serve with laver bread.

Pain d'Algues   Laver bread

4 portions

150 g (5 oz) fresh laver
150 g (5 oz) quick oats
600 ml (1 pint) water or milk
Salt and pepper
25 g (1 oz) bacon fat or butter

The Welsh name for this dish is *Bara lawr.* It is made from edible seaweed.

Laver bread and grilled bacon is a popular breakfast dish. The bread can also be served with fish or meat.

Soak the laver in running water for 3 hours. Place in clean water and boil gently for 2–3 hrs until tender.

Mince or chop the cooked laver to a fine purée. Blend with oats and recook in 600 ml (1 pint) water or milk for 6 minutes until thick

Season to taste. Cool the purée and divide into small cakes, 50 g (2 oz) each, heat the bacon fat or butter in a pan and fry the laver bread cakes on both sides until golden and crisp. Serve hot like fritters.

Thon Galloise   Baked tuna fish with strips of vegetables and herbs

4 portions

700 g (1 lb 8 oz) tuna fish
50 g (2 oz) butter
50 ml (2 fl oz) dry white wine
450 g (1 lb) carrots, leeks and
   celery, cut into thin strips
150 ml (5 fl oz) white wine
1 bouquet garni
15 ml (1 tbsp) chervil, basil, dill,
   and chives
Salt and ground black pepper

Bone and divide the fillet of tuna into four pieces.

Place in a shallow buttered baking tray. Season with salt and pepper. Sprinkle liberally with the vegetables and herbs. Add white wine and cover with aluminium foil in order to retain moisture.

Bake in a moderately hot oven 200°C, 400°F, gas mark 6, for 15 minutes, then serve.

Poulet au Fromage et Ciboulette   Farmhouse chicken breast with a Tiefi filling

4 portions

4 175 g (6 oz) chicken breasts
175 g (6 oz) Tiefi and chive
   cheese
2 eggs
300 ml (½ pint) milk
225 g (8 oz) white breadcrumbs
225 g (8 oz) white flour
Salt and ground black pepper
Vegetable oil for deep frying

Remove the fillet from the chicken and flatten slightly using a meat hammer. With a sharp knife, make a slit along the length of the chicken breast.

Divide the Tiefi into four equal portions and insert into the chicken. Cover the chicken fillet to make a good seal.

Whisk the eggs with the milk. Dip each chicken breast into the flour, then into the egg mixture and finally into the breadcrumbs.

Pat lightly and deep fry in hot vegetable oil until golden brown (about 10–12 minutes).

Pierre Jammet

Proprietor
Gérard Magnan, Chef de Cuisine
Pavillon Henri IV
21 Rue Thiers
St-Germain-en-Laye 78100
France
Tel: 1.34.51.61.62

Pierre Jammet became the Président Administrateur of the Paris Bristol Hotel, in succession to his father, in 1964. His grandfather, François, was chef of the Hôtel des Deux Mondes and then owned the famous restaurant Boeuf à la Mode in Paris. He later moved to Dublin in Ireland where Pierre's father was born in 1893. He eventually acquired the Jammet's in Dublin until he retired. In 1982 Pierre Jammet bought the Pavillon Henri IV and has transformed it into a sophisticated rendezvous of the Parisian epicurean clientele.

The chef de cuisine, Gérard Magnan, now in his 40s, was apprenticed at Albert Weischard and at Maxim's.

During his military service he was chef to General de Gaulle. He studied at Archestrate under M Sanderens. Continuing his career he worked for 4 years with Michel Guérard, and 7 years for the Chaîne PLM and two more reputable restaurants. Finally he was appointed head chef at the Pavillon.

Gérard Magnan is a magnificent culinarian and proud to work in the very place where the famous chef Collinet created the sauce Béarnaise and invented Pommes soufflées. He told us that his favourite dishes are bass and red mullet with vegetables raviolis. He has also perfected an old-style duck dish which, in its original form, was served to King Henri IV who lived in this château centuries ago.

The Pavillon was the birthplace of Louis XIV in 1668. In 1777, Louis gave the château to his brother, the Count of Artois, later King Charles X. The French Revolution destroyed it but it was rebuilt and rented to the famous chef Collinet. Prominent guests included Sarah Bernhardt, George Sand, Victor Hugo, and composers Gounod, Liszt, Massenet, and Offenbach. Alexander Dumas wrote his two famous novels while staying at the hotel. Sip champagne on the terrace at the Pavillon as the sun sets and watch the light play on the stunning view of Paris.

Dishes like Asparagus with mousseline sauce or Rhubarb beignets or Lamb's tongue or Sautéd crayfish have been served in both classic and modern styles. But whatever you may select, the great classic creation of the place is Châteaubriand, with Sauce Béarnaise and Pommes soufflées. It will always be featured by the present chef as a mark of respect for such a masterpiece.

Canard à l'Ancienne   Duck old style

4 portions

1 large duck 4 kg (8 lb)
75 ml (3 fl oz) cognac
1 bottle of white wine and half of
  water
4 sprigs of thyme
2 shallots, chopped
1 bunch of chervil, chopped
225 g (8 oz) streaky bacon
  rashers, diced
1 calf's foot
225 g (8 oz) lean bacon rashers
100 g (4 oz) butter
4 onions, sliced
4 carrots, sliced
6 cloves of garlic, crushed
Salt and pepper

Cut the duck into 4 portions on the bone.

Marinade them in a dish with ⅔ of the cognac and ⅔ of the wine with thyme, shallots and chopped chervil. After 2 hours remove and drain all the ingredients and retain the liquid for the sauce.

In another bowl macerate the diced bacon with the remaining ⅓ of wine and ⅓ of cognac and some chervil and shallots.

Boil the calf's foot with the lean bacon and its rind for 10 minutes. Refresh in cold water, drain. Bone the foot and dice the rashers.

Heat butter in a large sauté pan and brown the duck pieces for 10 minutes, turning each piece over once or twice.

Remove and place the duck pieces in a casserole dish with the calf's foot meat, diced bacon, sliced onion, carrots, and garlic, add the marinade liquid to these ingredients. Complete the liquid with a little water to immerse the meat. Cover with a lid and cook for 1 hour 30 minutes at 200°C, 400°F, gas mark 6, on the middle shelf. Remove surplus fat from the sauce.

Serve from the same dish with boiled cabbage, turnips and new potatoes. This was how King Henri IV liked the dish, and he mopped up the sauce with brown bread. He ate the whole duck as one portion in one sitting.

André and Jean-Paul Jeunet

Chefs/Proprietors
Hôtel de Paris
9 Rue de l'Hôtel de Ville
Arbois 39600
France
Tel: 84.66.05.67

André senior was a registered officer of the Epicurean Circle and listed in the *Gastronomic Tour de France* as far back as 1954. Since that time he has achieved well-deserved recognition as a grand master of cookery. He was previously a cookery lecturer at Thonon and was the best cook of the year in 1962. His son Jean-Paul was trained in Nice and, of course, by his own father. They both run the family hotel with great harmony, drawing the best of both worlds, classic and modern.

One look at the large menu is enough to convince you that you can still expect Tournedos Rossini to be served with real foie gras, and that Lobster Thermidor will be done with the best Bercy and Mornay sauce, with a tinge of Dijon mustard. I also noted a Pike soufflé with Nantua sauce (crayfish-flavoured), and Coq au vin jaune. This vin jaune is the local golden Arbois. We also noticed the morels, little spongy mushrooms which must be well cleaned to remove the sand inside them but which are so delicious.

This is the Jura, with lakes, waterfalls, caves, mountains, and lots of places to visit for fishing, riding, walking, and watching the annual feast of Arbois. In this old town the Hôtel de Paris with its timbered dining-room, deer head trophies on the wall, and old chimneys, looks like an old manor house. Yet the silver trolley is rolled to your table with a joint of venison or saddle of lamb, or even a rib of beef, all carved in front of you by M Jeunet himself.

Soufflé de Brochet aux Écrevisses   Pike soufflé with crayfish

6 portions

Brush the inside of 6 ramekin
   soufflé dishes of 150 ml
   (5 fl oz) capacity with soft
   butter.

Crayfish sauce
45 ml (3 tbsp) oil
4 crayfish or Dublin Bay prawns
   or king prawns
1 carrot and 1 onion, chopped
1 clove garlic, crushed
1 bouquet garni
30 ml (2 tbsp) tomato purée
2 saffron strands
150 ml (5 fl oz) water and as
   much white wine (or fish
   stock)
15 g (½ oz) ground rice
150 ml (5 fl oz) double cream
75 ml (3 fl oz) sherry
25 ml (1½ tbsp) brandy
Salt and pepper
Pinch cayenne

Soufflé mixture
150 g (5 oz) pike or white fish,
   skinned and filleted
2 egg yolks
4 egg whites
30 ml (2 tbsp) of the sauce
Salt and pepper
120 ml (8 tbsp) double cream

Sauce
Heat the oil in a sauté pan and stir-fry the crayfish or Dublin Bay
prawns. Remove them. Separate the tails from the heads. Place the
heads in the oil with carrot, onion, garlic, and bouquet garni, and stir-fry
for 3 minutes more. Add tomato purée, saffron, water and wine or fish
stock, and sherry and brandy, and boil for 25 minutes. Pass the mixture,
solid and liquid, through a moulinette, and strain again. Collect the fish
liquor in a saucepan and reboil for 10 minutes with cream. Season to
taste and it is ready.

Soufflé
Mince the fish and place in a bowl. Add egg yolks and cream 30 ml
(2 tbsp) only of the sauce. Check seasoning and blend well.
   In a separate bowl beat 3 egg whites with a pinch of salt until it is stiff.
Fold the meringue into the fish mixture lightly and thoroughly. Fill the
ramekin soufflé dishes to the brim, and bake at 200°C, 400°F,
gas mark 6, for 20 minutes.
   Serve the sauce separately.
   The crayfish tails are shelled and the flesh is diced and mixed into the
sauce as a garnish.

Jean-Louis Jolly

Chef de Cuisine/Proprietor
Hôtel de la Gloire
74 Avenue de Gaulle
Montargis 45000
France
Tel: 38.85.04.69

Jean-Louis Jolly is a master of fish gastronomy, yet his meat dishes are equally outstanding and harmonize well with the other items on a spectacular menu.

It includes Brill with fennel, Lobster in a jelly sauce, and Red mullet blushing with joy in a curry sauce, and Fish cassoulet.

The Blanquette de ris de veau with noodles had that classic look about it, in spite of the pasta garnish.

Jean-Louis Jolly has won a Michelin star and the hotel is rated one of the best in town. A place where you can also enjoy the famous wines of Sancerre and Chinon, particularly on a weekday, with his Blanquette de ris de veau — a perfect match.

The hotel is away from the centre of the town and looks grandiose. It has 17 rooms and a large restaurant in style with the period of the region.

Montargis is known as the Venice of Gatinais. It has 126 bridges over its many canals and waterways.

Blanquette de Ris de Veau   Sweetbread with noodles

4 portions

4 calves sweetbreads
50 g (2 oz) butter
150 g (5 oz) each of carrots, leeks,
   and celery, cut in small cubes
1 bouquet garni
300 ml (½ pint) water and as
   much white wine

Garnish
8 small button mushrooms
8 small spring onions
225 g (8 oz) cooked noodles
25 g (1 oz) Gruyère cheese, grated
1 small truffle

Thickening
100 ml (4 fl oz) double cream and
   5 ml (1 tsp) cornflour, mixed
Salt and pepper

Soak the sweetbreads in cold water for 1 hour. Put them in a saucepan, cover with water and blanch for 4 minutes. Discard the water and cool the sweetbreads until cold. Trim off the outer membranes and cut any fibrous bits away. Wrap them in a muslin cloth and press them under a heavy board.

Heat the butter in a sauté pan and brown the vegetables for 5 minutes. Place the sweetbreads and the bouquet garni in the pan. Season to taste and cook for another 6 minutes. Turn over half way through. Add water and wine. Cook for 20 minutes at low heat covered with a lid.

Clean mushrooms and onions, and parboil in water for 5 minutes. Drain.

Remove the sweetbreads. Slice them.

Now thicken the sauce by adding the mixture of cream and cornflour. Season to taste. Boil for 4 minutes and strain.

Blend a little of the sauce with the pasta. Check seasoning. Add milled black pepper and the grated Gruyère cheese.

On 4 plates, place a pool of the sauce, mushrooms, and onions. Add the slices of sweetbread and a little heap of pasta. Sprinkle a little julienne of truffles over the pasta.

Gary Allen Jones

Chef de Cuisine
Jenny's Restaurant
Portland Street
Britannia Building
Manchester M1 31A
Tel: (061) 228 2288

Gary Allen Jones attended a catering college in Bristol and gained his experience in that town with the Holiday Inn. Later he became sous-chef of the Royal Crescent in Bath. He now runs Jenny's Restaurant, a popular venue for youngsters and the young at heart who enjoy the choice of a large selection of well-garnished and nicely presented dishes.

The menu ranges from Flakes of salmon baked in foil to Medallions of pork brushed with Dijon mustard, to a lovely assortment of Italian salami, tender joint of beef and ham with a large selection of salads. Naturally there is also pizza topped with everything one can imagine. On our visit the Rib of beef and Braised shoulder of beef were the dishes of the day.

The atmosphere of Jenny's is that of the typical coffee house dining-room we find within the premises of large hotels all over the world. Food is served on polished tables with mats, and smiling waitresses attend to you with speed.

Boeuf Britannia   Scotch beef sirloin steaks crusted with pine kernels and green peppercorns

2 portions

100 g (4 oz) butter
2 sirloin steaks, each weighing
    12 oz (350 g)
Salt and freshly milled black
    pepper
350 ml (12 fl oz) white wine
600 ml (1 pint) beef stock
100 g (4 oz) breadcrumbs
15 ml (1 tbsp) olive oil
Pinch mixed herbs (tarragon and
    marjoram)
20 g (¾ oz) tinned green
    peppercorns
50 g (2 oz) chopped pine kernels
100 g (4 oz) parsley

Heat some of the butter and oil in a pan and cook sirloin steak for 8–10 minutes. Season and keep hot.

Deglaze the pan with the white wine and add the stock. Reduce, strain, and finish by whisking in the remaining butter.

Liquidize the breadcrumbs, olive oil, herbs, peppercorns, pine kernels, and the liquid from the tinned peppercorns.

Spread on top of the meat and brown under a hot grill. Serve with gratin of potatoes and leeks.

Emile Jung

Chef de Cuisine/Proprietor
Le Crocodile
10 Rue de l'Outre
Strasbourg 67000
France
Tel: 88.32.13.02

Emile Jung is rated one of the best specialists of Alsace gastronomy; and no wonder, for he was apprenticed at La Maison Rouge in Strasbourg and at the Mère Guy in Lyon, a famed house which no longer exists. For part of the year he works at the family restaurant. He blends the local Riesling wine with his river fish; his Medaillon de veau à la crème; and his Blanc de volaille et Saint Jacques aux coulis de poireaux. His *plat de résistance* is Chicken in Riesling.

There are Frogs in pastry, Hop shoots cooked as a vegetable like asparagus, Baked turbot served with sturgeon caviar, and real foie gras served hot or cold. Even the Guinea-fowl cooked in a pastry turnover had a distinctive style.

The restaurant is located near the cathedral, in a setting of such splendid luxury that it is patronized by all the leading politicians. Strasbourg is also near ski resorts and vineyards and there is much to see in the way of castles, curiosities, and museums.

Chausson de Pintade au Foie Gras et Truffle   Guinea-fowl turnover

4 portions

1 small guinea-fowl 1 kg
   (2 lb 4 oz)
50 g (2 oz) butter
200 g (8 oz) prepared puff pastry
100 g (4 oz) fresh raw goose liver,
   sliced
1 truffle, sliced
Salt and pepper
15 ml (1 tbsp) brandy

Season the guinea-fowl inside and out and roast it in a preheated oven at 220°C, 425°F, gas mark 7, for 25 minutes. Baste it with butter during cooking. Cool and carve into slices. Bone the legs, cutting the meat into thin slices. Cool.

Roll pastry to 3 mm (⅛ in) thick and cut 4 circles of 12 cm (5 in) diameter.

Brush each circle with water and place on it slices of guinea-fowl, a slice of goose liver and slices of truffle. Season with salt and black pepper. Pour on a little brandy and fold over in half-moon shape, like turnovers. Crimp edges to seal them tightly. Brush top with beaten egg and leave to rest for 30 minutes.

Bake in pre-heated oven at 220°C, 425°F, gas mark 7, for 20 minutes until golden. Serve hot or cold as a light entrée or picnic lunch.

Ahmed Laasri

Chef de Cuisine/Manager
Timgad
21 Rue Brunel
Paris 75017
France
Tel: 54.74.23.70

Ahmed Laasri attended the Ecole Hôtelière in Rabat. He progressed as a cook and served on the staff of the French Ambassador, Francois Poncet, in Morocco as a chef.

In 1964 he came to Paris and worked as head chef at the Domaine, Place de la Bastille. In 1971 he was engaged at the Timgad as head chef and was promoted to manager in 1981. He gained a Michelin star for his luxurious style of African cuisine.

If you fancy Arabic cuisine at its best we recommend Timgad. Ahmed Laasri is the proprietor, and has made this restaurant the best of its kind for northern African specialities.

A couscous is usually served with two sauces made from the broth of a hot-pot, where vegetables and chicken or lamb are boiled gently. The couscous is served on a separate plate with the meats and vegetables, and the broth is drunk as a soup first. Some claim it is the original of the Pot-au-feu of France. The Chicken in lemon sauce is not like the Greek version but is simpler and spicier. The Pigeon with almonds was the best I have eaten.

The restaurant has gained a Michelin star for its couscous and North African fare and you can be sure that if the French like it, it has to be good. The design of the restaurant is Moorish, with arched alcoves, tapestry on the walls, and tiled flooring.

Couscous de Mouton Timgad   Mutton couscous

6 portions

50 ml (2 fl oz) oil
2 kg (4 lb 6 oz) lean mutton meat
    cut into 2-cm cubes from the
    shoulder
4 medium onions, chopped
3 cloves of garlic, chopped
1 pinch turmeric
1 small red or green chilli, sliced
2 litres (3½ pints) water
2 courgettes or aubergines, diced
225 g (8 oz) pumpkin pulp, diced
4 large tomatoes, skinned, seeded
    and chopped
100 g (4 oz) marrow peas or
    chickpeas, precooked
2 sticks celery, sliced
1 stick fennel, sliced
2 leeks, sliced
15 ml (1 tbsp) tomato purée
Salt to taste

Garnish
225 g (8 oz) couscous semolina
50 g (2 oz) flaked almonds or
    peanuts
50 g (2 oz) seedless raisins
15 ml (1 tbsp) oil
30 ml (2 tbsp) butter
Salt and pepper

Heat the oil in a large sauté pan and brown the meat for 10 minutes. Add the onions and garlic, all the spices and chilli. Add the water and boil, and then simmer for 1½ hours. At this stage, add the courgettes, pumpkin, fresh tomatoes, and tomato purée, cooked chickpeas, leek, celery, and fennel. Cook for another 30 minutes until vegetables are tender. Remover any fat floating on top. Season with salt (no pepper is needed as the chilli is hot enough).

Garnish
Rub the semolina with 15 ml (1 tbsp) oil and 30 ml (2 tbsp) butter, and then add twice its weight of water and cook for 6 mins until mixture looks like dry crumbs. Season to taste.

Add the flaked almonds or peanuts and seedless raisins. Serve on separate plates with the mutton stew.

Note that couscous can be prepared in many ways with different meats, chicken, or fish.

Jean Lafon

Vice-President Cercle Epicurien
    Mondial/Owner
M. Galois, Chef de Cuisine
La Coupole
102 Boulevard du Montparnasse
Paris 75014
France
Tel: 1.43.20.14.20

Both M. Galois and his patissier M. Bourges have worked at La Coupole for 35 years.

The cuisine has always been classic with no gimmicks ever since this famous establishment opened in 1927. It has been patronized by the artistic and political world and has seen many famous feats, especially at Christmas and the New Year. For the past 60 years La Coupole has symbolized the spirit of festivity in every style. Famous specialities include Filet de sole, Homard cardinal, Canard à la presse and oysters by the dozen served from morning to late evening. There is a café atmosphere in which students can enjoy a beer and a Welsh rarebit or a dish of Tripes mode de Caen, yet a film star can be seated at the next table having caviar on toast! Anyone can enjoy a dozen oysters and a glass of Chablis at any time of the day.

La Coupole, in the centre of the Latin quarter, used to operate on three floors; the basement, with a night-club atmosphere; the ground floor, where 400 people could have a meal or a drink.

Sorbet au Café crème   Coffee sorbet with cream

12 portions

8 egg yolks
2 egg whites
50 g (2 oz) caster sugar
300 ml (½ pint) water
90 ml (3 fl oz) fresh coffee
    (brewed and chilled)
150 g (5 oz) granulated sugar
45 ml (3 tbsp) coffee liqueur
    (e.g. Tia Maria)
150 ml (5 fl oz) whipped cream
    for garnish

Put the egg yolks, egg whites, and caster sugar in a bowl and whisk with a balloon whisk for 4 minutes, over a tray of hot water.

Boil water and add the brewed coffee; do not allow to boil further. Add the granulated sugar and allow to dissolve. Strain.

Gradually blend the lukewarm coffee syrup and liqueur into the egg mixture and whisk until it begins to thicken like custard. Allow to cool.

Oil a wet mould and line it with greaseproof paper.

Fill with the mixture and freeze for 6 hours.

To serve, scoop the coffee sorbet into fluted glasses and pipe a rosette of whipped cream on top.

Serve with cigarette wafers.

If you have an ice-cream maker, the mixture can be frozen within 20 minutes and then served immediately afterwards.

You can add 2 raw egg whites to the cool coffee sorbet. This will help to stabilize the texture, resulting in a smoother sorbet.

The liqueur can also be added when the sorbet is almost frozen.

Presentation
Serve with cooked bananas and garnished with almond biscuits.

Denis Lecadre

Chef de Cuisine
Château de Locguénolé
Route de Port-Louis
Hennebont 56700
France
Tel: 97.76.29.04

Denis Lecadre, aged 30, took over the kitchen of this famous château in 1988. He was previously chef of a three-star Michelin restaurant at Vézelay in Yonne, the celebrated Espérance.

Denis Lecadre told us that the world was his oyster and being close to the sea, he certainly has all the fish and molluscs he needs at his disposal. 'After cooking in Burgundy wines I really enjoy myself using Muscadet and cider', he said. In his elaborate menu Denis has already modified the traditional Côtriade into a Marmite de poissons aux herbes provençales. The Foie gras pâté is lighter, the Crêpes Bretonne with crab and sweetbread is delicious and the baby turbot, baked and garnished, is a splendid dish to have for lunch. Our favourite is his recent creation of Hake fillet with an oriental ratatouille of aubergine, pepper, and courgettes slightly flavoured with basil and saffron.

The château has been in the same family for 500 years and the present owner is the Comte Bruno de la Sablière. It is located 4 km (2½ miles) south of Hennebont, and is surrounded by woodland and a lovely park. Nearby flows the river Blavet, which is a magnificent sight viewed from the château. It is a short distance from the beach and the famous resorts of Port-Louis, Carnac, and Quiberon.

Filets de Colin Pané au Citron et son Curry d'Aubergines

2 portions

Aubergine ratatouille
1 small aubergine, peeled and
   thickly sliced
90 ml (3 fl oz) oil
50 g (2 oz) onion, chopped
1 small red pepper, deseeded and
   chopped neatly
5 ml (1 tsp) Madras curry
   powder
1 large tomato, skinned, seeded
   and chopped
75 ml (3 fl oz) fish stock or water
Salt
5 ml (1 tsp) sugar or honey

Fish preparation
2 150 g (5 oz) fillets of hake
   without skin
15 ml (1 tbsp) seasoned flour
   mixed with a pinch curry
   powder and salt
2 eggs, beaten
50 g (2 oz) mixed crushed
   peanuts and breadcrumbs
Oil to shallow fry
8 slices of lime for decoration and
   16 basil herbs
30 ml (2 tbsp) mango chutney or,
   if in season, fresh mango, 1 for
   2 portions

Sprinkle salt over the peeled, sliced aubergines and leave for 30 minutes. Wash off the salt and drain. Dice the flesh into cubes.

Heat oil and stir-fry the onion for 1 minute, and then add red pepper and aubergine. Cook for 3 minutes, and then sprinkle with curry powder. Fry for 30 seconds to develop the flavour. At this stage add tomato and water or stock, and simmer the mixture to evaporate most of the liquid (about 30 minutes) to a sort of vegetable marmalade. Season with salt to taste. Add honey to counterbalance the acidity.

In a deep tray, coat the fish with seasoned flour. Shake off the surplus. Coat evenly in beaten egg, and then in the crumb and peanut mixture.

Heat oil in a deep pan and shallow fry for 3 minutes on each side until golden. Do not overcook.

To serve, arrange a pool of the aubergine mixture and the fish fillet. Decorate with slices of mango, slices of lime and a few basil leaves.

Marc Le Gros

Vice-Chairman, World Master
  Chefs Society
Royal Court Hotel
Sloane Square
London SW1W 8EG
Tel: 01-730 9191

Marc was apprenticed in Chartres at the Boeuf Couronne. He made his mark at the Inigo Garden in London, and was appointed head chef at the Brasserie St Quentin. In 1987 he was selected for the prestigious position of chef at Marlow.

Marc's style of cooking is exact, and precision being the hallmark of the perfectionist, we can vouch that the dishes he produces all have a personal touch.

Light liver in saffron sauce and Savoury fish terrine with salmon, sole, and prawns are typical masterpieces.

He cooks his veal with pink peppercorns not capsicums, for those who have never seen peppercorns of that colour. The point is worth making. The berries are first green, then turn red, and are then dried either black if the skin is left on or white if the skin is removed. Red peppercorns are kept in juice like green peppercorns and are softer and less pungent.

To end the meal you could try a Charlotte aux cassis.

Marc Le Gros now works at the Royal Court Hotel, London.

Medallion de Veau au Poivre rose   Veal loin in pink peppercorn sauce

2 portions

450 g (1 lb) rump or fillet of veal
Salt and pepper
100 ml (4 fl oz) white wine
5 ml (1 tsp) pink peppercorns
  (use green if unavailable)
150 ml (5 fl oz) double cream
25 g (1 oz) butter
Watercress or parsley to garnish

Cut the fillet into 6 very thin roundels. Season and pan-fry the veal until pink.

Discard fat and deglaze with a little white wine. Add the peppercorns and the cream and leave to reduce. Add the butter and salt if necessary and pour over the meat. Serve with a purée of celeriac or carrot.

Terrine de Pêcheur, Sauce verte   Mixed fish terrine marine style

12 portions

350 g (12 oz) fresh salmon,
  skinned and with black parts
  removed
Salt and pepper
8 egg whites
735–875 ml (1¼–1½ pints)
  double cream
50 g (2 oz) butter, melted
225 g (8 oz) sole fillet
Pinch saffron
350 g (12 oz) white scallops, with
  coral removed
10 large spinach leaves, lightly
  blanched
2 large carrots, cut into julienne
  strips and lightly blanched
1 white leek, cut into julienne
  strips and lightly blanched
2 sticks celery, cut into julienne
  strips and lightly blanched
150 g (5 oz) prawns, peeled and
  cooked

Sauce
2 small bunches watercress
1 small bunch chives
500 ml (18 fl oz) thick sour cream
a little white wine

Blend the salmon flesh in a processor. Add salt, pepper, a little egg white and 60 ml (4 tbsp) double cream. Blend again and add 10 g (½ oz) butter. Blend again until the mixture forms a smooth mousseline.
  Repeat the process with the sole fillet.
  Dry the scallops. Heat 425 ml (¾ pint) double cream with the saffron and 15 g (½ oz) butter. Lower the heat and cook until the cream feels tacky to the touch. Cool. Blend the scallops, add salt, pepper and the remaining egg whites, and then gradually cream.
  Assemble the terrine. Line the inside of the terrine with the spinach leaves. Fill ⅓ with the salmon mixture. Cover with the vegetables followed by a thin layer of the sole mixture. Then add the prawns in a layer and lastly the scallop mixture. Place spinach leaves on top. Cover with foil and bake in a deep tray half filled with water for about 50 minutes at 140°C, 275°F, gas mark 1.
  Make the sauce by liquidizing the watercress and chives. Mix together in a bowl with the sour cream and a little white wine. Season and serve on each plate with a slice of terrine on top.

Richard Lemoine

Chef de Cuisine/Proprietor
Le Nantais Restaurant
65 Rue Victor-Grignard
Cherbourg 50100
France
Tel: 33.93.11.60

Richard Lemoine learned cookery in Nantes. He worked at the fashionable seaside resort of La Baule and for 10 years worked in Paris at such places as La Truyère, Tante Louise, Air Maxim at Roissey, Le Jour et la Nuit on the Champs Elysées, and the Alsace Restaurant and many more, learning and saving to buy his own restaurant. He became a fish expert at an inn in Nantes, and as his wife was from Normandy, he moved to Cherbourg where he has performed miracles with seafood.

His restaurant is rustic and soberly decorated, but the atmosphere is frankly convivial and bistro-like. He offers three menus, including Pike and salmon terrine, a Fishermen's soup, Snails in butter, and Thin flank steak.

The charm of Cherbourg is the sea, golden beaches and the famous château. It has a yachting marina which brings in many tourists, and indeed the town has been well restored since the war.

Coquille Saint Jacques Nantaise   Scallops in Muscadet wine

4 portions

1 kg (2 lbs 2 oz) scallops, medium size
90 ml (3 fl oz) Orleans vinegar
150 ml (5 fl oz) Muscadet white wine
2 shallots, chopped
1 sprig thyme
Salt and pepper
225 g (8 oz) Normandy butter
Parsley, chopped
45 ml (3 tbsp) single cream

Open the scallops with a knife, or place them on top of a hot stove until the shells open. Remove the flesh. Discard the black sac and beard trimming. Use only white meat and coral. Wash and drain well. If too big, slice them laterally. Heat the vinegar and wine with shallots and a sprig of thyme. Boil to reduce by a third. Retain this liquor for the sauce. Poach the scallops for 2 minutes in this stock and strain again. Now reboil the stock liquor and whisk in the butter bit by bit, to form an emulsion. Season to taste, add cream, whisk mixture, and serve.

On 4 plates pour a pool of this foaming sauce. Sprinkle coarsely chopped parsley over the sauce and arrange the cooked scallops attractively in rosettes with the coral.

If you wish, you can use single cream in the sauce instead of butter. The sauce made with butter is called a *beurre blanc* sauce and is a speciality of Nantes.

Jean Lenoir

Chef/Proprietor
Hostellerie Lenoir
Auvillers-les-Forges
Maubert-Fontaine 08260
France
Tel: 24.54.30.11

Jean Lenoir is the son of a bistro owner. He attended the school of Namur in Belgium and then took the humble café of his parents, in this village where he had lived all his life, and transformed it into an inn of great character and simplicity, winning many gold medals. The Hostellerie is now a gastronomic rendezvous for the locals for miles around. To make a reputation off the beaten track is no mean feat in this work.

We noted on his menu Grand siècle, a Terrine de sole in pepper sauce and Gâteau de foie d'oie au miel (Honey and liver kidney and sweetbread with mint leaves). His huge menu is full of delicate preparations such as Truffles en surprise, Quails in port wine, and hot pâté of monkfish with sorrel sauce. There is a dish, however, particularly worth including, namely Wild duck with green peppercorn sauce.

The Hostellerie is located between Rocroi and Auvillers, almost in the Champagne region. It has 24 bedrooms with bath, and the restaurant has a terrace and garden for summer meals alfresco. It is now one of the most famous inns in the Ardennes region of France.

Maigret de Canard au Poivre Vert   Wild duck with green peppercorns

4 portions

2 trussed wild ducks (widgeon or
    mallard)
15 ml (1 tbsp) green peppercorns
A good pinch of salt
50 ml (2 fl oz) brandy or
    Armagnac
Juice of 1 lemon

Sauce
Ducks' bones
1 carrot
1 stick of celery
Bunch thyme
300 ml (½ pint) red wine
1 onion
2 cloves of garlic
1 bouquet garni
300 ml (½ pint) water
5 ml (1 tsp) cornflour mixed with
    25 ml (5 tsp) water to thicken
    the gravy
50 ml (2 fl oz) oil
60 ml (4 tbsp) double cream
5 ml (1 tsp) yeast extract or meat
    glaze

Garnish
100 g (4 oz) black grapes, seeded,
    or fresh raspberries or
    loganberries

Remove the skins of 2 trussed ducks. Cut off the legs, then very gently cut the breast away from the tip of the breast bone, make a slit and carve away the breast from the main carcass. If you remove the breast bone first it will be easier. Place the 4 skinned, boneless breasts in a polythene sheet, and then with a wooden mallet gently beat them thinner, as one does with escalopes, without crushing or breaking the meat.

Place the 4 breasts on a flat plate and cover with crushed green peppercorns. Sprinkle with salt, pepper, and about 25 ml (1 fl oz) Armagnac or brandy. Allow to marinate for 1 hour.

Meanwhile, prepare a stock by boiling the carcass and legs, with carrot, sliced celery stick, a bunch of thyme, water and red wine. Add 1 small chopped onion and clove of crushed garlic. After 1 hour, strain this liquor, which by now will be reduced to ½ its original volume. Reboil the stock for 10 minutes, and then add 1 tsp yeast extract or meat glaze. Thicken it slightly by adding the cornflour mixture and boiling for 4 minutes. Season with salt to taste.

When ready to serve the duck breasts, remove them from the marinade. Heat 60 ml (4 tbsp) oil in a sauté pan and cook for 4 minutes. Drain and keep hot. Discard the surplus oil and add green peppercorns and the gravy to the pan. Boil for 4 minutes. Add 60 ml (4 tbsp) cream and boil for 3 minutes more.

Pour a pool of sauce on to 4 plates, about 60 ml (4 tbsp) sauce per plate, and arrange a sliced breast steak on top of each pool. Decorate with seedless black grapes or fresh raspberries or loganberries and serve immediately.

Nicki McCann

Food Technologist
The Pasta Company
Units 4B/4C Harrier Road
Humber Bridge Industrial Estate
Barton-upon-Humber
South Humberside DN18 5RL
Tel: (0652) 660060

Nicki McCann is a qualified food technologist and a quality controller for a pasta company. She qualified at Bath College and expects to further her career in the field of research and development for food manufacturers. Nicki is part of a team which include Shona Richardson the marketing manager, Stuart Richardson, Nigel Stubley, and Mike Norton, who all left careers with large food companies to go into business on their own making pasta on a grand scale.

The Pasta Company has become a huge success, producing a range of domestic pasta with an authentic quality, so much so that they now export their products to Italy.

With their compliments we offer you: Spaghetti with fresh basil, pine nuts and cheese; Gnocchi with spicy carrot sauce; Chicken, fruit, and pasta salad; and a good Stir-fry of mixed vegetables with macaroni.

Les Pâtes au Basilic   Spaghetti with fresh basil, pine nuts and cheese

4 portions

225 g (8 oz) fresh spaghetti
15 ml (1 tbsp) olive oil
1 clove garlic, peeled and crushed
50 g (2 oz) basil leaves, chopped
    finely
Whole basil leaves for garnish
120 ml (4 fl oz) vegetable stock
25 g (1 oz) pine nuts, toasted
50 g (2 oz) pecorino cheese
    freshly grated (or Parmesan)
Salt and freshly ground black
    pepper

Heat oil in a frying pan, add the garlic and fry, stirring constantly, for about 30 seconds. Reduce the heat to low. Cook for about a further 30 seconds. Pour in the stock and simmer gently.

Meanwhile, cook spaghetti in 3 litres (5 pints) of fast-boiling water for 5 minutes, *al dente*. Drain the spaghetti and reheat with basil. Toss. Mix in the pine nuts, cheese, and seasoning, and toss again. Serve immediately, garnished with fresh whole basil leaves.

George McCartney

Master Butcher/Officer of the
   Cercle Epicurien Mondial for
   Northern Ireland
58 Main Street
Moira
County Down
Northern Ireland
Tel: (0846) 611422

George is the second generation of a family of butchers who have made their name for the excellent quality of their sausages. Indeed, he is a champion sausage maker, having won the International Prix d'Excellence awarded by the Epicurean Circle in London at the Marriott Hotel in March 1988.

He produces gluten- and additive-free sausages made to order.

His range of speciality sausages reads like a cookery book: with herbs; Italian beef; beef curry; thick beef bangers; with tomato and onion; with leek; and a low-fat pork Cumberland-style sausage.

To help readers understand the making of a sausage we give you the French version of this favourite pork delicacy.

Saucisses à la Charcutière   French pork sausages

6 portions

450 g (1 lb) pork meat from neck
   (only 20% fat)
25 g (1 oz) white breadcrumbs
50 ml (2 fl oz) double cream
5 ml (1 tsp) horseradish cream
10 ml (2 tsp) salt
A pinch sugar
5 ml (1 tsp) honey
1.25 ml (¼ tsp) white pepper
15 g (½ oz) chopped shallots
1 whole egg
1 pinch grated nutmeg
30 ml (2 tbsp) fresh chopped
   parsley
30 ml (2 tbsp) flour
Oil for frying or grilling

Mince the meat with the shallots and breadcrumbs. Collect the mixture and blend it in a bowl with the remaining ingredients. Cover with a clean cloth and leave overnight in a refrigerator.

On the following day, divide the forcemeat into 12 balls. Coat with seasoned flour and shape into cylindrical forms or into burgers. No skin is needed.

Heat the oil in a pan and fry for 5 minutes until golden. Or brush with oil and grill.

For kebabs, make 18 smaller balls. Put them on a skewer with onion layers and peppers and grill for 6 minutes.

Perfect for salads.

Gordon McGuiness

Chef de Cuisine
Midland International Bank
Directors' Catering
City of London
110 Cannon Street
London EC4
Tel: 01-260-4530

Gordon McGuiness was born in the West of Scotland, and has worked in several British Transport hotels north of the border, including the celebrated Gleneagles at Auchterarder and St Enochs Hotel, Glasgow. He was for a number of years senior sous-chef at the Baron of Beef in the City of London and later became head chef at the Norfolk Hotel in Kensington. Gordon has been cooking for important financiers from all over the world in the Midland Bank's kitchen for many years.

The food varies from expensive joints of venison, saddle of lamb or veal, to ribs of Scottish beef, carved in front of the guests. Gordon is proud to be Scottish and to have been trained using the finest meat and game available from Britain, and we reproduce here that Royal dish, Fillet of beef Bonnie Prince Charlie. The beef is roasted *underdone*, then cooled and coated in mushroom mixture, flavoured with Drambuie liqueur, wrapped in spinach leaves and then in brioche dough and finally baked until golden. It can be served hot or cold, for the buffet or dinner.

The City of London employs many catering companies, which manage its executive dining-rooms to a very high standard. The chefs of these dining-room units are highly trained and can undertake any culinary banquet with great skill.

Boeuf en Brioche à la Bonnie Prince Charlie   Beef baked in brioche

6 portions

Brioche dough
225 g 8 oz bread flour
10 g (½ oz) fresh yeast
100 ml (4 fl oz) tepid milk
2.5 ml (½ tsp) salt
2 eggs, beaten
50 g (2 oz) butter, melted
1 beaten egg for brushing

Main ingredients
450 g (1 lb) beef fillet, trimmed,
    skinned and tied up with string
50 ml (2 fl oz) oil for quick searing

Brioche
Place the flour and salt in a stainless steel basin and warm it for 5 minutes in the oven. Meanwhile, dilute the yeast with warm milk at 27°C, 80°F.

Remove the flour. Make a well in the centre and pour in the yeast liquor. Sprinkle with a little flour and leave to ferment for 10 minutes, until it begins to froth.

Blend the beaten eggs and melted butter into the mixture and beat dough for 6 minutes until it stiffens and remains in one piece and has a smooth elastic consistency. If you use an electric mixer with a dough hook, this operation will take only 3 minutes.

Place the dough inside an oiled polythene bag until it doubles in size (40 minutes).

Filling

50 g (2 oz) oil
4 shallots, chopped
150 g (5 oz) mushrooms, washed,
    drained and chopped
30 ml (2 tbsp) mixed fresh herbs,
    chopped
75 g (3 oz) minced raw liver
    (calf or chicken)
25 g (1 oz) breadcrumbs
30 ml (2 tbsp) Drambuie liqueur
    or whisky
Salt, pepper and a good pinch of
    ground mace

Gravy

150 ml (5 fl oz) port wine
150 ml (5 fl oz) beef stock
    (see Antoine Benoit's recipe for
    pot-au-feu)
50 g (2 oz) mushroom stalks
1 clove garlic, chopped
2 shallots, chopped
1 small sprig of thyme
Salt and black pepper
15 ml (1 tbsp) Drambuie liqueur
    or whisky
5 ml (1 tsp) cornflour and 45 ml
    (3 tbsp) double cream, mixed,
    to thicken gravy

Wrapping

24 spinach leaves, 450 g (1 lb)

Meat

Meanwhile, heat 50 ml (2 fl oz) oil in a large frying pan or roasting tray and sear the trimmed fillet of beef, browning it all over for 4 minutes.

Roast it in a tray for 15–20 minutes, in a preheated oven at 225°C, 430°F, gas mark 7–8. Then remove the meat from the roasting tray. Place it in a deep dish to cool completely and remove the string from the meat. Meanwhile prepare the gravy.

Gravy

Discard some of the oil from the tray, leaving only the beef juice. Add shallots, garlic, thyme, mushroom stalks, port, and beef stock, and then boil down to reduce it by half. Pour in the mixed cornflour and cream to thicken the gravy. Cook for 4 minutes more. Season to taste. Add 15 ml (1 tbsp) Drambuie or whisky to the gravy. Strain the sauce and keep warm on top of the stove or in a bain-marie.

Filling

Heat the butter in a sauté pan and stir-fry the shallots and mushrooms for 2 minutes. Bind the mixture with the raw minced liver and cook for 3 minutes more. Add mixed herbs, salt, and pepper. Stir in 15 ml (1 tbsp) Drambuie liqueur or whisky for extra flavour. Lastly blend in the breadcrumbs. Remove from heat and cool.

Finishing the dish

Scald 24 spinach leaves for 5 seconds, remove and drain on a dry cloth. Cool. By now the brioche dough has swollen and needs to be knocked back by kneading. Roll it out into an oblong on a dusted pastry board, so that it is wide enough to wrap the beef. Brush the pastry edges with beaten egg. Spread the mushroom and liver pâté mixture over the top of the beef fillet. Wrap it with spinach leaves, and then place this parcel over the piece of rolled brioche pastry. Wrap uniformly to obtain an oblong loaf. Mark it with the prongs of a fork in a criss-cross pattern and place it on a greased baking tray. Brush the top with beaten egg.

Leave to rest for 20 minutes, then bake in a preheated oven at 225°C, 430°F, gas mark 7–8, for 30 minutes like a bread loaf. Carve in front of your guests and serve the gravy separately. Note: On removing the cold beef, collect the juice which has escaped from the meat during cooling and add to the made gravy. Reheat it and pour a small pool of the gravy on 6 plates and serve 2 slices of beef in brioche per portion.

Albert Mackay

Chef de Cuisine
The Carlton Highland Hotel
North Bridge
Edinburgh EH1 1SD
Scotland
Tel: (031) 556 7277

Born in Scotland, Albert Mackay has lived most of his life on the Isle of Skye. He was brought up on fine food such as Angus beef, which was provided by his father, himself a butcher. His mother was a baker, and this combination led Albert to learn the craft of cookery. He was trained as a chef to a high standard at the Gleneagles and, having learned a great deal, became a head chef in Aviemore, Scotland's premier ski resort. During that time he represented Britain at the Festival Britannica in Florence. He opened the Carlton Highland Hotel in 1984, using the best of the styles he had learned, and created the 'Auld Alliance', which is well typified in the dishes shown on the lavish menu of the Quills Restaurant of the hotel.

For the first course he recommends a dish of Foie gras and salmon presented in parcel-like morsels and served with sherry sauce. The main dish of Saddle of venison with pears and redcurrants in port wine was truly royal, and would have graced the table of Mary Stuart.

Scotland is a land of game, fish and confectionery. The magnificent turreted Scottish baronial style of the exterior of the Carlton Highland, flagship of this hotel group, has been the inspiration for its interior design. The atmosphere of the two restaurants which lead from the open area of the cocktail bar and lounge is very welcoming.

The Quills Restaurant takes a library as its theme, in which oak panelling and wooden beams revealed in the ceiling help to suggest a reading room.

The operation director in charge of the Scottish Highland Hotels is Paul Murray-Smith, a graduate of the Ecole Hôtelière. He is also the patron of the Scottish branch of our Epicurean Circle.

Roselade de Saumon au Foie gras   Parcel of River Spey salmon with foie gras

4 portions

4 slices salmon 5 mm (¼ in)
  thick, 10 cm (4 in) square
4 slices fresh foie gras
Salt and pepper
15 ml (1 tbsp) oil
25 g (1 oz) unsalted butter
300 ml (½ pint) fish stock
150 ml (¼ pint) double cream
50 ml (2 fl oz) dry sherry
100 g (4 oz) mixed strips of root
  vegetables
25 g (1 oz) fresh chives

Place the slice of foie gras in the middle of each slice of salmon. Season well, wrap the foie gras with salmon to make 4 parcels.

Heat the oil and half the butter and sauté the 4 parcels gently for 4 minutes. Turn only once. The fish should be only slightly coloured. Remove the salmon and keep it warm. Tip off the fat, add the remaining butter, and stir-fry the vegetables until crisp.

Put the fish stock and dry sherry into another pan and reduce by two-thirds. Add the cream and reduce by a half or until thick. Add chives and seasoning.

Pour sauce on to a hot plate, add the drained vegetables, and place salmon parcels on top.

Mignon de Venaison aux Poires et Groseilles   Saddle of venison with pears and redcurrants, served with port wine

4 portions

12 chestnuts
100 g (4 oz) sugar
50 g (2 oz) butter
50 ml (2 fl oz) oil
12 50 g (2 oz) pieces of saddle of
  venison (boned, skinned, and
  de-sinewed)
120 ml (4 fl oz) port
30 ml (1 fl oz) brandy
15 ml (1 tbsp) redcurrant jelly
5 ml (1 tsp) tomato purée
2 pears, skinned and poached
600 ml (1 pint) good game stock
12 bread croûtes
50 g (2 oz) fresh redcurrants
Salt and pepper

Poach the chestnuts in a little stock with sugar and 25 g (1 oz) butter until they take on a good dark brown glaze.

Heat the oil in a pan and cook the venison — 2 minutes on either side should be sufficient. Drain off oil and pour on the port, brandy, and redcurrant jelly. Reduce over a high heat. Add the tomato purée, blending well. Pour in the game stock and reduce quickly until it takes on a thicker, sticky consistency.

Poach pears, cut them in a fan shape and keep warm.

Strain the sauce into a pan. Garnish it with fresh redcurrants.

On to each plate place 3 small croûtes. Place venison on top of each one. Place the fanned poached pear at the apex of the three and a chestnut on top of each piece of venison. Arrange sauce around the plate.

Graham M. Maloney

Executive Chef
Coatham Hotel
Mindeville
Near Darlington
County Durham DL1 3LU
Tel: (0325) 300400

Graham gained experience at the Europa, where he was head chef from 1975 to 1978. There then followed a succession of prestigious positions at the Dragonara, Middlesborough and the Potto Hall Hotel, where he won the Mouton-Cadet's competition of Northallerton in Yorkshire, the majestic Adelphi Hotel in Liverpool, and finally at the Coatham Hotel.

All the dishes of his menu reflect a French style. For example there are Foie gras and langoustines tossed or poached lightly and served as salades tièdes on a variety of radicchio and lettuce leaves. I remarked to Graham that it is amazing how few people know of that medley of wild herbs like dandelion, radicchio, oak leaves, and nasturtium flowers called a *mesclun*. 'You learn something new every day,' he replied, 'but between you and me, good old rump steak grilled on charcoal and a plain green Belgian salad with walnuts would do me as well.'

Assiette savoyarde en soufflé avec son bouquet hivernal

Two small cheese soufflés encased in trimmed pancakes, served garnished with a winter salad, lightly basted by a raspberry vinaigrette

4 portions

Pancake mixture
2 eggs
100 g (4 oz) flour
300 ml (½ pint) milk
Pinch of salt

Main ingredients
100 g (4 oz) Roquefort cheese
100 g (4 oz) Pont-l'Evêque
   cheese, or Camembert
100 ml (4 fl oz) milk
Pinch of celery salt
2 egg yolks
8 egg whites

Garnish
A selection of winter lettuce
   leaves, such as radicchio,
   winter rose, oak leaf, curly
   endive, white dandelion, celery
   leaves, etc.

Dressing
25 g (1 oz) raspberries
75 ml (3 fl oz) rosé wine vinegar
25 ml (1 fl oz) olive oil
Pinch of black pepper

Prepare the pancake mixture and make 8 12-cm (4½-in) diameter pancakes. Allow to cool.

Place the first cheese in one saucepan and the second cheese in another. Add a little milk and a pinch of celery salt to both pans.

Melt the cheese until soft. Remove the pans from the heat and allow to cool a little. Whisk the egg whites until stiff. Fold half the egg whites into each pan. Spoon some of the mixture into the middle of each pancake, and fold them over. Bake the pancakes in a moderate oven for approximately 3–5 minutes. In the meantime, prepare the winter salad.

Wash and mix lettuce leaves together on the side of 4 suitable dessert platters. Push raspberries through a sieve into a bowl and add the purée to the vinegar, oil, and pepper. Whisk ingredients well together and spoon a little dressing over each bunch of mixed lettuce leaves. Refrigerate until required.

Presentation
Remove dishes from the fridge. Remove the pancake soufflés from the oven and arrange them 2 of each kind per plate, facing each other. Serve immediately.

Antonio Mancini

Executive Head Chef
Hotel Piccadilly
PL Box 107
Piccadilly Plaza
Manchester M60 1QR
Tel: (061) 236 8414

Antonio is Italian and has a contagious enthusiasm for the beautiful aspect of food. He recently won nine gold medals and two silver trophies at Olympia and holds many other awards. He previously worked for the Britannia and the Holiday Inn Crown Plaza in Manchester.

Antonio's Chartreuse of asparagus with lime mousse is made with two sauces, one pink and one green. We could not resist the opportunity to have a dish of pasta, and his Ravioli of sweetbread with morels is a chef-d'oeuvre. The simple but well-presented Pear bavarois in caramel was a sheer delight.

Chartreuse Antonio

Asparagus and lime mousse on a bed of 2 sauces: blood orange and raspberry mayonnaise; and fresh herb, lavender honey, and yoghurt mayonnaise

4 portions

225 g (8 oz) fresh asparagus
100 g (4 oz) smoked salmon
5 ml (1 tsp) Pomméry mustard
100 g (4 oz) real mayonnaise
Grated zest of one lime
Juice of 1 lemon
Sprig of chervil
25 g (1 oz) peeled cucumber, grated
50 ml (2 fl oz) vegetable stock
Juice of 1 shallot
Pinch of black pepper
6 leaves of gelatine

First sauce
2 blood oranges
50 g (2 oz) fresh raspberries
Pinch of black pepper
25 ml (1 fl oz) raspberry vinegar
50 ml (2 fl oz) real mayonnaise

Second sauce
50 ml (2 fl oz) water
15 ml (1 tbsp) lavender honey
Juice of 1 lime
50 ml (2 fl oz) plain yoghurt
50 ml (2 fl oz) real mayonnaise

Garnish
2 sweet red peppers
Chervil sprigs
Asparagus tips
Pinch of poppy seeds

Use a vegetable knife to cut and scrape the asparagus tips. Peel the rest of the stalks, and boil them in salted water until tender. Allow to cool.

Blend the asparagus stalks into a fine purée, and place in a mixing bowl. Boil the asparagus tips in salted water, cool them, and chill until required.

Push the smoked salmon through a fine sieve or mince it, and add to the mixing bowl. Add also the Pomméry mustard, grated lime zest, juice of lime, chervil, black pepper, juice of 1 shallot, and grated cucumber. Fold the ingredients together well. Blend in the mayonnaise. Soak the gelatine leaves in vegetable stock, and when dissolved add it to the mixing bowl. Stir the ingredients well. Spoon the mixture into 4 suitable dariole moulds or ramekin dishes, and refrigerate until required (approximately 40 minutes).

First sauce
Place the fresh raspberries in a blender with the raspberry vinegar, black pepper, and juice of 2 blood oranges, and liquidize to a sauce. Put the mayonnaise in a mixing bowl, and mix in the raspberry and orange sauce. Refrigerate until required.

Second sauce
Put the honey, water, and juice of 1 lime in a suitable saucepan and bring to the boil. Take the pan off the heat and allow to cool a little. Then fold in the yoghurt and lastly the mayonnaise. Refrigerate until required.

Garnish
Cut the sweet peppers into fine strips, and blanch them in salted water for a few seconds. Allow to cool and refrigerate.

Presentation
Spoon the raspberry mayonnaise sauce into the centre of each platter. Spoon the honey mayonnaise sauce round the first sauce to cover the base of the platters.

Turn the asparagus and lime mousse out of the moulds, and place one in the centre of each platter.

Arrange the julienne of red peppers and asparagus tips round each mousse. On the inside edge of each platter, arrange chervil sprigs on to the sauces, and sprinkle each dish with the poppy seeds. Serve when required.

Guy Martin

Chef de Cuisine/Director
Relais Château de Divonne
Divonne-les-Bains 01220
Near Genève
Switzerland
Tel: 50.20.00.32

Born at Lens in 1957, Guy qualified with distinction in 1976. He was promoted to chef de cuisine at L'Etoile d'Or in La Plagne in 1981, and very soon this gifted cook was appointed at the Château de Coudrée in Sciez (Douvaine) and, in 1984, at the Château d'Esclimont (Ile-de-France) until he obtained his present position by Lake Léman.

Guy Martin offers a large selection of starters such as Frogs' legs with shrimp fritters, Salmon roulade, and Smoked scallops with honey-flavoured potato salad.

The fish section lists many lake delicacies such as Féra and other local fish, but it also includes Lobster with sea-urchin sauce.

We were pleased to see Scottish Angus beef featured (the most expensive item on his menu). There was also Tartare de boeuf (raw minced beef) served with horseradish sauce. The Canard de Challans was a duck dish served in two parts: the breasts with fresh figs and the legs served with salads.

The desserts included Millefeuille de banane with rum-flavoured ice cream, and a Soup of fresh berries and pear with red wine. Apart from the usual sorbets, the bill of fare was well balanced and showed a great deal of originality from this young master chef. We have selected for his contribution a sweetbread described as Ris de veau de lait au asperges sauvages, in preference to the Féra fish with oyster raviolis, which was also listed in this splendid menu.

The château is located in its own grounds, 15 minutes away from Geneva, against a backcloth of green hills, with a magnificent view of Lake Léman. There is an 18-hole golf course and you can enjoy a trip on the lake as well as gambling at the casino. This elegant nineteenth-century residence is beautifully furnished, and visitors are made to feel at home by a dedicated staff under the guidance of our maestro, Guy Martin.

Ris de Veau de Lait aux Asperges sauvages et à la Roussette de Savoie

4 portions

4 calves' sweetbreads
100 g (4 oz) seasoned flour
2 egg yolks and 30 ml (2 tbsp) oil
  mixed
100 g (4 oz) white breadcrumbs
Salt and pepper
75 g (3 oz) butter

Sauce
300 ml (½ pint) veal or chicken
  stock
150 ml (5 fl oz) white wine
150 ml (5 fl oz) vermouth
20 asparagus stalks (reserve the
  tips for garnish)
100 ml (4 fl oz) double cream

Soak the sweetbreads in running water for 30 minutes. Drain and remove the outer membranes. Cut the sweetbreads into escalopes (3 slices per sweetbread, approximately).

Coat each slice in seasoned flour, shake off surplus then dip into the mixture of beaten egg yolks and oil. Finally, coat them in breadcrumbs. Stand by to fry them at the last minute.

Blanch the asparagus for 4 minutes, refresh in cold water and drain. Keep the tips for garnish and liquidize the stalks. Heat the purée in a saucepan and blend in the cream. Keep warm. Boil the wine, vermouth, and chicken stock together until the sauce is richer in flavour and a third of its original volume. Mix the sauce with the asparagus stalk purée. Season to taste.

When ready to serve, fry the sweetbread escalopes in clarified butter for 4 minutes until golden. Remove and drain. Discard the butter. Pour a pool of the sauce onto 4 plates and arrange the sweetbread pieces on the sauce with asparagus tips as a light garnish.

Aimé Mettetal

Chef de Cuisine/Proprietor
La Dinanderie
Avrille 85440
Vendée
France
Tel: 51.22.32.15

Highly skilled in cookery, Aimé Mettetal has travelled the world of gastronomy, picking up his vast repertoire of dishes, which he now handles with the precision of a chemist.

The menu is simple but varied, according to the market. The sea is not far away and you can always begin a meal with oysters or a scampi salad.

The entrée can be as light as Papeton of pheasant, a pudding made of eggs and sliced pheasant (for which we give you the recipe) or it can be as rustic as Mougetas vendéenne, a sort of casserole with beans.

These little villages with good inns and restaurants are a relief from the bustle of the seaside resorts with their boarding-houses which often overcharge and do not always deliver the goods.

At the Dinanderie the atmosphere is peaceful. The silver bells adorning the well-garnished plates of food glitter in the candlelight on the tables. You sip a vermouth and cassis aperitif or a champagne cocktail, and await the dishes with appetite and anticipation. And you are not disappointed when the food arrives, piping hot, for it is perfect and princely.

Papeton de Faisan aux Aubergines   Pheasant pie with aubergines

6 portions

6 medium-sized aubergines
75 ml (3 fl oz) olive oil
2 cloves of garlic
150 g (5 oz) cooked pheasant
  (or chicken) breast, minced
6 medium eggs
150 ml (5 fl oz) single cream
1 kg (2 lb 2 oz) fresh tomatoes
  skinned, seeded, and chopped
5 basil leaves, chopped
Salt and pepper

Peel and dice the aubergines. Sprinkle salt over them and leave for 30 minutes to remove their bitter juice. Wash, rinse, and drain, and then dry with a cloth. Sprinkle with 45 ml (3 tbsp) of flour and shake off any surplus. Heat some of the oil and stir-fry the aubergine pieces for 5–8 minutes until soft. Drain well and mince them to a purée with the cooked, minced pheasant. Add 1 clove of crushed garlic, seasoning, and chopped basil.

Blend the beaten eggs and cream into the purée. Fill 6 150 ml (5 fl oz) capacity china earthenware ramekins with this mixture. Place them on a deep tray half filled with water and bake in a preheated oven at 200°C, 400°F, gas mark 6, for 45 minutes, on the middle shelf of the oven.

Prepare a fresh tomato coulis by heating 30 ml (2 tbsp) of oil and cooking the tomatoes and 1 clove of chopped garlic for 8 minutes. Season to taste and strain.

To serve, pour a pool of the sauce on to 6 plates and unmould the 'puddings' in the centre of each plate. Sprinkle with chopped basil or use whole leaves as decoration. Serve hot as a light entrée.

Michel Million

Chef de Cuisine/Proprietor
Château d'Adomenil
Renhainviller
Lunéville 54300
France
Tel: 83.74.04.81

Jean Million was a famous restauranteur at Vislones in Meuse, where Michel was trained under the paternal beady eye. In 1966 Michel, determined to show his skill and talent, purchased the Voltaire at Lunéville, where he gained his first Michelin star in 1977. A year later he became the proud owner of the splendid château d'Adomenil, with a lake filled with frogs and fish ready to be caught for the table. Michel claims to be a classic cook, yet he tends to use the modern style of presentation. On his menu the expensive items such as foie gras, lobster, turbot, deer, and lamb are featured in various ways and shapes.

Located 3 km (2 miles) from Lunéville, the festive château hides its guests within the privacy of the dining-room, overlooking the pastoral beauty of a splendidly renovated park. A horse-and-carriage will bring you to this lovely residence and a young and cheerful staff will make your stay pleasant and memorable.

Grenouilles Sauce verte Frogs' legs in green sauce

4 portions

4 dozen frogs' legs (in England use
   frozen packs)
225 g (8 oz) fish bones from
   salmon or trout
300 ml (½ pint) water and wine
   mixed
1 onion, sliced,
1 carrot, sliced
1 bouquet garni
1 sprig of mint

Sauce
15 ml (1 tbsp) cider or sherry
   vinegar
15 ml (1 tbsp) shallot, chopped
6 mint leaves, chopped
3 spinach leaves, chopped
1 sprig parsley, chopped
100 ml (4 fl oz) double cream
Salt and pepper

Boil the stock ingredients in the wine and water for 25 minutes and strain into another saucepan.

Poach the frogs' legs for 5 minutes in the stock, remove and keep warm. Add mint, parsley, and spinach, and liquidize the ingredients. Reheat and add cream and seasoning. Barely boil for 2 minutes.

Pour a pool of the sauce on to 4 plates and arrange the frogs' legs, allowing 12 per portion.

Serve as a starter.

Christian Morisset

Chef de Cuisine
Hôtel Juana
La Pinède
Avenue Général de Gaulle
Juan-les-Pins 06160
France
Tel: 93.61.08.70

Like all well-trained culinarians, Christian Morisset began his career by gaining the certificate of Patissier-Confiseur Glacier, then the certificate in cookery, and finally the master's degree in pastry. For 8 years he worked in the pastry shops at Lizant, Rocadis and Arles. He took on the cookery side of the business at the Mas d'Artigny in St Paul-de-Vence. Next he was promoted to chef de cuisine at La Bonne Auberge in Antibes. After a spell at the Moulin with Verge, he became head chef at the Altiport Hotel Meribel in Les Allues. He returned as sous chef to Verge, and became head chef at the Château d'Esclimont in Saint-Symphorien-le-Château. Finally, in 1987, he was appointed chef de cuisine of the Juana Hotel and soon was awarded 2 Michelin stars.

The menu and the dishes he presents are a revelation to many culinarians who can evaluate the work involved in a ravioli stuffed crab or chicken served with courgettes filled with a light mousseline. Indeed the recipe he gives us reflects the skill of the patissier and the cook — Filet de lapereau fermier, mijoté aux cebettes, avec son foie chaud et tagliatelle frâiches aux blettes (Rabbit with chard leaves, foie gras and pasta). A light Mediterranean dish with the Italian touch maybe, but how original!

Hôtel Juana lies in a garden fringed with palm-trees. The clientele can have a swim in the pool and drink their cocktails oblivious of the world outside. In the distance the Lérins Islands are silhouetted on the horizon. The building, massive and white, is sheltered from the powerful wind of the south. At night, all rooms and the garden terrace are illuminated, and this brightness, in contrast to the black night, is like a scene from Walpurgisnacht in *Faust*.

Three generations of the Barache family have run this elegant and sumptuous hotel, the most luxurious in Juan-les-Pins.

Filet de Lapereau fermier, mijoté aux Cebettes, avec son Foie gras chaud et Tagliatelle frâiches aux Blettes

Rabbit with chard leaves, foie gras and pasta

4 portions

100 g (4 oz) butter (divided for three uses)
4 saddles of rabbit, completely boned and filleted but retaining the under-fillets
50 g (2 oz) raw chicken meat from breast
30 ml (1 fl oz) double cream
1 litre (1¾ pint) chicken stock
4 small beets (not the red ones), peeled and sliced
4 chard leaves
225 g (8 oz) goose liver (or duck liver)
30 ml (2 tbsp) oil

Pasta
300 g (10 oz) flour
3 eggs, beaten
5 ml (1 tsp) salt
4 chard leaves, cut in shreds

In a sauté pan, heat some of the butter and sauté the rabbit fillets for 3 minutes, just to sear the meat. Season and remove. Cool until cold.

Prepare a forcemeat with the chicken meat. Mince it and blend it in a bowl with cream and seasoning. Coat the rabbit with this chicken paste.

Scald the chard leaves for 10 seconds in boiling salted water. Drain and wipe dry on a cloth. Wrap the 8 fillets of rabbit with the chard leaves to form green parcels.

Make the dough for the pasta. Mix the flour, eggs, and salt and knead it a little. Wrap it in a polythene bag and rest it for 1 hour. Then roll it to 4 mm (¼ in) on a floured pastry board. If you have a noodle machine pass the paste through. Otherwise roll it and cut it into ribbons 5 mm (¼ in) wide.

Prepare a sauce. In a sauté pan, heat 30 ml (2 tbsp) oil and fry the rabbit bones and trimmings. Stir in the chicken stock, add the small beets (cebettes) and cook on a low heat for 30 minutes. Strain the reduced stock. Place the rabbit fillets on to a shallow dish, cover with the reduced stock and cook for 5 minutes in a hot oven, 200°C, 400°F, gas mark 6.

Lastly, boil the tagliatelle in salted water for 5 minutes. Drain and reheat with 2 tbsp of butter and blend in the shredded raw chard leaves. Then quickly sauté the liver slices, for 4 minutes, 1 per portion, in the remaining butter. Season to taste.

Serve 2 fillets per portion, with some tagliatelle, a slice of liver, and the sauce seasoned to taste.

Ray Morrison

Chef/Proprietor
The Old Hoops
15 King Street
Saffron Walden CB10 1HE
Essex
Tel: (0799) 22813

Ray and his wife bought this charming eating place in 1985 after a successful period at the Oxford and Cambridge Club in London, where we first met him. He has now firmly established a leading position for himself throughout Essex, and his specialities reflect the talent of an enthusiastic English chef.

Watercress soup with mussels, Calves' liver with cassis, Lamb with light mustard sauce and a light dessert of Almond biscuit with passion fruit are an exquisite 'ensemble' for a perfect meal.

Ray began his career in 1958 by taking a City and Guilds course full time at Hendon Technical College. He worked for British Transport Hotels for almost 20 years with the positions of chef saucier at the Charing Cross Hotel, London, sous-chef at the Manor House Hotel, Devon, and chef de cuisine at the Great Northern Hotel, London.

Ray is a practical man whose hobbies nevertheless include astronomy and art. A founder member of the Society of Master Chefs, he always brings to the Committee a common-sense approach to everything. This extends to the way he runs his kitchen as well, with no fuss but a mixture of dry humour and authority that is efficiency plus.

Crème Cressonnière et Moules   Mussel and watercress soup

4 portions

600 ml (1 pint) mussels
300 ml (½ pint) white wine
300 ml (½ pint) fish stock
1 medium onion, finely chopped
1 stick celery, finely chopped
300 ml (½ pint) whipping or
    double cream
1 medium-sized potato, peeled
    and diced fairly small
½ bunch of watercress
salt and pepper

Wash and de-beard the mussels and place in a saucepan, adding the white wine, fish stock, onion, and celery. Cover and bring to the boil until all the mussels are open.

Strain off the juice, and put the mussels to one side. Add the cream to the juice and bring back to the boil. Reduce gently by about a third. Add diced potato and cook for a further 10 minutes.

Taste for seasoning, then add the shelled mussels and the watercress chopped at the last minute. Finish with a knob of butter.

Serve with fresh granary bread.

Bernard Müller

Chef de Cuisine
Hôtel des Trois Epis
Blumenrain 8
Basel 4000
Switzerland
Tel: 19.41.61.28.52.52

Bernard Müller began his career at the Negresco in Nice and at the Palace in St Moritz. In 1961 he became chef patissier at Ciba-Geigy near Basel, in Switzerland. In 1977 he joined the luxury hotel Les Trois Epis. Bernard Müller is French and has worked most of his life in Switzerland where he is acknowledged as the grand master of his craft. His menu reflects the quality of the fare in a splendid manner: Salmon in coriander seeds, Terrine of game with foie gras, Duck consommé with quail eggs, Crêpes aux deux caviars, and the local lake fish with noodles. Strange as it may seem, he also does a dish of veal with crawfish. The patisserie in Switzerland is the best in the world, and the sweet trolley is a picture of delicate, fruity, and tempting desserts for children and adults alike.

From such a unique menu, whose items change according to the market and season, we decided to produce a recipe based on the delicate terrine. The winter sports bring the jet set from England, and because of their catholic taste in gastronomy, we substituted turkey for the game used in one terrine. Here you have a culinary adaptation which can easily revert to game, according to the wish of the guest.

The Hôtel des Trois Epis is a Michelin star hotel. The manager is Roman Steiner.

This is a city full of history. It is most influenced by German culture, although the population can speak two or three languages. The zoo, museums, the cathedral and the fish market are all worth visiting. Basel is on the Rhine, which brings boatloads of tourists from many parts.

Terrine de Dinde   Turkey terrine

10 portions

150 g (5 oz) French beans

150 g (5 oz) carrots, peeled, cut
  into thin sticks and halved
  lengthwise

8 cabbage leaves, rib part
  removed, blanched for
  30 seconds and refreshed

Forcemeat

300 g (10 oz) raw breast of turkey,
  skinless, minced

50 g (2 oz) turkey liver or calves'
  liver, skinless, cleaned, minus
  gall bladder

50 g (2 oz) back bacon rasher,
  rindless with a little of the fat

2 whole eggs, beaten

120 ml (8 tbsp) double cream

30 ml (2 tbsp) brandy, gin, or
  whisky

5 ml (1 tsp) salt

1.25 ml (¼ tsp) crushed black
  peppercorns

5 ml (1 tsp) ground gelatine
  soaked in 120 ml (8 tbsp)
  stock (cold then reheated to
  dissolve)

Garnish

100 g (4 oz) fresh cranberries and
  a few vine leaves or mint leaves

Aspic

300 ml (½ pint) amber colour
  aspic made from clear turkey
  or chicken stock

½ tsp (15 g) ground gelatine

Blanch the beans (head and tailed, cut to the same length) and carrots for just 2 minutes, refresh in cold water, and pat dry in a cloth.

Mince the turkey, liver, and bacon together. In a bowl blend the mixture with beaten eggs, cream, and brandy, gin, or even whisky. Season with 5 ml (1 tsp) salt and crushed peppercorns.

Dissolve the 5 ml (1 tsp) gelatine in stock. Cool and blend it with the forcemeat.

Butter a 1¼-litre (2-pint) capacity oblong earthenware terrine with soft butter and line the bottom and sides with cling film, then blanched, diced cabbage leaves.

Place a layer of the forcemeat 2 cm (¾ in) thick in the bottom, then a layer of the carrot, then a layer of the beans. Repeat the layers until the terrine is full. Cover with cabbage leaves. Place the terrine in a deep tray half filled with water and bake in a preheated oven 200°C, 400°F, gas mark 6, middle shelf, for 40 minutes.

Remove. Cool and chill overnight.

To serve

Prepare a good transparent aspic by dissolving 15 g (½ oz) of ground gelatine in the hot turkey or chicken stock. Cool. When nearly cold, pour the aspic on to plates. This will form a skin that looks like a skating rink when it has set firmly.

Turn out the terrine on to a pastry board for cutting. With a knife dipped in hot water, cut slices (1 cm) (½ in) thick and place one on each plate. Decorate with cranberries and mint leaves or vine leaves.

Any type of poultry or feathered game can be used for this recipe instead of turkey.

Graham Newbold

Chef de Cuisine
Inverlochy Castle
Torlundy
Fort William
Highlands PH33 6SN
Scotland
Tel: (0397) 2177

Graham Newbold was recently chef to the Prince and Princess of Wales, for 4 years previous to his employment at Inverlochy Castle. Trained at Wakefield College in 1966, this young chef has already achieved eminence in the starlit world of cookery. He was also a cook at Buckingham Palace for three years and moved with the Royal Family to all the other stately establishments at the service of Her Majesty. He then gained valuable experience at the Connaught Hotel and is now ruling his own domain.

Three of his specialities are in line with this grand style: a Game consommé flavoured with lovage, a Salmon and wild mushroom pie to represent Scottish fare, and Turban of smoked haddock with pink champagne sauce — all dishes which would have tickled the palate of Mary, Queen of Scots, who was a great eater.

Inverlochy was built by Lord Abinger in 1863, and Queen Victoria, who stayed there, wrote that the spot was enchanting and romantic. This luxurious castle stands amongst the foothills of Ben Nevis, in 500 acres of land.

The owner is Mrs Grete Hobbs and the managing director is Michael Leonard.

Consommé au Pigeon   Consommé of wood pigeon scented with lovage

6 portions

3 breasts of pigeons, boned, skinned and cooked
225 g (8 oz) minced raw chicken
225 g (8 oz) minced raw pigeon (from legs)
Bouquet garni
6 black peppercorns
150 g (6 oz) minced mixed vegetables (carrot, celery, leek, and onion)
1 good bunch of lovage
100 ml (4 fl oz) port wine
4 egg whites
Salt
1¼ litres (2 pints) good chicken stock (cold)

Mix the chicken, pigeon, washed minced vegetables, bouquet garni, and peppercorns with the egg whites, then add the cold chicken stock and the bunch of lovage. Place in a thick-bottomed pan and bring to the boil slowly, stirring occasionally to prevent burning. When a crust has formed on the top of the soup simmer for 1½ hours, taking care not to disturb the crust on top or this may make the soup cloudy. Strain the soup carefully through fine muslin, removing any fat that has settled on top with kitchen paper. Correct the seasoning with salt and add the port wine, chop a little cooked pigeon breast to place in the soup bowls as a garnish. Serve piping hot and place a small lovage leaf on top.

Couronne d'Eglefin   Turban of smoked haddock with pink champagne sauce

4 portions

Mousse
100 g (4 oz) lemon sole fillets,
  skinned
100 g (4 oz) scallops
100 g (4 oz) smoked haddock
  fillets, boned and skinned
1 egg white
300 ml (10 fl oz) double cream
Salt and cayenne pepper

Filling
350 ml (12 fl oz) skinned smoked
  haddock fillets (diced)
300 ml (10 fl oz) double cream

Champagne sauce
3 Dover sole bones
300 ml (10 fl oz) dry white wine
600 ml (1 pint) fish stock
50 g (2 oz) shallots, sliced
25 g (1 oz) button mushrooms,
  sliced
200 ml (6 fl oz) pink champagne
300 ml (10 fl oz) double cream
Pinch of sugar

Garnish
16 Queen scallops, grilled
2 tomatoes skinned, deseeded,
  and chopped
Chervil

Mousse
Blend the sole, scallops, and smoked haddock in a processor with egg white, then pass through a fine sieve. Pour into a bowl and gradually beat in the double cream and season with salt and cayenne pepper. Carefully spoon the mousse into four individual buttered turban moulds, then cover with buttered greaseproof paper and aluminium foil. Cook in a bain-marie in an oven pre-heated to 180°C, 350°F, gas mark 4, for 10–15 minutes, until firm to the touch.

Filling
Boil the double cream to reduce it by half, add the haddock and cook for approximately 1 minute, correct the seasoning.

Champagne sauce
Place the sole bones, white wine, fish stock, shallots, mushrooms and sugar into a saucepan. Bring to the boil and reduce the liquid to one-fifth. Add the cream and reduce by one-third. Complete with the pink champagne. Check the seasoning and strain the sauce. Keep the sauce warm.

To serve
Turn out the haddock mousse on to a plate, coat lightly with the champagne sauce. Place the haddock filling into the centre, garnish around with the grilled Queen scallops, chopped tomato and sprigs of chervil.

Alain Nonnet

Chef de Cuisine/Proprietor
La Cognette
Issoudun 36100
France
Tèl: 54.91.91.83

Born in La Châtre near Issoudun, Alain Nonnet attended the Ecole Hôtelière of Thonon-les-Bains. He progressed rapidly in star restaurants such as le Chateaubriant, La Marée and The Ritz in Paris. He was a winner of the best cook competition of France, and he is the Président des Tables Gourmandes du Berry and medallist of the Ministry of Agriculture. He now runs La Cognette with great enthusiasm, ably assisted by his wife Nicole and daughter Isabelle.

Perusing his many menus is like studying the gastronomy of the Berry province. His dishes include Terrine de lièvre, Poulet en barbouille Raviolis de langoustines, and Filet mignon au thé et badiane. Imagine the tenderloin under-fillet or the tail end of beef flavoured with tea and star anis; one is inclined to wonder whether this odd mixture will give the right taste. But we can assure you it does.

We noted Snail turnovers as well as Pike with nettles. The sweet trolley was as exciting, with Gâteau Tante Yema, Tulipe glacée au marc, Roasted figs, and Pancake soufflés with pears. Naturally all the Loire wines were available, including Chinon and Couly to name but two.

Described by Honoré de Balzac in his book *La Barbouilleuse*, this venerable auberge dating from 1836 has kept its Napoleonic style.

The hotel is located 27 km (16½ miles) from Châteauroux, in a region that was dear to George Sand, the writer. It is a gastronomic restaurant par excellence, highly rated and approved by local gourmets as well. This place was opened by a man called Père Cognet whose wife was nicknamed 'Cognette'. Was it because she was a first class *cordon bleu*? From that time on the reputation grew and the rest is history. Apart from the best of meats, the region also produces lentils and the rivers abound in carp.

Carpe à la Bérichonne   Carp Berry-style in red wine

4 portions

300 ml (½ pint) red wine
1 onion, sliced
1 bouquet garni
1 clove of garlic, crushed
1 carp 1.25 kg (3 lb) scaled,
    gutted, and cut into steaks
    across the bone
15 ml (1 tbsp) flour + 15 ml
    (1 tbsp) butter (for thickening)
30 ml (2 tbsp) oil
4 slices of crustless bread, cut into
    triangles
12 spring onions, sliced
Salt and pepper

Boil the wine with the onions, garlic and bouquet garni for 10 minutes, then cool.

Place the carp pieces in an earthenware dish and cover with the cold stock.

Bake in the oven at 220°C, 425°F, gas mark 7, for 15 minutes, covered with a lid.

Strain the fish liquor into a saucepan and thicken it with a paste of flour and butter. Season to taste and simmer for 8 minutes. Strain the sauce.

Fry the bread in oil until golden.

Place the fish on flat dish coated with the sauce and surrounded with the fried croûtons.

Filet mignon au Thé et Badiane   Tender tail beef fillet with star anis and tea

4 portions

1 anis star (badiane)
1 tea bag
300 ml (½ pint) boiling water
4 fillets of beef, preferably the tail
    end, flattened thin like
    escalopes
15 ml (1 tbsp) soya sauce or
    Worcester sauce
6 black peppercorns, crushed
45 ml (3 tbsp) oil
4 mushrooms, sliced
2 shallots
Salt and pepper

Brew the tea and anis star in boiling water in a teapot for 4 minutes and strain.

Season the beef fillets and sprinkle with soya sauce or Worcester sauce. Add the crushed peppercorns. Leave to soak for 20 minutes.

Heat some of the oil in a frying pan and stir-fry shallots and mushrooms for 2 minutes. Remove with a slotted spoon. With the rest of the oil, pan-fry the steaks, according to requirement, rare or medium, for about 2 minutes. Remove from the pan. Now add the brew and bring it to the boil with the cooked mushrooms and shallots for 1 minute. Season with salt. Pour just enough gravy on to 4 plates and place the steaks on it. Surplus sauce can be used again.

Note: Veal or pork can also be cooked in this way.

Christopher John Oakes

Chef de Cuisine/Proprietor
Oakes Restaurant
169 Slad Road
Stroud
Gloucestershire GL5 1RG
Tel: (04536) 79950

Christopher Oakes is one of those British chefs who can take any challenge in cookery in their stride. His menu reflects a man with taste, talent, and the ability to please his clients without fuss.

He was trained at two colleges, Ipswich and Essex, to an advanced level of cookery. He became head chef of the Castle at Taunton, famed for its high standards. He completed his apprenticeship in many other places, including the Talbooth in Essex and a spell in Switzerland. Christopher is one of the great English chefs who have made their mark in recent years.

His four menus at different prices include a selection of innovative cuisine. Typical dishes are Potted pork with pumpkin conserve, Lentil soup with fish in saffron, Marinaded trout in yoghurt sauce, and a modern Salade tiède with pine nuts and pigeon.

The main courses are just as exciting: Breast of chicken with smoked ham and vegetable mousse, or Fillet of brill with anis seed sauce, and Loin of venison with cranberries and apple.

We found his Hot soufflé in cinnamon spice with Drambuie cream to rank with the best English sweets. He also does a light Bread and butter pudding with an apricot sauce, and a Pear in butterscotch. And he makes his own crispy bread rolls.

Oakes Restaurant is an early nineteenth-century Cotswold stone house with mullioned windows, which was previously a finishing-school, but has now been transformed into a family restaurant. It is located in Stroud, a town famed for its cloth industry in the Arcadian setting of the southern Cotswolds and the Golden Valley.

Caroline Oakes, and Nowell and Jean Scott run the restaurant while Christopher officiates in his kitchen.

Soufflé à la Cannelle   Cinnamon soufflé with Drambuie cream

4 portions

620 g (1 lb 6 oz) ripe pears,
    peeled, cored, and diced
600 ml (1 pint) water
5 ml (1 tsp) cornflour
30 ml (2 tbsp) water
5 ml (1 tsp) cinnamon
75 g (3 oz) granulated sugar
5 egg whites

Decoration
300 ml (½ pint) whipping cream
15 g (½ oz) sugar
30 ml (1 fl oz) Drambuie

Note: Any fruit can be used similarly.

Purée
Place pears in saucepan, barely cover with water and cook until soft.
    Liquidize to a purée and recook until thick, stirring occasionally (approximately 5 minutes). Mix the cornflour and water together and stir into the pear mixture and cook on a low heat for a further 10 minutes. Flavour with cinnamon. The purée should now have a finer texture.
    This purée can now be used immediately or kept in the fridge for later use.

Cream
Whisk the cream until it peaks. Sprinkle on sugar and add Drambuie to taste. Chill in a sauceboat.

Soufflé
Warm the purée gently in a bain-marie.
    Whisk the egg whites with a pinch of salt in a copper bowl until they peak. Add sugar a little at a time, beating between each addition until it is firm again to a meringue texture.
    Blend a spoonful of the meringue into the pear purée, and then fold in the rest gently and thoroughly.
    Butter ramekin moulds and sprinkle sugar inside the moulds.
    Spoon in the soufflé mixture up to the rim. Smooth off around the edge with a palette knife, finishing with a flat top.
    Place on a baking sheet in a pre-heated oven at 220°C, 425°F, gas mark 7, for approximately 10–12 minutes.
    Dust with icing sugar and serve immediately, with the sauceboat of whipped cream.

Patrick Pages

Chef de Cuisine/Proprietor
Hostellerie Chantoiseau
Vialas 48220
Le Pont de Monvert
France
Tel: 66.61.00.02

Patrick Pages is one of those fabulous characters who endears himself by his sheer enthusiasm in teaching his customers gastronomy. A former student of the Ecole Hôtelière of Grenoble, with a good foundation in all departments, he now teaches his art to his own clientele. Patrick has been honoured by his colleagues too. He and his wife welcomed President Mitterand on a recent visit to Chantoiseau and the former German Chancellor Willy Brandt has tasted his fare many times. This is the success story of a man who, since 1975, has established his own place on a par with the top inns of France. This is also the man who won the Grand Prix Nationale de Cuisine.

The menu is not another large piece of gold cardboard, but a little book which guests can take with them after eating and drinking. We have selected a few examples: his own pâté for which a recipe is given; then Quails with blueberries, asparagus and three types of mushrooms and three sauces; Carp with spinach; Monkfish with pasta; Tripe with wine; Leg of mutton with beans; Chicken and chestnuts; all the goat cheese of the region; and old-fashioned tarts. As for the local Languedoc wines, we have Banyuls Grenache, Muscat de Lunel, some young, some old, and all very good.

This is an exciting region, not far from the famous Gorges du Tarn. Against a background of mountains, the hotel stands like a fortress, with its long garden bordering the road, its flag flapping in the wind, as if a festival were in perpetual progress. The sign outside under a canopy of red roof tiles spells the name 'Chantoiseau'. All around, the woodlands are thick with chestnut trees, and the meadows full of wild mushrooms. Near the National Park, this old hotel has become a monument. The dining-room's stone walls are a reminder of the age of the place, for the building dates from the seventeenth century. The huge chimney in the dining-room, the timbered ceiling, the copper pans on the wall, shining in the light, and the candles on the table at night give the place a vibrant atmosphere, which reflects the happy mood of the people.

Terrine de Foies de Volaille   Chicken liver pâté

12 portions

8 thin slices cooked ham
50 g (2 oz) farm butter or lard
450 g (1 lb) lean veal
450 g (1 lb) lean pork
450 g (1 lb) chicken liver
15 g (½ oz) salt and 4 ml (¾ tsp)
    black pepper
30 ml (2 tbsp) gin
5 eggs
150 g (6 oz) field mushrooms,
    chopped
3 shallots, chopped
25 g (1 oz) flour
100 ml (4 fl oz) white port
6 sheets gelatine

This pâté will freeze well and it can also be used as a forcemeat for chicken or turkey.

Clean the liver and be sure to remove the gall without bursting it. Wash and drain.

Mince the port, veal, and liver, and blend the forcemeat in a mixing bowl. Add beaten eggs, chopped shallots, flour, chopped raw mushrooms, gin, port wine, salt, and pepper. Mix well. Leave the mixture in the refrigerator for 2 hours to allow for flavour development.

Line a terrine with cling film and grease it with soft butter or lard and stick the ham slices on the wall of the mould. Soak 6 sheets of gelatine in cold water for 10 minutes. When soft blend with the meat mixture and fill the mould to the top.

Place the mould on a deep baking tray with hot water and bake at 180°C, 350°F, gas mark 4, middle shelf, for 1 hour 45 minutes.

Cool. When cold, unmould and cut into slices and serve with lettuce leaves on smaller plates.

Store the pâté in a refrigerator for further use.

Note: Instead of pork meat you can use sausage meat.

The soaked gelatine sheets can be placed between the two layers of forcemeat with a few on top. This will produce a succulent aspic jelly with the juice of the meat.

Albert R. Parveaux

Proprietor
Château de Castel-Novel
Varetz 19240
Corrèze
France
Tel: 55.85.00.01

Albert Parveaux learned bakery, pâtisseries, general management, and cookery at the famed Ecole Hôtelière of Paris. Four generations have succeeded one other in the Parveaux family. The great-grandfather opened a modest café, which became a hotel, and eventually his successors rose to higher status when they acquired this fabulous château in Corrèze. Assisted by his wife Christine, Albert runs this castle every summer season, and another one in winter, Château de Puy-Robert at Montignac.

The menu has a choice of 100 items. From Foie gras de canard to a simple Neck of goose meat wrapped in cabbage leaves as a starter; the local soups especially attracted our attention. We noted Tourain à l'ail and Crème de la jatte a l'oseille. Other regional specialities we noted include Hot-pot of duck, Civet of pork, Flan of guinea-fowl with salsify, Beef steak with mustard sauce, and Rhubarb compote.

All the poetry of this cheerful Corrèze countryside gives this château-citadel, with its pink-stone turrets, the appearance of an elegant country residence in a park of 100-year-old oak trees, cedars, and beeches.

Poêlée de Foie au Cidre   Liver in cider

4 portions

150 ml (5 fl oz) butter and oil for
    stir-frying
4 × 150 g (5 oz) pieces of calves'
    liver
30 ml (2 tbsp) flour seasoned with
    salt and black pepper
150 ml (5 fl oz) milk

Cider sauce
2 shallots, chopped
30 ml (2 tbsp) butter and oil
150 ml (5 fl oz) dry cider
Salt, pepper, and mace
75 ml (3 fl oz) double cream

Garnish
4 small Cox's apples poached in
    cider.

First prepare the liver. Soak in 150 ml (¼ pint) of milk and marinade for 5 minutes. Drain and coat with seasoned flour, shaking off the surplus.

Heat the butter and oil and stir-fry the livers for 4 minutes, keeping them juicy. Remove livers and keep warm.

In the same pan, fry shallots for 4 minutes. Slowly add the cider and boil for 4 minutes to reduce. Season and blend in the cream while whisking the sauce. Strain and pour on to 4 plates. Add the cooked livers and garnish with 1 whole poached apple per person.

Martyn J. Pearn

Chef de Cuisine
Buckland Manor
Buckland
Gloucestershire WR12 7LY
Tel: (0386) 852626

Martyn Pearn is a graduate with distinction of the City and Guilds of London Institute. He progressed at the Hyatt Carlton in Knightsbridge and then at the Connaught Hotel in Mayfair. On the strength of such experience he was appointed chef de cuisine at the Hôtel la Réserve, Pessac in Bordeaux — no mean achievement for an English chef! He has managed the kitchen of Buckland Manor since 1986.

His menu has the simplicity of perfection with six starters to choose from on a handwritten bill of fare. We were interested to notice a pickled duck cured like ham and served with a Roquefort cheese. A Millefeuille de champignons had a touch of fantasy about it, highly suitable for vegetarian gourmets. Martyn Pearn seems to have a liking for blue cheese dressing — another item was made up of a mousse of blue cheese inside a breast of guinea-fowl. Original idea, we thought.

His talent oozes from the style of his recipes. Délice de truite de mer et sole cooked in a terrine of leeks would be our favourite as a starter. The Duck in a sweet and sour sauce with onions was redolent of the Italina agro dolce dishes so well celebrated by the masters of Chinese cuisine, and introduced to Italy by Marco Polo. And finally we come to the pudding, no doubt a popular one with children and lusty epicureans, in the form of Mousse de chocolate blanc et Cointreau. This sweet has been called Marquise by many chefs and mousse by the more conservative culinarians, for mousse it is. Originally served in prewar days in France in small pots known as *petits pots au chocolat*. The fact that you can choose dark, milky and white chocolate only makes it more versatile, and as for the liqueur, chefs have used also Grand Marnier, rum or brandy as well as Cointreau.

Buckland Manor is owned by Adrienne and Barry Berman, two sophisticated gourmets who have transformed this delightful residence into one of Britain's most luxurious hotels. It lies in the village of Buckland, nestling in a valley midway between Cheltenham and Stratford-upon-Avon. The site was first mentioned in about AD 600 when the land was given by Kynred, King of the Mercians, to the Abbey of Gloucester.

Guests are pampered and cosseted like royal visitors, and the Manor has many acres of garden, and all kinds of amenities including horse riding and golf.

Délice de Truite de Mer et Sole au Coeur de Poireaux Trout and sole terrine

8 portions

1.2 kg (3 lb) sea trout, skinned
   and filleted
3 large Dover sole, 400 g (14 oz)
   each, skinned and filleted
1 kg (2 lb 2 oz) blanched baby
   leeks
25 g (1 oz) chopped parsley,
   tarragon, basil, and chervil
200 ml (6 fl oz) hazelnut oil
50 ml (2 fl oz) lemon juice

Line a 25-cm (10-in) oblong terrine with good-quality oven-proof cling-film and cover the entire terrine with fillets of sole, boneside down with the head and tail ends of the fish hanging over the edge of the terrine. Layer the terrine with the blanched leeks, season, fillet of sea trout, season, then the remaining sole. Repeat until all the fish and leeks have been used. Finish by folding over the sole fillets and cook in a bain-marie for just 25 minutes in a moderate oven 180°C, 350°F, gas mark 4. When cooked, remove and place a weighted object on top of the terrine to press the fish down in order that the natural gelatine will set the terrine. Refrigerate for 24 hours and serve accompanied by a fresh herb vinaigrette.

Caneton rôti et sa Marmelade d'Oignon Roast duck and onion

4 portions

2.5 kg (5½ lb) domestic duck
Salt and pepper
4 medium onions, thinly sliced
100 g (4 oz) butter
180 g (6 oz) good-quality honey
200 ml (7 fl oz) red wine vinegar
½ bottle claret
600 ml (1 pint) good dark duck
   stock
Chervil
Mirepoix of 1 onion, 2 carrots,
   ½ heart celery, all chopped
   uniformly

In a hot oven roast the seasoned duck for 45 minutes, keeping it quite pink. In a solid-bottomed pan, stew the onion with half the butter and vinegar. When the vinegar has been absorbed, add the honey and cook, covered, for 1½ hours, stirring from time to time. When cooked it should resemble a rich marmalade. Keep the duck warm.

Remove fat from roasting tray, add the *mirepoix*; colour slightly. Add the red wine and boil, scraping the bottom of the tray to remove all sediment. Reduce by half, add the duck stock, reduce again by half and pour through a fine sieve into a saucepan. Whisk in the remaining butter.

To serve
Remove the 2 legs and keep warm. Remove the 2 breasts lengthways. Pile the marmalade into a buttered dariole mould and tip out to one side of a large dinner plate. Arrange the sliced breast cascading off the marmalade, with the legs, trimmed to remove the knuckle, placed on the opposite side of the plate. Flash under the grill, reheat the sauce and coat the pieces. Garnish with chervil and serve.

Michel Philippe

Chef de Cuisine/Proprietor
Hostellerie des Bas-Rupts
Gérardmer 88400
Vosges
France
Tel: 29.63.09.25

Michel Philippe began his career at the Capucin Gourmand in Nancy, where his first job was to clean mussels, a bivalve he had never seen before. He learned to make ice cream, using a hand-mixing/freezing machine. Nowadays, with an electric ice-cream machine, this task is done in 5 minutes. His next experience was to work on the stove, roasting meat and birds of all sizes.

He completed his training as a chef in Paris at the sophisticated Fouquet's on the Champs-Elysées. In 1960 he bought the Hostellerie, in this delightful part of the Vosges on the slopes of a mountain, and won a Michelin star. It was there he trained his daughter to cook. He has participated as a culinary competitor in many gastronomic events, lecturing on his local cuisine.

In the autumn, he offers a large selection of game, wild mushrooms, and pike from the lake of Gérardmer. In the spring he cooks asparagus, assorted salades tièdes, young goat meat, and frogs.

Bas-Rupts Hostellerie is a few kilometres from Gérardmer in the Vosges. This region is well known for its winter sports. The hotel looks like a Swiss chalet set in the snow-covered hills. The Hostellerie has five dining-rooms and full amenities for children.

Michotte aux Mirabelles   Golden plum pizza

6 portions

3 whole eggs, beaten
200g (8 oz) caster sugar
600 ml (1 pint) milk or single
　cream
250 g (8 oz) self-raising flour
3 drops of vanilla essence
20 golden plums (the French
　variety called mirabelles),
　stoned
30 ml (2 tbsp) mirabelle liqueur

Butter a deep metal cake mould 2 cm (¾ in) high.

Beat the eggs and sugar in a bowl for 5 minutes, then stir in the milk or cream, and blend in the flour. Flavour with vanilla essence.

Place the stoned mirabelle plums in the mould and drizzle the liqueur over them. Pour in the batter to cover the plums completely as if it were a Yorkshire batter pudding. Bake in a moderate oven at 180°C, 350°F, gas mark 4, for 45 minutes. The texture should be like a set custard. Serve with cream.

Patrick Pommier

Chef de Cuisine/Director
Le Petit Coq aux Champs
Campigny 27500
France
Tèl: 32.41.04.19

Patrick Pommier, aged 39, initially learned his craft from his father Francis, who was trained in Paris at the famous Larue Restaurant. Francis was also head chef at the Bristol and for 22 years owned Le Petit Coq, 16 Rue de Budapest, Paris. When the lease ran out the family moved to Campigny, where for the past 22 years they have brought a ray of gastronomic sunshine to Normandy. This is the typical example of a fourth generation of *cuisiniers* which inspired us to produce a book based on their family heritage.

Their menu contains a list of the best of both worlds in modern and classic Norman dishes, where calvados suitably replaces brandy in almost every recipe. Steak de lotte aux petits oignons confits, Le paletot de Barbarie au cidre, and Les escargots petit gris en feuilleté are recipes which have been formulated by this father-and-son team.

The restaurant is located outside the Forêt de Orée, close to a large park. It has a swimming pool and a lawn where the game of *boules* can be played. All other sports amenities, including tennis and golf, are available nearby.

It is located within reach of many important Norman towns, including Bayeux, with its tapestry, Rouen with its churches and chapels, and various seaside resorts such as Honfleur, Deauville, and Etretat.

Inside the dining-room there is a rustic atmosphere with high chimney and beams across the ceiling. Tables with candles are rather stylish in the evening.

In the summer the meals are served in the garden to the sound of music.

Côte de Veau Vallée d'Auge   Veal cutlets with apples

4 portions

100 g (4 oz) butter and oil
4 veal cutlets, trimmed and
    chined
15 ml (1 tbsp) seasoned flour
2 apples, peeled, cored, and
    quartered
60 ml (4 tbsp) calvados
100 ml (4 fl oz) double cream of
    Normandie
Salt and pepper

Heat butter and oil in a large sauté pan. Cook apples for 3 minutes, remove and keep warm on a dish.

Rub each cutlet in seasoned flour, shake off surplus and pan-fry gently in the same fat used for apples. After 12 minutes remove surplus fat and flame in calvados, extinguish the flames immediately by stirring in the cream. Boil for 4 minutes. Season to taste.

Pour a pool of sauce on to 4 plates, place a veal cutlet on each plate and garnish with 4 apple segments.

Steak de Requin au Calvados aux petits Oignons confits   Shark fish with onions and prawns

4 portions

4 200 g (6 oz) shark fish fillets
50 ml (2 fl oz) Calvados

Stock
450 g (1 lb) fish bones
1 onion and 1 carrot, sliced
1 bouquet garni
450 ml (¾ pint) plus 150 ml (¼
   pint) white wine
3 crushed peppercorns
1 clove of garlic, crushed and a
   sprig of parsley

Cream thickening
2 egg yolks
90 ml (3 fl oz) double cream
15 ml (1 tbsp) chives, chopped

Garnish
225 g (8 oz) button onions
50 g (2 oz) butter
5 ml (1 tsp) honey
Salt and pepper
4 Dublin Bay prawns
1 raw carrot, thinly sliced on the
   slant and scalded, for
   decoration
Chervil or parsley, chopped
Chives, snipped

Boil the stock ingredients for 20 minutes. Add the prawns and boil for 5 minutes more. Remove the prawns and strain the liquor for sauce-making. Shell the prawns for garnish.

Place the stock in a deep tray and poach the fish for 8–10 minutes. Season to taste. Remove and keep warm.

Boil the stock again and reduce to half its original volume.

In a bowl, blend egg yolks and cream, and then gradually stir in about a cup of the reduced stock. Pour back this mixture and reheat it to effect a liaison like a custard sauce. Do not boil.

Check seasoning.

Pour a pool of the sauce on to 4 plates. Arrange a fillet on each one with a prawn, 3 slices of carrot, and a sprig of green chervil or parsley for decoration. Sprinkle the fish with chopped or snipped chives.

Shell the prawns and reheat in the sauce.

Garnish
Heat butter and stir-fry the onions without too much coloration. Cover with water and boil for 6 minutes, until water evaporates. Add honey and simmer for 2 minutes until it is like butterscotch. Stir in the calvados. Set it alight and serve on the side of the fish.

Pierre Pontis

Chef de Cuisine
Le Plaisance
Quai Arthur Rimbaud
Saint-Cyprien
France
Tel: 68.21.14.34

Pierre Pontis was a pupil of André Daguin of the Hôtel de France. He gained further experience with Michel Bellaton at Perpignan.

Pierre offers a short but interesting menu with starters such as Smoked salmon mousse with asparagus and a light Bass soufflé with raspberry vinaigrette flavour (optional).

Saint-Cyprien is a new 150-acre government development in this relatively unknown part of France. It is the perfect setting for a family holiday. You can enjoy all the Languedoc specialities — the Roussillon, the Caez, and Jonquères d'Oriolo wines in particular.

The port of Saint-Cyprien pleases holidaymakers with the traditional fishing activity which is the main attraction of this new resort — the arrival and departure of the fishing boats and the sale of fresh fish on the spot. There is also the beach and casino.

Rouget au Saffran   Red mullet in saffron

2 portions

4 medium-sized red mullets,
  scalded, gutted, with head left
  on
2 large tomatoes, skinned,
  seeded, and chopped
8 strands of saffron
8 coriander seeds
2 sticks of fennel, thinly sliced
  across
2 cloves of garlic, chopped
150 ml (5 fl oz) local red wine or
  rosé
15 ml (1 tbsp) vinegar
60 ml (4 tbsp) olive oil
1 sprig of thyme and basil
Salt and pepper

Garnish
Chicory
Lettuce
Sliced lemon
Black olives, stoned

Place the red mullet in a shallow ovenproof serving dish. Season with salt and pepper and cover with tomatoes, wine, fennel, saffron, and coriander seeds. Bake in a preheated oven at 200°C, 400°F, gas mark 6, for 15 minutes. Cool and serve chilled with chicory, lettuce, and a slice of lemon on each fish. The fish can also be garnished with stoned black olives.

Guy Poyer

Chef de Cuisine/Proprietor
Le Petit Bedon Restaurant
37 Rue Louis Brindeau
Le Havre 76600
France
Tel: 35.41.36.81

Guy Poyer was born in Londinières, Normandy. He learned his craft in the same town at the Auberge du Pont. He developed his skill at the Plaza Athenée in Paris, and was chef at the Sofitel and other gastronomic hotels, before buying the present restaurant.

From an extensive à la carte menu, featuring mainly fish, we selected Turban of scampi and oysters with mushrooms and rice. The famous Norman recipes with lashings of cream might be a thing of the past, but somehow we felt confident that Guy Poyer was really conveying a more modern approach to this fine style of cookery. Even the dessert of Almond blancmange with a coffee sabayon had some sophistication.

Turban de Langoustines Havraise   Rice pilaf with scampi, oysters, and mushrooms in wine

4 portions

50 g (2 oz) butter
1 onion, chopped
100 g (4 oz) Patna rice
300 ml (½ pint) fish stock
5 ml (1 tsp) turmeric or 3 strands of saffron
1 pinch paprika
Salt and pepper
12 scampi or peeled raw prawns
12 oysters
150 g (5 oz) mushrooms, sliced

Sauce
50 g (2 oz) butter
75 g (3 oz) mixture of chopped onion, carrot, and celery
15 ml (1 tbsp) tomato purée
300 ml (½ pint) fish stock used to poach the scampi and oysters
150 g (5 oz) mushrooms, sliced
45 ml (3 tbsp) cognac
Seasoning to taste
100 ml (4 fl oz) double cream
Chopped parsley

Heat 50 g (2 oz) butter and stir-fry the onion for 2 minutes until translucent, add the rice and let it soak up the butter for 30 seconds then pour on water and boil for 17 mintues. Add turmeric or saffron to make the rice yellow. Season to taste. Remove from heat and keep hot.

Poach the scampi for 3 minutes in the fish stock and add the oysters for 30 seconds. Remove and keep hot in some of the stock, strain the remaining stock to be used in the sauce.

Sauce
Heat 25 g (1 oz) of the butter and stir-fry the onion, carrot, and celery mixture for 3 minutes. Add the tomato purée and stock and boil for 10 minutes. Strain this sauce.

Heat the remaining butter and toss the sliced mushrooms for 2 minutes. Flame with brandy and stir in the sauce and cream. Season to taste. Boil for 4 minutes.

Reheat the scampi and oysters in this sauce.

To serve
Mould some rice in individual crown moulds (well oiled). Turn out on to 4 plates and fill the centre with scampi and oysters and the sauce. Sprinkle over a little coarsely chopped parsley.

Paul Reed

Chef de Cuisine
The Chester Grosvenor Hotel
Eastgate Street
Chester
Cheshire CH1 1LT
Tel: (0244) 24024

Paul Reed is a perfectionist who was apprenticed at the Dorchester and the Hilton in London. Paul heads a 36-strong team and his menu reflects the style of an able and talented culinarian.

Fish, meat, and poultry appeared in the *nouvelle cuisine* style. The dish we have chosen to illustrate here has a stamp of originality: Filet de pigeon de Norfolk poché aux légumes du marché (Poached pigeon hot-pot with assorted vegetables). The intricacy of preparation shows the skill of the chef. The pigeon breasts are stuffed with a mousseline, wrapped in a caul like a faggot, and poached in a fresh vegetable broth.

Under the management of Jonathan Slater, a new era of elegance and charm has dawned at this Tudor inn, certainly the best in Cheshire.

Cheshire is, of course, cheese country. Chester, the Roman Deva, was the headquarters of the famous XXth Roman Legion. The fourteenth-century cathedral dominates this picturesque town. The Dee Bridge with its distinctive seven arches was built in 1280.

Filet de Pigeon de Norfolk poché aux Légumes du Marché   Stuffed pigeon with vegetables

2 portions

1 squab pigeon (march pigeon)
25 g (1 oz) calves' sweetbreads (finely diced)
15 g (½ oz) each of finely diced carrot, shallot, leek, courgette, and tomato flesh
15 g (½ oz) turned carrot, 2.5 cm (1 in) long
15 g (½ oz) turned courgette, 2.5 cm (1 in) long
3 button onions
3 asparagus tips
50 ml (2 fl oz) double cream
225 ml (8 fl oz) pigeon broth, clarified
15 g (½ fl oz) brandy
15 g (½ oz) basil
25 g (1 oz) pig's caul fat
Salt, pepper, and mace

Remove the breasts from the squab. Remove the skin from the breast and wing bone.

Make a mousseline from the leg meat, finely diced sweetbreads, finely diced vegetables, cream, and brandy, adding salt and pepper to taste.

Remove the fillet and flatten it with a cutlet bat. Slit the breast open to form a purse shape from the fillet side, fold back and fill with the mousseline.

Reshape the breast to its original form and place fillet on the underside. On the skin side place a leaf of basil and encompass the breast in caul fat. Refrigerate for 1 hour to allow the mousse to settle.

Poach the breast in 75 ml (3 fl oz) broth for approximately 5 minutes.

Blanch all the vegetables and drain.

Reheat the rest of the broth and blanched vegetables, and season to taste.

Serve the poached breasts in hot individual soup tureens. Pour in broth and small vegetables and diced tomato flesh, and decorate with basil leaves.

Carlo Renzi

Chef de Cuisine
M.V. *Orient Express* Liner
British Ferries Ltd
Sea Containers House
20 Upper Ground
London SE1 9PF
Tel: 01-928 6969
Reservations: 01-928 6000

Carlo Renzi started work at the age of 14 as an apprentice pastry-cook with the Lloyd Triestina Lines, which had routes to the Far East, Australia, India, and South Africa.

During his 30 years' service on first-class Italian passenger liners such as the *Galileo Galilei* and *Gulielmo Marconi* he gained considerable experience in presenting sumptuous buffets.

From four restaurants on the M.V. *Orient Express* there is cuisine to match every mood. The exclusive Orient Express restaurant has a gorgeous à la carte menu; there is also the conviviality of the Savani restaurant, where you can sample delicious Italian pasta entrées; or you can enjoy alfresco meals at the Lido and the Bosphorus Café. You may have Pasta with salmon or Chicken flamed in cognac, for which Carlo has contributed the recipes, or may just want caviar on toast.

Poulet al Pepe Rosa   Supreme of chicken 'Al Pepe Rosa' with red peppercorns

4 portions

50 g (2 oz) butter
4 breasts of chicken, dusted with
  flour
75 ml (3 fl oz) cognac
100 ml (4 fl oz) whipped cream
Salt, red pepper in grains
5 ml (1 tsp) yeast extract
Parsley, chopped

Heat the butter and fry the breasts of chicken. When half cooked add a pinch of salt and pepper. Pour ignited cognac over the contents of the pan. Add whipped cream and the yeast extract, and cook until ready to serve. Sprinkle with parsley and red peppercorns.

Les Pâtes au Saumon   Pasta with salmon

4 portions

300 g (10 oz) fettuccine
150 g (5 oz) smoked salmon
100 g (4 oz) butter
50 g (2 oz) onions, sliced
1 glass of vodka
100 ml (4 fl oz) 'panna'
  (whipped cream)
Salt and pepper
Parsley, cut into small pieces

Cook the fettuccine, keeping them *al dente* (slightly firm). In a pan, fry the onion in the butter. When cooked add the salmon, cut into slices. After 1 minute ignite the vodka and pour over the contents of the pan. Add the whipped cream, pepper, and a pinch of salt. Cook until the sauce is sufficiently thickened. At this point add the fettuccine and mix. Sprinkle with parsley and serve.

Jean-Luc Rousseau

Chef de Cuisine/Proprietor
Restaurant l'Halbran
86 Rue du Président-de-Gaulle
La Roche-sur-Yon 85000
France
Tel: 51.07.08.09

Jean-Luc attended the Ecole Ferrandi in Paris, and for 16 years was head chef at the Hôtel Les Cols Verts. He won the gold medal for fish cookery and was admitted to the Académie Culinaire de France. He now runs his own restaurant, which he bought in 1984, and specializes mostly in fish and local dishes.

His menu is made up of semi-classic and regional dishes according to market supplies. The combination of lightly poached oysters on a bed of red and green lettuce, with thin slices of smoked wild duck, might appear to be far-fetched to some gourmets, but it is worth trying. The French word *l'halbran* means 'wild duck'.

The restaurant itself is simply furnished and would appeal to a large family group wanting to enjoy a good meal at a reasonable price.

Roche-sur-Yon, originally called Bourbon-Vendée, and later Napoléon-Vendée, has not lost its old charm. There is enough to see within a few miles' radius, with seaside resorts and many places of historic interest inland.

Pied de Cheval Grillerois   Large oysters with leeks

4 portions

8 large shallow oysters
   (Portuguese)
200 g (8 oz) leeks, white part only
50 g (2 oz) shallots, chopped
100 g (4 oz) girolles
   (wild mushrooms)
100 ml (4 fl oz) single cream
25 g (1 oz) butter
100 ml (4 fl oz) Pineau des
   Charentes (a local aperitif
   wine)
Salt and pepper

Open the oysters, strain and retain the liquid in a bowl.

Wash and slice the leeks, and then wash and drain them again.

Heat the butter in a pan and cook the leeks for 6 minutes until soft. Remove and keep warm.

Poach the oysters in wine in a pan for 1 minute, with shallots and mushrooms. Add the oyster liquid. Remove the oysters and keep warm. Add the cream and boil for 8 minutes.

Wash the shallow oyster shells. Fill each one with leek purée. Arrange 1 or 2 oysters on top. Coat with the well-reduced sauce, which should be seasoned to taste.

George Robert Saint

Manager
The Chequers Inn
Redbourn
Hertfordshire AL3 7AD
Tel: (058285) 2359

Born at Birtley, County Durham, George Saint joined the Royal Air Force catering service in 1964 and worked for 6 years in the kitchen. He qualified with the City and Guilds at Framwellgate Moor Catering College with distinction. He gained further experience as the head chef of the New Inn at Iveston and in 1985 joined the Grand Metropolitan. He now acts as general manager. The head chef, Pasquale Chiappenelli, produces delectable meals of very wide appeal.

The chef has worked at the Chequers for 15 years and attracts a regular clientele. Prior to this he was at the King William in St Albans. The head waitress, Mrs Cindy Turner, has served at the Chequers for 25 years. This record speaks for itself.

There is a wide choice of popular items on the menu, from grilled sardines and whitebait to classic entrées. The whole Lobster thermidor is tempting. The Sole Véronique and T-bone steaks are available on demand, along with many other English-style grills. The entrées are prepared to perfections. Tournedos Rossini, Veal Zingara, Beef Stroganoff as well as Chicken à la Kiev. Even garlic bread is served. The Sunday lunch joints vary, but you are sure to enjoy the Roast topside of beef with Yorkshire pudding, or you could try the Steak and kidney pudding with a sauce enriched with brown beer.

Set on the A5 on the outskirts of Redbourn near St Albans, the Chequers is better than a tavern and as cheerful as a fancy French restaurant. Facilities in the area are many, including golfing, fishing and gliding.

Elizabeth Beef Pudding in Stout

6 portions

Egg paste
225 g (8 oz) plain flour
15 g (½ oz) baking powder
1.25 ml (¼ tsp) salt
100 g (4 oz) vegetable margarine
2 eggs, beaten
15 ml (1 tbsp) water

Prepare the egg paste by blending all the dry ingredients, rub in the margarine until it produces a crumble, and finally stir in the eggs to form a pliable dough. Leave it to rest for 10 minutes.

Roll the paste out to 4 mm (¼ in) thick. Cut 8 circles to cover the insides of the 7-cm (3-in) moulds. Fit the circles inside the moulds and press with fingers to apply the paste smoothly without creasing it. Now cut 8 circles for topping the puddings after they have been filled to the brim with the beef mixture.

Filling

225 g (8 oz) topside of beef, or
thick flank or fillet
150 g (5 oz) ox kidney
50 g (2 oz) onion, chopped
15 ml (1 tbsp) parsley, chopped
15 ml (1 tbsp) Worcester sauce
100 ml (4 fl oz) stout or brown ale
Pinch of ground black pepper
Salt to taste
15 ml (1 tbsp) flour

Stock

450 g (1 lb) beef bones
1 litre (1¾ pints) water
1 carrot
1 stick of celery
1 bouquet garni

Mushroom sauce

25 g (1 oz) oil
25 g (1 oz) onion, chopped
5 ml (1 tsp) tomato purée
5 ml (1 tsp) meat glaze or yeast
extract
150 ml (5 fl oz) stout or brown ale
150 ml (5 fl oz) beef stock
Salt, pepper and ground mace for
seasoning to taste
150 g (5 oz) mushrooms, sliced
5 ml (1 tsp) cornflour mixed to a
paste with 60 ml (4 tbsp) water for
thickening sauce
Parsley for garnish

Filling

Remove fat and sinews from kidney and meat and cut into 1-cm
(½-inch) cubes. Place the meat in a basin, and add the onion, parsley,
seasoning, beer, Worcester sauce, and flour. Mix well and leave for 30
minutes to marinade. Fill each mould with the beef mixture after
draining it a little. The juice can be saved for the sauce which is made
separately. Put the tops on the filled puddings (first wet the edges and
then press with thumb and forefinger). Wrap the tops of puddings with
greased paper and greased foil. Steam for 2½ hours.

Meanwhile prepare a good beef stock.

Brown 450 g (1 lb) beef bones in the oven and add 1 litre (1¾ pints)
of water, 1 carrot, 1 bouquet garni and a stick of celery. Boil the stock
for 2 hours, then strain.

Sauce

Heat the oil and stir-fry the onion for 2 minutes. Add tomato purée,
meat glaze or yeast extract, 150 ml (5 fl oz) of reduced beef stock and as
much stout or brown ale. Boil for 15 minutes. Season to taste. Blend in
the cornflour paste to thicken the sauce. Add the sliced mushrooms and
simmer for 4 minutes only.

To serve

Pour a pool of the mushroom sauce on to 6 plates. Turn out the meat
puddings upside down like sand castles. Be sure to ease them out with
the point of a knife.

Now arrange sprigs of parsley all around, and if you want to design a
pattern use the sliced mushrooms overlapping each other around each
pudding, or use button mushrooms.

Gérard Salle

Chef de Cuisine
Hôtel Normandie
2 Rue Edmond Blanc
Deauville 14800
France
Tél: 31.88.09.21

Gérard Salle was born in Villemomble. He has worked in many of the most famous restaurants in Paris: Le Doyen, Le Vert Galant and the Hôtel Bristol, to name but a few. His first position as head chef was at the Congrès in Paris. He then moved to Deauville at the Hôtel du Golf quickly to be head-hunted by Fred Welke, the dynamic German-born manager, himself a keen epicure and able administrator with a record of important managerial posts.

Traditionally Norman dishes include Foie de canard, Mussels in cream and Veal flambé in calvados. As Mr Welke told us, *nouvelle cuisine* has had its time and we must move forward a little to the new classic cuisine which has more taste and refinement. Mr Welke, whose French wife is a *cordon bleu*, told us that he likes a good Coq au vin. But Chef Salle was invited to contribute to this debate, and we agreed that his Dublin Bay prawns cooked with asparagus and cabbage in a light creamy sauce were a revelation. The main courses from his menu that we have chosen to feature here are Breast of chicken set alight in calvados, in true Norman style, and Hot pheasant mousseline wrapped in sauerkraut, in the German style preferred by Mr Welke. What a good composition!

Deauville in Calvados and the neighbouring towns of Trouville and Le Havre are all affluent seaside resorts. They continue to draw the rich and the poor to the amenities of beach, casinos, good fish restaurants and luxurious hotels like the Normandy, where the jet-set descend during the season. The racing also pulls in tourists.

The Deauville Casino owns this wooden-gabled Normandy hotel, whose steeply pitched roof and half-timbered walls with balconies, makes this place the focus of attention.

Crépinette de Faisan au Chou vert   Pheasant sausage wrapped in cabbage leaves

6 portions

1 × 1.35 kg (3 lb) pheasant
3 rashers of mildly pickled bacon belly, rindless and diced
2 whole eggs, beaten
200 ml (6 fl oz) white port
Salt, pepper, and grated mace
1 small cabbage (green)
300 g (11 oz) sauerkraut (pickled cabbage, available tinned)
4 pig's cauls or thin slices of cooked ham
50 g (2 oz) butter
300 ml (½ pint) water and dry cider
6 juniper berries or 15 ml (1 tbsp) gin
15 ml (1 tbsp) yeast or meat extract

Separate the legs and breasts from the carcass. Remove the skin, bone the breasts and legs and mince the meat with the bacon rashers to obtain a forcemeat. Blend the mixture in a bowl with eggs, wine, and seasoning (about 3ml (½ tsp) salt, 1.25 ml (¼ tsp) pepper and a good pinch of mace).

Blanch 6 cabbage leaves. Refresh in cold water until cold and drain well. Pat dry each leaf with a cloth. Take 50 g (2 oz) of the mixture, shape into a dumpling with a little of the sauerkraut, and wrap like a parcel with a cabbage leaf. Repeat until all the mixture is used and then wrap each cabbage parcel with a slice of pig's caul or thin slice of ham.

Grease a deep tray with butter and arrange the parcels in rows.

Now boil the bones, skin, and neck of pheasant in the dry cider and water for about 20 minutes. Add 15 ml (1 tbsp) yeast or meat extract. Season to taste. Add a few juniper berries or 15 ml (1 tbsp) gin for flavouring. Strain the stock and pour over the cabbage parcels. Cover with a lid and bake in an oven for 20 minutes.

Note: The game stock must be made first to synchronize the operation.

Jean-Pierre Sedon

Chef de Cuisine/Proprietor
La Marine
Au pied du pont D 982
Tancarville 76684
France
Tèl: 35.39.77.15

Jean-Pierre Sedon has established one of the finest restaurants of the region, near Le Havre in Normandy, where he specializes in seafood. Highly talented, this outstanding culinarian has led the field in modernizing traditional recipes into healthier dishes with less fat and starch while still retaining the real flavour of the originals.

The menu is large, with over 65 items to choose from, ranging from starters to sweets. It includes Soup with scallops and leeks. We like the Turbot stuffed with a mousse of sole and caviar, and garnished with prime vegetables carved into olive shapes. Vol-au-vent, shaped like boats and filled with mussels and spinach was tempting as a light entrée. As for sweets, he offers Pear flavoured with the local Norman liqueur, Bénédictine, as well as many other sweets with apples and Almond cream in pastry.

The restaurant is located close to the mouth of the Seine, in front of the Bridge of Tancarville. The town has a festive holiday atmosphere and attracts tourists in large numbers. You can enjoy all the beach amenities and visits to local castles and churches. Although this part of Normandy was badly bombed during the war it has been completely reconstructed in the old style.

La Soupière Saint-Jacques   Scallops tureen Tancarville

2 portions

8 large scallops, white meat and
   red coral only
1 egg
225 g (8 oz) puff pastry, prepared
   in advance
1 leek, white only, sliced
150 m (5 fl oz) double cream
250 g (9 oz) white mushrooms or
   ceps, sliced
50 g (2 oz) butter
1 sprig of parsley, trimmed,
   washed, drained, stalks
   removed and chopped
2 shallots, chopped

Tureen with leek
Wash the scallops and slice them vertically. Divide half of them between 2 individual earthenware tureens. Add the leek and the cream. Roll the pastry 4 mm (¼ in) thick and cut rounds to fit the diameter of the tureens, as for a pie. Place a round over each tureen and seal it hermetically. Crimp edges to hold the pastry firmly on to the brim. Brush the tops with beaten egg. Rest for 30 minutes. When ready, bake like a pie for 15–20 minutes at 200°C, 400°F, gas mark 6.

Tureen with mushrooms
Heat butter in sauté pan and toss the mushrooms for 1 minute with the shallots. Add the chopped parsley.

Cool and fill 2 other individual bowls with the mushrooms and the other half of scallops. Cover with rounds of pastry as for the first tureen. Rest and bake as for the first tureen. Serve 2 tureens per portion.

Les Filets de Sole en Aumonière de Moules du Mont St Michel

4 portions

Stock
300 ml (½ pint) water
300 ml (½ pint) white wine
1 bouquet garni
450 g (1 lb) of fish bones from the
    soles
1 onion

Main ingredients
20 mussels, about 225 g (8 oz)
    net weight
4 large lettuce leaves
50 g (2 oz) butter used as needed
1 shallot, chopped
4 large white mushrooms, sliced
8 sole fillets, cut in small strips
    6 cm (2½ in) long
100 ml (4 fl oz) double cream
Salt and pepper

Boil the stock ingredients for 20 minutes and strain.

Boil the cleaned mussels for 3 minutes in the stock and remove. Discard mussels which do not open. Shell the mussels, reserving 4 shells for garnish. Strain the stock again.

Blanch lettuce leaves for 3 seconds. Drain and pat dry.

Wrap 4 mussels per lettuce leaf to form parcels and reserve 4 for garnish.

Heat butter and stir-fry the shallot for 2 minutes, add the mushrooms and small strips of fish. Cook for 4 minutes. Stir the stock and poach for 3 minutes more. Then remove the sole and mushrooms. Strain the stock again into another saucepan to complete the sauce.

Boil the stock to reduce it by half and blend in the cream. Season to taste. Place a parcel of mussels on each of 4 plates together with the mixture of sole and mushrooms and a cordon of sauce.

Decorate each portion with one mussel replaced in its shell.

John Sherry

Chef de Cuisine/Proprietor
The Highland Welcome Hotel
Manchester Road
Chequebent
Westhoughton
Greater Manchester
Tel: (922) 8111 446

John Sherry is the picture of a perfect host, with a round face, happy smile, and portly appearance. He practises what he preaches — to eat and drink well — for he has achieved his ambition to own a hotel-restaurant.

He trained at the Malmaison Central Hotel in Glasgow, reputed to be the best in town for fine French/Scottish cuisine.

John admits that his specialities are the food of Scotland: salmon, game, Angus beef, and all the Highland snacks that people take on trips — pies, puddings, and smoked salmon sandwiches. He feels that the perfect snack is one which you can eat with your fingers, such as a sausage roll, a good pastry, or crab turnover, or better still grouse or wild duck in flaky pastry. All of these, he thinks, make perfect partners for a glass of strong stout. He gave us the recipe for the last of these, which can be made with salmon instead of wild duck or grouse.

The Highland Welcome Hotel is a family hotel, catering for locals and motorists. The bar of the hotel is popular with the residents of this suburban town, and the fact that the landlord is also chef is an added bonus for the clientele, who can always count on sophisticated cuisine.

Chausson de Coq de Bruyère   Highland turnover

2 portions

1 grouse, boned, filleted and
   skinned
150 ml (5 fl oz) port wine
50 g (2 oz) oil and butter
2 rindless back rashers of bacon,
   diced
50 g (2 oz) chicken liver
50 g (2 oz) mushrooms, chopped
15 ml (1 tbsp) flour
225 g (8 oz) puff pastry
1 egg, beaten
Salt and pepper

Marinade the grouse meat in port wine for 2 hours. Heat the butter and oil and pan-fry the grouse meat for 8 minutes to seal the juice in. Remove and cool.

In the same pan, fry the bacon rasher for 1 minute only. Remove and cool. Mince the liver and bacon together. Season to taste and add mushrooms. Heat 30 ml (2 tbsp) oil in a pan and cook this mixture 3 minutes only to dry it more. Blend with 15 ml (1 tbsp) flour, and season to taste.

Roll the pastry 4 mm (¼ in) thick and cut 2 rounds, 14 cm (5½ in) in diameter. Place the rounds on a greased tray and fill the centre with sliced grouse meat with a spoonful of liver mixture heaped on top. Wet the edges with water and fold the pastry into a half-moon shape, like a turnover. Crimp the edges of each turnover by pressing together and brush the top with beaten egg. Leave them to rest for 20 minutes, and then bake in a preheated oven at 210°C, 410°F, gas mark 6–7, for 16 minutes, or so. Eat hot or cold.

Note: A gravy can be made by boiling the port wine with grouse bones and skin, a little water, and a few shallots.

Richard Sturgeon

Chef de Cuisine
The Marine Highland Hotel
Crosbie Road
Troon
Ayrshire KA10 6HE
Tel: (0292) 314444

Richard Sturgeon started his career at Dudley Hotel, Hove. He served a full 4-year apprenticeship at the Dorchester in London, and went as sous-chef to the Marine Hotel at Troon. He became head chef at the same hotel two years later, after spending a brief spell in France to master *nouvelle cuisine*. He also taught at Glasgow Catering College for one day a week for many years.

In his menu he features a light Sole mousse with salmon served with lobster sauce, the popular Best end of lamb with pine kernels and a Marinaded salmon, which is served raw with mustard sauce — this has been well adapted from the Gravlax of Scandinavian gastronomy. The Escalope of venison with green peppercorn is as good, if not better than, the version with beef. As for a sweet we are glad to see a real Drambuie syllabub on the menu — a genuine Scottish speciality.

The Marine Highland stands in the heart of Burns country. A superb leisure club is a feature of the hotel, with indoor swimming pool, jacuzzi, sauna, steam room, solarium, squash courts, snooker room and beauty salon. There are seven golf courses in the surrounding area.

The chef is a keen angler and catches the elusive lobster.

Escalopes de Venaison au Poivre vert

Escalopes of venison in a whisky and green peppercorn sauce

4 portions

8 escalopes of venison, 75 g (3 oz) each
25 g (1 oz) butter
Salt and freshly ground black pepper
2 shallots, finely chopped
7 g (¼ oz) soft green peppercorns
75 ml (3 fl oz) whisky
225 ml (8 fl oz) double cream
5 ml (1 tsp) parsley, chopped

Lightly season the escalopes and sauté in hot butter until lightly cooked and pink, remove from the pan and keep warm.

Pour off surplus fat, add the finely chopped shallots and sauté until transparent. Add the soft green peppercorns and a little of the brine from the peppercorns. Flame with 50 ml (2 fl oz) of the whisky.

Add double cream, reduce to required consistency, add chopped parsley and the remainder of the whisky, reboil, and check seasoning.

Place the escalopes in a serving dish, pour the sauce over them and serve.

André Surmain

Chef de Cuisine/Proprietor
Le Relais à Mougins
Place de la Mairie
Mougins 06250
France
Tel: 93.90.03.47

André Surmain has also created other restaurants bearing the same name in New York and in Palm Beach, Florida, and together with his own chef, Dominique Louis, has made Le Relais à Mougins an international eating place.

Dominique's previous employment was at the Normandy Hotel at Deauville, and the Hôtel Nikko in Paris. He gained further experience and promotion as sous-chef at the Cairo Concorde Hotel and at the Hôtel Beaurivage at Geneva. He is now in his third year at the Relais. This formidable team presents a great challenge to Roger Verge's two establishments in the same village, which attracts more gourmets than do the larger towns of the Riviera.

As may be expected, the menu is large and well planned, with such items as Ravioles aux huitres and Dodine de canards aux crustaces, an adventurous mixture of duck and crustaceans. But our choice was a lamb dish of superb quality garnished with foie gras and ceps.

Mougins, a typical village perched in the hills above Cannes on the Côte d'Azur, is the site for Le Relais à Mougins, a charming restaurant situated right on the village square.

From the terraces, where one can lunch or dine leisurely, and where the only noise is that of the fountains (Mougins is traffic-free), one has an overall view of this romantic fifteenth-century village.

Le Relais à Mougins offers several different arrangements for groups of up to 120 diners.

Noisette d'Agneau en Chemise au Foie gras Loin of lamb and liver wrapped in pancakes

6 portions

Main ingredients
2.5 kg (5 lb) saddle of lamb,
    boned and trimmed
30 ml (2 tbsp) oil
150 ml (¼ pint) single cream
20 g (¾ oz) butter
Salt and pepper
450 g (1 lb) raw goose liver

Stock
30 ml (2 tbsp) oil
2 carrots, cut into small cubes
1 stick of celery, sliced
450 g (1 lb) bones and trimming
    of lamb
1 clove of garlic, crushed
2 sprigs of thyme and tarragon

Pancake mixture
2 eggs
300 ml (½ pint) milk
225 g (8 oz) plain flour
15 ml (1 tbsp) oil
Pinch salt
15 ml (1 tbsp) fresh chopped
    parsley and tarragon, and a few
    rosemary leaves.

Heat 30 ml (2 tbsp) oil in a sauté pan and shallow-fry the vegetables, meat trimmings and bones until brown. Stir from time to time, add garlic and the herbs at the last minute. Just cover with water and boil for 45 minutes to obtain a well-flavoured gravy. Remove fat and strain.

Meanwhile blend the ingredients of the pancake mixture to a smooth batter. Rest it for 30 minutes and then add a little chopped parsley, tarragon, and rosemary to flavour this batter.

Cut the two loins of the saddle into 18 small escalopes (noisettes), 100 g (4 oz) each at the most. Flatten then thinly with a mallet. Heat 30 ml (2 tbsp) oil in a pan and seal them quickly for 2 minutes, then cool.

Heat the butter and cook 18 12-cm (4½-in) diameter pancakes (make sure each pancake is very thin). If the batter is a little too thick add cold water.

Wrap each lamb piece with a little liver on top in each pancake until all the fillings have been used.

Boil the gravy to reduce it by half from ½ litre (1 pint). Add cream to the reduced gravy and seasoning. When it has boiled for another 4 minutes and is syrupy, pour a pool of the sauce on to 6 plates and place 3 pancakes on each plate. Decorate with a little sprig of tarragon or rosemary in the centre.

Jacques-Henri Tachet

Chef de Cuisine/Proprietor
Les Pigeons Blancs
110 Rue Jules Brisson
Cognac 16100
France
Tel: 16.45.82.16.36

Jacques-Henri Tachet is the pupil of Raymond Oliver, who is the owner of the Grand Véfour in Paris, a TV personality, and a well-known cookery writer. Jacques' cooking is highly personalized, and his wife Catherine and his son welcome you to Les Pigeons Blancs.

It would be natural to expect every dish to be flambéd in Cognac, for this is the region of the finest brandies. In general, it is hard to escape the temptation to be generous with the 'water of life'. Bisques of shellfish, Steak Diane, Coq au vin, Jugged hare and good Liver pâté are all marinated in a little brandy. Even Crêpes Suzette is flamed in such spirits. In perusing the menu of this charming little place, we noticed that Fillet of beef was served with a St Emilion sauce, a rare distinction as usually the name of the wine is not credited.

Jacques-Henri is a grand master of cookery, and whether you want a Foie gras en gelée, a chicken garnished with crayfish, or a Terrine de poisson au vinaigre de framboise, food on the buffet table is presented with great panache.

The Pigeons Blancs was a seventeenth-century posthouse, and is located on the outskirts of the town. It is an old inn, which has kept its charm and hospitality, making this family house worth a visit. The dining-room has an old-fashioned fireplace with a log fire in the winter, and there is a garden terrace where you can drink your aperitifs in peace.

In summer, one of the features is to serve barbecue dinners by candlelight, outside on the terrace. The barbecue fireplace has been constructed in stone and you can watch your steaks or kebabs or fish being grilled alfresco.

All the great Cognac houses allow visitors to sample their products. Charente, as famous for its butter as its Cognac, has received gastronomic gifts from all the regions around. This is the Land of Kings, the country of transition and the province of contrasts. But the real wealth and fame of this region lies around Cognac, the prime brandy of the whole world, produced according to ancient traditions and methods that have remained unchanged for generations.

Francois I lived at the Castle of Cognac, which houses the great reserves of the precious brandy. Visit the castle and park, also the Chais of Cognac.

Mouclade au vin de Bordeaux et Cognac   Mussels in wine and brandy

4 portions

50 g (2 oz) butter
2 shallots, chopped
1 pinch curry powder
1 clove garlic, chopped
300 ml (½ pint) white Bordeaux
   wine
1 bouquet garni
1 sprig of thyme
2 litres (4 pints) mussels, cleaned,
   scraped, and washed
45 ml (3 tbsp) brandy
50 ml (2 fl oz) double cream
30 ml (2 tbsp) parsley, chopped

In a large saucepan, heat the butter and gently stir-fry the shallots and garlic for 30 seconds. Add the wine, bouquet garni, and curry powder, and 3 turns of the pepper mill. Boil for 4 minutes. Add the mussels. Cover with a lid and boil for 6 minutes. Add brandy. Strain the sauce into another saucepan. Add cream and boil for 3 minutes. Remove 1 shell only from each mussel and place the mussels in 4 soup plates. Cover with the liquor and sprinkle chopped parsley on serving.

Note: Allow ½ litre (1 pint) (8 in number) of large mussels per portion.

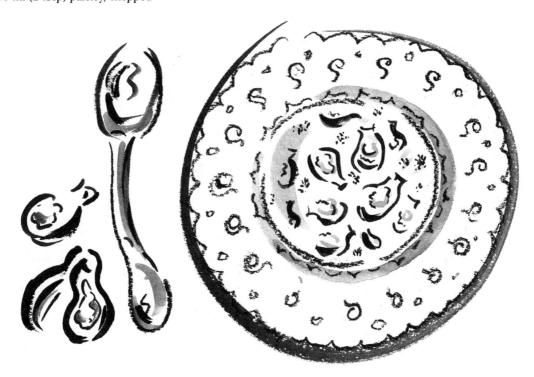

Lucette Thémelin

Chef de Cuisine/Proprietor
L'Etable du Pregnoux
La Bourboule 63150
France
Tel: 73.81.14.36

Lucette Thémelin learnt her craft from her grandfather, a chef of great distinction who worked on the *Queen Mary* in prewar years and owned a smart little bistro restaurant in Paris, near Les Halles, afterwards.

'I don't go for this *bagatelle* of pretty dishes on a plate with mini portions', she said, in her heavy Auvergne *patois*. 'My meals are made up of robust food, good enough to satisfy a regiment of hungry customers.'

All the food is served in dishes and tureens from which the clients help themselves as if they were at home: Braised belly of bacon with cabbage, Veal fricassee of sweetbread, Coq au vin with chestnuts, Duck stuffed with mushrooms, Tripe cooked in red wine, a potato dish with truffles and L'alicot, a simple dish of mashed potato with garlic and cream. All the puddings and tarts you can dream of were featured on her seasonal menu.

Pregnoux is a little village outside Bourboule in the Auvergne. Lucette Thémelin's modest inn has been established for many years and is always full during the summer season. It is near the Parc Fenestre and the Roche Vendeiz, where the meandering river caresses the shores planted with chestnut trees. Prehistoric man walked in this valley 40,000 years ago.

Le Ragoût limousin Bacon and chestnut hot-pot

6 portions

30 ml (2 tbsp) lard or oil
750 g (1 lb 12 oz) neck or
   shoulder piece of green bacon,
   desalted in water
1 bouquet garni
2 cloves of garlic
1½ litres (2½ pints) water
3 peppercorns, crushed
450 g (1 lb) peeled chestnuts,
   hard skin removed (or use
   canned)
1 onion, studded with 2 cloves

Heat the lard or oil in a metal casserole pot and brown the joint of bacon all over for 10 minutes. Remove the fat to be used later for a roux. To the bacon, add bouquet garni, studded onion and water. Season only with crushed peppercorns. Bring to the boil, remove scum as it rises, and then simmer gently for 1½ hours. About 20 minutes before the meat is cooked, add the chestnuts.

Sauce
Remove 500 ml of the stock and separately thicken it with a roux made by blending 25 g (1 oz) flour and the same amount of the fat used for the meat. Cook this paste for 2 minutes to develop flavour. Dissolve the paste in the stock and stir until the sauce is smooth. Boil for 10 minutes and strain. Carve the meat and serve it coated with this plain sauce, with the chestnuts as garnish.

Yves Thuries

Chef de Cuisine/Proprietor
Le Grand Ecuyer
Cordes 81170
Tarn
France
Tel: 63.56.01.03

In this medieval abode, rated not only one of the best restaurants of the region but also of the whole of France, Yves Thuries has improved all regional recipes beyond comparison. This grand master has produced the most outstanding work on cookery of our times — in eight volumes.

Born in Lempaut in the Tarn in 1938, Yves grew up amongst the herbs and woodland of the country. His parents were bakers.

Yves was apprenticed in Castres then processed in two of the best patisserie shops in Toulouse. After various posts as a patissier in Deauville, Paris, Strasbourg, and in Switzerland, he purchased his own pastry shop and eventually travelled all over the world to demonstrate the art of his profession, winning gold medals by the score. In 1980 he acquired Le Grand Ecuyer and restored it to its splendid original design.

His menu reads more like a book on art than a cookery work; it is a gastronomic treasure. We read with awe and enchantment as each dish is lyrically described: for example, Noisettes de melon au filet d'oie et saumon fumé; Goose and smoked salmon with melon and strawberry. Then there is a succession of dishes all garnished with fruits in the true style of Fraîcheur, such as: Scallops with grapes; Monkfish with blueberries; Salmon with pink peppercorns; Bass with pears; Mackerel with rhubarb. The same applies to the meat course: Wild duck with melon; Goose liver with medley of mixed fruits; Sweetbread with orange segments; Rabbit with mango; Calves' liver with redcurrants.

Sixteen cooks assist him and a school of students watches his every move to learn and benefit.

Other dishes on his menu we noted were Guinea-fowl; Goat meat with salad; Snail stew with raisins; Crayfish with noodles and truffles; and Breast of duck with honeyed apple. But best of all these are sweets to please all the children of the world.

This ancient house was the home of the powerful Comtes de Toulouse, who ruled the southern region like kings for centuries from 1222. Every house in Cordes stands as a memorial to the past, reflecting Italian and Spanish culture. Visit the market on a busy weekday and walk along the Promenade de la Bride, which has a unique panoramic view. There is also a campsite of 8 hectares (20 acres), with woodland.

Filet de maquereaux au trois marmelades   Mackerel with rhubarb, tomatoes, and pickled onions

4 portions

Rhubarb chutney
450 g (1 lb) rhubarb, peeled and
    sliced
50 g (2 oz) sugar
45 ml (3 tbsp) double cream
Salt and pepper

Onion chutney
30 ml (2 tbsp) oil
450 g (1 lb) onions, sliced
30 ml (2 tbsp) each of sugar,
    vinegar and white wine
Salt and pepper

Green tomato chutney
450 g (1 lb) green tomatoes,
    quartered
45 ml (3 tbsp) each of sugar and
    vinegar

Red tomato sauce
30 ml (2 tbsp) oil
1 shallot, chopped
225 g (8 oz) red tomatoes,
    skinned, seeded and chopped
15 ml (1 tbsp) tomato purée
300 ml (½ pint) fish stock

Main ingredients
30 ml (2 tbsp) flour
Salt and pepper
45 ml (3 tbsp) oil
4 mackerels, filleted, washed, and
    wiped dry

Rhubarb chutney
Boil rhubarb and sugar until thick, season with salt and pepper and blend in the double cream.

Onion chutney
Heat oil and fry the onions until soft, blend in the sugar, vinegar, and wine and boil until thick, season with salt and pepper.

Green tomato chutney
Boil all ingredients together until thick like jam.

Tomato sauce
Heat oil, stir-fry the shallots until soft, add tomatoes, tomato purée and fish stock, boil for 10 minutes, season to taste, and strain.

Fish
Season the mackerel with salt and pepper, coat with flour, brush with a little oil and grill for 8 minutes.

To serve
Pour a pool of the tomato sauce on to 4 plates, arrange one fillet on the side of the plate and garnish with one scoop of each chutney side by side.

Simon Traynor

Executive Sous-Chef
Marriott Hotel
ABC Strasse 52
2000 Hamburg 36
West Germany
Tel: 49.40.35.050

It was during a judging session at the Marriott Hotel that we met Simon Traynor, who was on the panel of judges examining the quality of sausages. We were more impressed by the quality and professionalism of Simon than the range of 100 sausages we had been tasting all morning. Simon is the epitome of what an executive sous-chef should be, and many of his cooks have blessed the days they were lucky enough to work with him. A sous-chef is like the Chief of Staff in a large brigade of cooks. Simon was previously sous-chef at the Savoy Hotel, and at the Grosvenor House Hotel, where he was highly regarded by M Louis Outhier and Jean Georges Vongerichten of Strasbourg. We wish him well in his new post at the Marriott Hotel in Hamburg.

Saumon au Coulis de Betterave

Planked pink salmon on shredded beetroot with Cabernet Sauvignon wine sauce

1 portion

150 g (5 oz) salmon fillet
4 sprigs of chervil and dill
50 g (2 oz) beetroot, peeled and
   shredded
6 button onions in red wine
1 glass wine
15 ml (½ fl oz) enriched stock
25 g (1 oz) butter
5 ml (1 tsp) chive, in strips
5 ml (1 tsp) button mushroom, in
   strips

Garnish the salmon fillet with chervil and dill and cook on plank in a hot oven at 220°C, 425°F, gas mark 7, for 10 minutes.

Reduce beetroot, wine, and stock in a saucepan. Add onion and blend with butter.

Place beetroot at the centre of a plate, arrange onions around this and flood with sauce. Place the fish on the beetroot.

Garnish with chives and mushrooms.

M Tuccinardi

Chef de Cuisine/Proprietor
Pavillon de l'Ermitage
Chavoires Lac d'Annecy
Veyrier-du-Lac 74290
France
Tel: 50.60.11.09

M Tuccinardi was apprenticed at Pont de Claix in Grenoble. Then he worked at Mère Brazier, at Col de la Luère, and finally bought the present establishment, which he has run successfully for 22 years.

His specialities are Swiss oriented in style; for example, Omble chevalier (the local trout-like fish from the lake), Pike soufflé, and Poularde de Bresse Chavoisienne have been his most popular dishes for a long time.

The hotel is situated almost on the lake shore, with a wooded garden terrace and a jetty from which it is most pleasant for guests to view the waterway traffic.

Poularde de Bresse Chavoisienne   Chicken steamed over a vegetable broth

6 portions

1 plump fowl, trussed and all fat
  removed
6 small slices of goose liver

Broth
Chicken giblets (neck, gizzard,
  winglets, etc.)
2 litres (3½ pints) water
1 onion, studded with 3 cloves
2 small leeks, cleaned and tied
  with string
2 sticks of celery
4 carrots, left whole
Salt and 6 crushed peppercorns

Garnish
2 carrots
2 turnips
1 cucumber
50 g (2 oz) butter
150 g (5 oz) rice
1 small onion, chopped
1 small red pepper, split,
  deseeded, and diced
4 strands saffron
Salt and pepper

Sauce
5 ml (1 tsp) sherry vinegar
5 ml (1 tsp) port wine
150 ml (5 fl oz) double cream
15 g (1 tbsp) truffle, cut in strips
6 small slices of goose liver

Prepare a strong chicken broth with chicken giblets, water and the listed vegetables. Cook for 2 hours.

Place the fowl on the top steamer of the pot and steam for 45 minutes. The broth will flavour the fowl.

Garnish
Cook carrots, turnips, and cucumber separately, all cut into fingers or olive shapes. Cook the carrots for 8 minutes, the turnips for 4 minutes and the cucumber for 2 minutes. Poach the slices of liver in the chicken broth for 3 minutes.

Rice garnish
Heat the butter and stir-fry the onion until translucent. Add rice to soak up the fat for 30 seconds, and then add 300 ml (½ pint) water or broth and saffron. Cook for 20 minutes. Season to taste and add blanched red peppers (blanched for only 30 seconds).

To serve
Arrange the vegetables which have been cooked separately on 6 plates with a piece of breast or leg, minus skin, and a slice of goose liver. The breast can be carved in thin slices. Pour on a little of the broth. Serve the rice separately on a side plate, or moulded in individual savarin dishes and turned out upside down on to plates. Serve the sauce separately.

The broth and roughly cut vegetables can be liquidized to produce a tasty soup.

Sauce
In a saucepan, boil the sherry vinegar and port wine for 1 minute. Add cream, seasoning, and truffle. Boil for 5 minutes.

Jean-Michel Turin

Chef de Cuisine/Proprietor
Château de Vauchoux
Port-sur-Saône 70170
France
Tél: 84.91.53.55

Jean-Michel Turin has twice been the winner of the culinary competition in Paris — in 1972 and 1976. Since that time he has not looked back, nor rested on his laurels, but has transformed his French château into a temple of gastronomy. His wife won the first prize at the Chariot d'Or competition in 1982 for a cocktail composed of champagne, Grand Marnier and a pear liqueur.

The large menu is a revelation both in its gastronomic language and in the originality of dishes. Bass becomes Le petit basset, a diminutive, no doubt, for a small bass (one per portion). We give the recipe for the larger bass steamed in seaweed stock with a vermouth sauce. There was also L'effeuillé de ris de veau à l'ancienne for sweetbread in cream sauce over a medley of salad leaves. The classic duck salmis becomes Le fondant de canard aux champignons des bois. The Marquise, that ubiquitous chocolate mousse, has found its way to the sweet section again. But how about Les feuilles de chêne en folie au vinaigre de Xérès — this is sheer poetry as a description of oak-leaf salad with sherry vinegar dressing. The salmon is cooked in champagne and there are also classic favourites — Les oeufs à la neige is one of them, but l'Eclance de mon père must remain a surprise.

The château is located in its own green park. It is a few miles from Vesoul and Gray, with vineyards, forests, lakes, plateaux and waterfalls to enchant you. The region is crossed by the river Saône in this lush valley.

This is a land of good cheeses, fish and game, particularly the hazel-grouse. Plums and cherries are made into liqueurs. The town itself is small, with 2700 inhabitants. There is also a large campsite with all the sports amenities.

Bar cuit à la Vapeur des Algues, Sauce Vermouth   Bass steamed with vermouth sauce

4 portions

Stock for steaming fish
50 g (2 oz) dry kelp or seaweed
1 bouquet garni
15 ml (1 tbsp) dried mixed herbs
1 pinch anis seed
1 litre (2 pints) water

Parcel of fish
4 fillets of bass, skinned
4 large scallops, cleaned, white
  meat and coral only
8 large spinach leaves
30 ml (2 tbsp) oil

Sauce
Bones and skin of the fish
150 ml (5 fl oz) vermouth and as
  much water
25 g (1 oz) butter and oil
2 shallots
1 large tomato, skinned, seeded,
  and chopped
2 strands saffron
150 ml (5 fl oz) double cream in a
  bowl
2 egg yolks
Salt and pepper and a pinch of
  ground ginger

Garnish
Sprig of dill or tarragon
Slices of lime

First prepare the aromatic stock for steaming the fish by boiling the seaweed, bouquet garni, and anis seeds in the water. Place the top steamer over the pot. A porridge saucepan would be ideal.

Season each fish fillet and the scallops. If the scallops are too big, cut them laterally into slices.

Place the spinach leaves on a board. Brush them with oil to make them pliable. Place 1 scallop on top of each fish fillet and wrap in a spinach leaf like a parcel. (As an alternative to brushing with oil you may blanch the spinach leaf for 10 seconds, refresh and dry with a cloth, but this is rather more tedious).

Now wrap the fish again in very well greased foil and place these parcels in the top container of the steamer when the stock is boiling. Steam for 5 minutes only with lid on.

The sauce
Place the bones and skin of fish in 150 ml (5 fl oz) vermouth and as much water with 1 onion and bouquet garni and a carrot. Boil for 20 minutes until the liquid has reduced by half. Strain and transfer the strained liquid into a small saucepan and thicken it by whisking in cream and egg yolks which have first been mixed together in a bowl.

Simmer the sauce.

Now heat 25 g (1 oz) butter and oil and stir-fry the shallots for 1 minute. Then add tomato and saffron and cook for 4 minutes. Add this mixture to the finished sauce. Season to taste and flavour the sauce with a little ground ginger.

To serve
Pour a pool of the sauce over 4 plates, and place the green parcels on the sauce. Decorate with a slice of lime and a sprig of dill or tarragon.

Susilahwati Ukkah

Head Cook/Caterer
Stephenson Hall
85c Highbury Park
London N5 1UD
Tel: 01-354 2337

Susilahwati Ukkah was born in Sintang, Kalimantan, Indonesia. She trained in the hotel and catering industry in Japan, at the Keio Plaza Hotel. There she learned the principles of Japanese cuisine.

She then returned to Jakarta, Indonesia, where she worked at the Borobudur Continental Hotel, as the Assistant Manager of their Keio Restaurant.

She moved to London in 1979 where she ran an Indonesian restaurant 'Matahari' for two years.

In 1982 she was appointed as a residential cook for Stephenson Hall, the National Children's Home, where she has since gained a high reputation for the superb food served there.

Diners are getting to know the charm of Indonesian cuisine, and Susila (as she is known by the patrons of the NCH dining-room) has contributed much to making this style of cooking popular amongst the staff and guests.

Many of the dishes offered are of vegetarian composition, with peanut sauce and other spicy vegetable mixtures. Coconut is used a great deal in flavouring. Among the many dishes are: Sayur Lodeh, which is a cabbage and coconut soup; Ikan Goreng, fish marinated in tamarind sauce and deep fried; Bakmi Goreng, which is fried noodles: Nasi Goreng, a sort of pork and chicken pilau with prawns; and a shredded omelette to enrich it as a complete meal by itself.

Susila's assistant, Desmond McEnery, is an experienced chef. He worked for 5 years at the Honourable Society of the Inner Temple as head chef, and for 2 years at Simpsons, in the Strand.

The dining-room at Stephenson Hall displays a variety of exciting food, the menus being changed daily. In the evenings many special dinners are organized for distinguished visitors and residents.

Poulet à l'Indonésienne   Chicken with cumin and coriander

4 portions

900 g (2 lb), 4 pieces, boneless
    and skinless chicken breasts
5 ml (1 tsp) cumin powder
5 ml (1 tsp) coriander
3 ml (½ tsp) cinnamon
10 ml (2 tsp) tomato purée
15 ml (1 tbsp) thin soy sauce
1 medium onion, finely chopped
1 clove garlic, finely chopped
15 ml (1 tbsp) cornflour, mixed in
    45 ml (3 tbsp) water
30 ml (1 fl oz) oil
Salt and pepper to taste

Rice
450 g (1 lb) rice

Cut the chicken into cubes.

Mix all the other ingredients except the oil into a paste with the cornflour and water.

Marinate the chicken overnight in the paste.

Heat the oil in a pan, add the marinated chicken and fry.

Shake the pan during cooking to prevent sticking, cook until the chicken is golden brown. Serve the chicken on rice, or with boiled potatoes.

Garnish with cucumber and parsley.

Rice
Wash the rice and change the water 4 or 5 times. Put the rice in saucepan with 600 ml (1 pint) fresh water. Cook on a medium heat until all the water is absorbed. Turn off the heat and leave the rice for 10 minutes with the lid on. The rice should be fluffy and intact.

Gérard Veissière

Chef de Cuisine/Proprietor
Capucin Gourmand
31 Rue Gambetta
Nancy 54000
France
Tel: 83.35.26.98

Gérard Veissière was trained at the Restaurant Lion Vert at Luxeuil. He progressed to the Grand Hotel in Nancy, and then moved to Paris to work at Le Fouquet's and the Pré Catelan — two famous places. He became chef de cuisine of the Royal at Metz, and later acquired his first restaurant, Les Trois Lapins, at Luxeuil-les-Bains, where he won his first Michelin star, which he kept at the Capucin Gourmand, the restaurant he now owns. He has an impressive list of VIP visitors.

The menu card is not flamboyant. The names are those of simple and popular dishes. He offers you fruit juice cocktail without alcohol; there is a selection of salades tièdes, with foie gras, scallops or langoustes; and turbot is one of his specialities. Among the entrées are Hot foie gras charlotte, served with apples in a honey sour sauce, Lamb baked in salt crust, and a Truffle turnover. All the sweets are made to order.

The dining-room is luxuriously furnished and carpeted.

Nancy is the capital of the Duchy of Lorraine, which became part of France only in 1766. It is a really beautiful town, with a magnificent park, museums, and squares with fountains. Not far away, you will find the small village of Domrémy, where Joan of Arc was born.

La Charlotte de Pommes au Foie Gras   Duck or goose liver and apple

4 portions

4 Cox's apples, cored, peeled, and
  sliced into wedges
50 g (2 oz) butter
25 g (1 oz) sugar
225 g (8 oz) duck or goose liver,
  cleaned and cut into 16 slices
20 ml (4 tsp) honey
20 ml (4 tsp) vinegar of acacia or
  cider
1 bunch of mint leaves for
  decoration
300 ml (½ pint) chicken broth

Heat the butter and sugar for 1 minute and toss the apple wedges for 1 minute. Remove when golden but still firm. Cool.

Poach the liver in chicken broth for 2 minutes. Cool.

Take a 48-cm (18-inch) diameter pastry cutter. Place it on one plate, as if it were a mould, and make a fan-like design with the apple and liver inside the ring, alternating the liver and apple. Fill the mould and remove. The ring is used to help shape the design.

Repeat this with other plates.

Boil the honey and vinegar for 15 seconds and pour over the Charlotte to glaze the ingredients.

Gratin de Poireaux   Leek mousse

2 portions

50 g (2 oz) butter
225 g (8 oz) leek white part only,
  cleaned, washed and sliced
1 egg, beaten and 15 ml (1 tbsp)
  cream, mixed
25 g (1 oz) grated cheese
Salt and pepper

Heat the butter and gently cook the leeks for 6 minutes until soft. Season and blend in the egg and cream to bind the mixture. Simmer gently for 3 minutes more. Place in a ramekin dish and sprinkle with grated cheese. Brown under the grill to melt the cheese. Sprinkle with grated nutmeg and serve with grilled trout.

Roger Vergé

Chef de Cuisine/Proprietor
L'Amandier de Mougins, the
    Moulin
Mougins 06250
France
Tel: 93.75.78.24

Roger Vergé is the Picasso of the culinary world. He is talented, highly personable and extremely erudite in gastronomic matters.

Born in Commentry in 1930, he learned his craft locally and completed his apprenticeship at the Tour d'Argent and the Hôtel Plaza-Athenée in Paris. He went as a head chef to Africa, where the tropical sun shone on him for 8 years. He learned the properties of unusual vegetables and fruits, and this inspired him to create his own style of cookery. When he returned to the South of France he managed the kitchen of the famed 'Club' at Cavalière for 8 years, and gained a 2-star recognition by Michelin.

He now runs two restaurants at Mougins: the Moulin and L'Amandier de Mougins, both multi-starred restaurants. He has written two outstanding books.

His very large menu contains a wealth of dishes reflecting his genius. The dishes are meridional and the accent is on salads of wild herbs known as *mesclun*. The Soupes de poissons are classic and are composed of shellfish and small fish which are rich in calcium. The flesh and bones can be eaten after the soup has been sieved, liquidized and strained. 'The most important point in making my fish soups is to use fresh fish', he writes. 'There is no need to wash or gut the small fish', he affirms with assurance. Indeed, this famous chef also gives cookery lessons to foreign visitors, and all the meridional soups are on his syllabus.

The Moulin was renovated by Roger Vergé in 1966, in a building which has been built as an olive press in the sixteenth century, and was still being used as such in 1960 when Vergé bought it. L'Amandier was opened in 1977 and is equally successful. The hotel school above is always booked and there is a long waiting-list.

La Soupe de Poisson Fish soup.

In view of the complexity of this recipe and difficulty of obtaining the fish ingredients, we have produced our own version of this soup, but the principles are based on Roger Vergé's tuition.

8 portions

Soup

1 kg (2 lb 2 oz) mixture of small
    fish: smelt, whiting, sardines,
    red mullet, gurnard, tiny crabs,
    fresh prawns, or shrimps
2 litres (3½ pints) water
150 g (5 oz) onion, chopped
4 cloves of garlic, chopped
2 large tomatoes, skinned,
    seeded, and chopped
2 sticks of dried fennel or dill
    sticks
1 sprig of thyme
4 strands of saffron
15 ml (1 tbsp) tomato paste
75 ml (3 fl oz) olive oil

Rouille sauce

100 g (4 oz) stale crusty bread
25 g (1 oz) (5 cloves) garlic,
    skinned
75 ml (3 fl oz) olive oil
½ chilli, sliced
100 ml (4 fl oz) fish soup
Salt and pepper
8 slices French bread, toasted

Soup

Scale, gut, wash and drain all the fish, and cut them into small pieces.

Heat the oil in a large (2.3-litre (4-pint) capacity) heavy-bottomed pan. Sauté the onion until pale golden. Pile the fish on top, stir with a wooden spoon and then blend in all the other ingredients and herbs. Stir-fry for 12 minutes to develop the flavour. Then add 2 litres (3½ pints) of water and boil the soup fast for 20 minutes. Only at the last minute do you add the seasoning and the saffron, as this would lose its pungency if added earlier.

The hard work now begins. Liquidize the mixture and then pass it through a sieve, getting as much fish through as possible, and finally strain it.

Rouille sauce

The purists from Languedoc claim that rouille does not need an egg in it, but just bread, oil, and garlic, pounded to a paste, with chilli and saffron and a little of the soup to make it softish, like the consistency of a dip. Roger Vergé adds an egg to his rouille. Some chefs do likewise, but others also blend in mashed potatoes, and the most sophisticated epicures of the Côte d'Azur even use sea-urchin flesh in their rouille. All these experts claim the divine right to know the 'right' recipe. Here we give you the real century-old Languedoc recipe.

Soak the stale bread in a cup of soup (check quantities from listed ingredients).

Place this bread paste in a liquidizer with garlic, saffron, and chilli, and gradually, while the machine is working, pour in the olive oil in a small thread to obtain an emulsified sauce, the consistency of a dip. Check salt seasoning, no pepper is required.

This sauce is served separately with snippets of toasted French bread.

Jean-Louis Viale

Chef de Cuisine/Manager
Les Antilles
12 Rue de Siam
Brest 29200
Brittany
France
Tel: 98.46.05.52

Jean-Louis Viale, whose father was an hotelier in the Ile du Levant off Lavandou in the south of France, was awarded the Diploma of the Ecole Hôtelière of Nice, which is a qualification in general catering. He managed the Vatel in Brest for 4 years and then moved to Les Antilles, where he has been manager since 1976. He has participated in a presentation of the Brittany Fish Fair in Paris and was the host at the reception of British tourists from Plymouth, a town which is twinned with Brest. He came to Britain to demonstrate his own specialities at the Mayflower Hotel during a gastronomic festival week.

The 3 fine dishes he recommends from his large menu are Scallops cooked with artichoke hearts, Mackerel wrapped with ham in pastry, as he calls it, and his most interesting fish dish, a sort of fish sausage of 3 fish, monkfish, salmon, and sole, wrapped in sausage casings or pig's caul. This last dish is made with a lovely sauce and seaweed-flavoured stock.

Les Antilles has a seaside atmosphere, epitomizing the Breton town of Brest, populated with sailors. There are palm-trees everywhere and a fishtank full of crayfish as well as other shellfish. This *restaurant-loisirs*, as it is called, is the kind of place one selects for a lazy lunch or dinner.

Brest is a military port where the entire fleet of the Western Command is assembled in the large bay.

Artichauts aux Saint Jacques Scallops with artichokes

4 portions

600 ml (1 pint) water and white wine
450 g (1 lb) mixed white fish bones
1 onion, sliced
1 bouquet garni
300 g (12 oz) nori or kelp (dried seaweed)
4 fresh globe artichokes
Juice of 1 lemon
8 medium scallops, white meat and orange coral only
50 g (2 oz) butter
60 ml (4 tbsp) calvados (apple-jack)
2 egg yolks
60 ml (4 tbsp) sour cream
3 ml (½ tsp) cornflour
Salt, pepper, and cayenne pepper
50 g (2 oz) grated Gruyère cheese

(Fresh artichokes are a bit more expensive in Britain than in Brittany, but canned, prepared artichokes are available in supermarkets.)

First prepare a fish stock by boiling 450 g (1 lb) fish heads and white fish bones together with a sliced onion and a bouquet garni in 600 ml (1 pint) of water. After 25 minutes strain the liquid.

Next prepare 6 fresh globe artichokes as follows. Remove all leaves. Use only the bottom parts, which you must trim with a stainless steel knife since an ordinary knife will cause the artichokes to blacken on heating. Boil the artichoke bottoms with 15 ml (1 tbsp) oil and half the lemon juice for 15 minutes and drain well.

Lastly, clean 6 fresh scallops. Use only the white flesh and the orange coral. Slice the white flesh horizontally.

Now heat 50 g (2 oz) butter in a sauté pan and stir-fry the scallop meat for 1 minute. Flame the meat in about 60 ml (4 tbsp) calvados. Remove the meat, and then reduce the stock by a third, by rapid boiling. In a cup, mix the egg yolks, cornflour, and sour cream. Add this mixture gradually to the stock, and then reheat gently until the new mixture thickens like a thin custard. If it becomes too thick, add a little more fish stock. Season to taste. Add the juice of half a lemon and a pinch of cayenne pepper.

Arrange the artichokes on 4 plates (gratin egg dishes). Add a few slices of scallop and cover with the egg sauce. Sprinkle with grated Gruyère, and brown under the grill of your cooker if you want to have a golden glaze. Serve with nori.

M. Viale recommends a glass of chilled Muscadet with a few drops of blackcurrant syrup as an aperitif.

Crépinette de l'océan Brestoise   Seafood sausages

6 portions

Stock
600 ml (1 pint) white wine and
    water
500 g (1 lb 2 oz) fish bones
1 onion, sliced
1 carrot, sliced
1 bouquet garni
25 g (1 oz) dry seaweed (nori or
    kelp) boiled separately,
    chopped
3 peppercorns, crushed

Main ingredients
50 g (2 oz) butter
50 g (2 oz) flour
225 g (8 oz) sole fillets
225 g (8 oz) monkfish
225 g (8 oz) salmon or mackerel
    fillets
6 scallops, orange coral and white
    meat only
6 pig's cauls or sausage skins made
    from alginates
2 whole eggs
2 egg yolks
½ cup milk
30 ml (2 tbsp) cream
White wine for poaching scallops

Boil the stock ingredients (excluding the seaweed) for 25 minutes, and
then strain. Heat 50 g (2 oz) butter and add the flour. Cook for
2 minutes and stir in the stock, making sure the sauce does not become
too lumpy. Boil for 12 minutes and strain. Dilute with ½ cup milk to
produce a thinner consistency. Season. Cool half of the sauce.

  Mince the fish, and in a bowl blend it with 2 whole eggs and 1 cup of
cold sauce (*velouté*).

  Boil the seaweed for 12 minutes and drain. Blend it into the minced
fish. Season to taste.

  Divide the mixture into 6 dumplings and shape them like sausages.
Wrap each one with a pig's caul or fill sausage skins with the mixture.
Poach them in water for 12 minutes.

Sauce
Add a little seaweed to the remaining sauce as well as 30 ml (2 tbsp)
cream and 2 egg yolks.

  Poach the scallops in white wine for 2 minutes.

To serve
Pour a pool of sauce on to 6 plates and add 1 crépinette (fish sausage),
1 scallop and a sprig of broccoli, asparagus, or samphire (scalded 30
seconds only) to each plate.

Robert Vrignon

Chef de Cuisine/Proprietor
Aux Chouans Gourmands
6 Rue des Halles
Fontenay-le-Comte 85200
France
Tel: 51.69.55.92

Robert Vrignon trained in the region at the Hôtel Tranchant in Parthenay and at the Hôtel du Faisan in Limoges. He was promoted at Lyons, then appointed head chef at the Buffet de la Gare in Thionville, where he stayed for 2 years, and for a further 6 years at the Restaurant Le Concorde. Finally he joined the Auberge Cheval Blanc at Varreddes, near Meaux, before he acquired his own restaurant at Fontenay-le-Comte, which he has run since 1979.

The menu is comprehensive with a good selection of seafood and river fish, all types of game and poultry, and some good local specialities such a Foie gras de canard and Canette braisée au mareuil et cassis.

The Restaurant Aux Chouans Gourmands derived its name from the term applied to the people of the region who fought against the republicans during the French Revolution.

The town is the administrative headquarters of the region. All around there are many sights, castles, forests, and other amenities for all tourists. Swimming, riding, fishing, and hunting are among the sports available. On market day you can taste the fresh butter from the farmers' wives before you buy it.

Aiguillettes de Pigeons au Vin de Vendée Slivers of pigeon in wine

4 portions

4 tender pigeons (corn-fed)
75 ml (3 fl oz) local spirit
　(eau-de-vie)
Salt and ground black pepper
1 carrot, sliced
1 medium onion, sliced
1 stick celery, sliced
1 bunch of thyme
300 ml (½ pint) rosé wine
300 ml (½ pint) water
5 ml (1 tsp) meat or yeast extract
50 g (2 oz) butter
50 g (2 oz) butter and oil, mixed
15 ml (1 tbsp) sesame seeds

Remove the skin of 4 pigeons already trussed and eviscerated. With a sharp knife remove the breast of each bird. Flatten the breasts with a wooden escalope mallet or rolling-pin. Season with salt and pepper and sprinkle with 75 ml (3 fl oz) of local spirit to add flavour. Allow the breasts to marinade for 20 minutes in a shallow dish while you prepare the stock and sauce.

Place the legs, bones, and skin with the onion, carrot, celery, and a bunch of thyme in a saucepan with 300 ml (½ pint) of rosé wine and 1 cup of water. Boil for 40 minutes. Strain the liquor. Add 5 ml (1 tsp) of meat or yeast extract to the stock. Boil the gravy for 15 minutes. Add 50 g (2 oz) of butter to the sauce and whisk to emulsify it. Check seasoning. Now the sauce is almost ready.

Pan-fry the pigeon escalopes in 50 g (2 oz) of a half-and-half mixture of butter and oil for 6 minutes. Then remove them from the pan and place on plates. Add a little of the well-reduced gravy. Sprinkle with toasted sesame seeds.

Garnish with an artichoke egg custard (see next recipe).

Artichoke Custard

450 g (1 lb) Jerusalem artichokes
50 ml (2 fl oz) cream
Salt and pepper
2 eggs, beaten
Butter

Peel, slice and boil the artichokes for 2 minutes, then purée. Blend 2 beaten eggs into the purée of artichokes. Season to taste. Grease 4 ramekin dishes with butter. Fill them with this mixture. Place in a tray half filled with hot water and bake for 30 minutes in a preheated oven at 200°C, 400°F, gas mark 6. Leave them to rest for 10 minutes and then cut round the edges with a knife. Ease the mixture loose, and then turn it on to 4 plates as a garnish for the pigeon slices.

Robert Webster

Chef de Cuisine
Shoppenhangers Manor
Manor Lane
Maidenhead
Berkshire SL6 2RA
Tel: (0628) 23444

Robert has been head chef at Shoppenhangers Manor since October 1984, having arrived at Maidenhead from Crest's award-winning Plough and Harrow Hotel in Birmingham.

Born in 1954 and educated in Sheffield, Robert left school at the age of 15 to join the Savoy Banqueting Halls in Birmingham where his family had moved.

When the Savoy, a subsidiary of Bass, was sold and transformed into a casino, Robert, by now aged 17, joined the Plough and Harrow, as First Commis Chef in the Larder.

Amongst his hobbies Robert includes a keen interest in gardening, English furniture, and eighteenth-century architecture.

Shoppenhangers today is a luxury establishment and the menu reflects a style of cuisine as refined as the best château in France.

You may start a meal with a Salad of two types of asparagus in a nest of multi-coloured lettuce leaves, and enjoy Bass stuffed with salmon mousse flavoured with a vermouth sauce. Or tuck into a Tenderloin of lamb with morel mushrooms (belonging to the genus Morchella — they look like a sponge — so delicious with cheese).

For dessert Robert makes a sorbet out of mulberries from the old bush growing outside, but he told me he also uses the berries for venison sauce.

We noted Pears stuffed with chocolate and nuts, served with a ginger sabayon as an interesting ending of a well-composed menu.

The manager of this stately country hotel is Nick Seever. Crest Hotels are the owners. Shoppenhangers Manor recaptures the days of gracious living. Earthy shades of traditional furnishings complement the peaceful garden setting to produce a venue that is simply unique.

Maidenhead is situated near Cliveden Reach and Boulter's Lock on the Thames. There are boating and fishing facilities, while the neighbourhood is rich in historical associations. It is only 26 miles from London.

Longe d'Agneau roti aux Morilles   Roast tenderloin fillet of lamb with morels

1 portion

5 large morel mushrooms — dried
   or fresh
75 g (3 oz) raw chicken, minced
1 egg white
15 ml (1 tbsp) double cream
4 basil leaves
50 g (2 oz) butter
25 g (1 oz) shallot, chopped
100 g (4 fl oz) white wine
50 ml (2 fl oz) brandy
150 ml (¼ pint) veal stock
Salt and pepper
175 g (6 oz) fillet of lamb taken
   from the best end

Dry mushrooms must be soaked in water to remove all sand and grit. Rinse well before using. This applies to fresh morels as well. Remove the stalks.

Chop basil and add to chicken, egg white, and cream. Using a small plain piping nozzle fill the morels with the chicken mixture.

Heat the butter and fry shallots for 1 minute. Add morel stalks and white wine. Cook for 4 minutes and flame with brandy. Stir in (150 ml) (¼ pint) veal stock and reboil to reduce by half. Add butter and cream to the sauce while whisking it, to produce an emulsified sauce. Season and strain.

Season the fillet of lamb, and cook on top of the stove, remove from heat and leave to rest.

Poach the filled morels in a little light chicken stock. Drain, season, and gently sauté in butter

To finish
Slice the lamb fillet and arrange on a plate. Cut morels in half lengthways. Use the 5 largest halves to interspace with the lamb. Arrange the rest of the morels in the centre of the plate. Gently season the cut surface of the meat. Pour the sauce around.

Note: If desired, for presentation, add extra morels to a filo pastry basket, made by using a greased fluted mould.

This moulded pastry is deep fried until the mould is detached, the pastry looks like a basket and can be used as a case, which can be filled with mushrooms.

Stephen T. Whitney

Chef de Cuisine
The Copper Inn
Church Road
Pangbourne
Berkshire RG8 7AR
Tel: (07357) 2244

Stephen Whitney came to this famous inn from the Savoy Hotel, where he had been senior sous-chef. He had previously gained experience in modern cuisine at the Dorchester and in Washington, USA. His amicable personality and imaginative gastronomy are his greatest assets.

We sampled a splendid meal while dining with him one evening and were impressed by the simplicity and taste of the fare. The dinner consisted of a starter of Poached apple and cream cheese, followed by a light Mousseline of pike in saffron sauce; and then Maigret of duck in fruit and tender Loin cutlets in rosemary. The meal was perfectly cooked and presented. Steve is as much at home with Oxtail and carrots, Fillet of beef Wellington, and Steak and kidney puddings, all of which are served to regular clients and are as good as those prepared at the Dorchester.

The Copper Inn is owned by the Resort Hotel Group.

The hotel is a nineteenth-century coaching inn converted to modern style.

All sports facilities are available locally.

The French manager is Mr Michel Rosso, who was trained on the Riviera.

Nougat glacé Iced nougat

6 portions

50 g (2 oz) caster sugar
80 g (3 oz) flaked almonds
3 egg whites
60 g (2½ oz) sugar
Pinch of coriander
600 ml (1 pint) whipped cream
450 g (1 lb) honey
50 g (2 oz) chopped cherries and
  angelica
4 drops coffee essence

First make a lightly-coloured caramel by boiling 30 g (1¼ oz) of sugar with a little water until a light caramel colour is reached. Away from the heat add half the almonds and pour on to a greased metal tray. Allow to cool completely and grind to a fine powder.

Next make a dark caramel. Follow the above procedure but allow the caramel to become a rich dark brown colour, without lettting it burn. Mix in the remaining almonds. Pour on to a greased metal tray, cool, and grind to a fine powder.

In a saucepan, mix the egg whites with the caster sugar and coriander over a very low heat until all the sugar has dissolved. You must stir vigorously so as not to cook the egg whites. When all the sugar has dissolved whisk in a bowl, preferably using an electric mixer, until the meringue forms stiff peaks.

Gently heat the honey to blood heat. Gently fold into the meringue. Fold in whipped cream gently.

Place half the mixture in a separate bowl and add sufficient chopped cherries and angelica to give a good colour. To the remaining half of the mixture add the coffee essence and the dark caramel powder.

Line a terrine with cling-film or greaseproof paper.

Sprinkle the bottom of a terrine with the light caramel. Using a piping bag with a large nozzle, pipe in the mixture with the cherries and angelica until the terrine is half full. Sprinkle over a little more of the light caramel. Using a clean piping bag, pipe in the darker mixture until the terrine is full. Level off the top with a palette-knife. Put at the bottom of a chest freezer for at least 6 hours. To turn out, dip the terrine into a tray of hot water for a few seconds and turn out on to a tray. Cut into slices.

Lea Xhauflair

Chef de Cuisine/Joint proprietor
  with Victor Xhauflair
L'Ecurie Royale
33 Rue de Vauban
Antibes 06600
France
Tel: 93.34.76.20

Lea Xhauflair is one of these leading *cordon bleu* cooks who runs her kitchen so professionally that she has acquired a well-deserved reputation all over France. She was rated the first lady chef of Belgium in 1964 and was awarded a Michelin star in 1970. The family moved to the South of France in 1965 and she was made a chevalier du Club Prosper Montagné.

In 1977, with her husband Victor, she bought L'Ecurie Royale in Antibes and soon gained another Michelin star. By now their son had joined the kitchen. Victor manages the restaurant, looks after the cellar, and welcomes the gourmets.

The handwritten menus include: Veal chop in port wine, Kidneys sautéd with a sauce composed of 3 types of mustard, Fillet of beef with foie gras, various wild birds, like quail, guinea fowl and pigeons. And, this being the south of France, there was a large selection of fish including the Bouillabaisse de lotte et rouget and Grilled bass with Pernod and butter.

The dining-room of this restaurant is intimate, with well-decorated furniture, and designed so as to look inviting without ostentation. Cap d'Antibes is one of the most exclusive spots on the Riviera. It is the centre of commercial flower production, and the local market is still alive with fresh produce: fish caught that day, cackling poultry and aromatic vegetables and fruits. The town is noted for the Musée Picasso and the Château Grimaldi, both of which deserve a visit.

Bouillabaisse de Lotte et Rouget   Monkfish and red mullet soup

4 portions

225 g (8 oz) monkfish, cleaned,
    filleted, skinned, and cubed
225 g (8 oz) red mullet, cleaned,
    filleted, skinned, and cubed
450 g (1 lb) of the fish bones and
    heads for stock
1 litre (2 pints) water
300 ml (½ pint) white wine
4 strands saffron
30 ml (2 tbsp) tomato purée
2 tomatoes, skinned, deseeded,
    and chopped
1 large onion, chopped
3 cloves of garlic
1 sliced chilli pepper
1 bouquet garni

Garnish
4 croûtons of French bread
75 g (3 oz) garlic mayonnaise
25 g (1 oz) mashed potato

Break the fish bones and heads and boil them in the water with sliced onion, garlic, chilli, saffron, and bouquet garni for 20 minutes. Then strain the liquor into another saucepan.

Add the white wine, the chopped tomatoes, and the fish cubes. Poach for 5 minutes and serve in individual dishes. Season to taste with salt, pepper, and cayenne.

Combine the thick garlic mayonnaise with the mashed potatoes and spread this mixture on rounds of toasted French bread. Allow 1 per portion.

This is a simplified version of the most complicated meridional recipe, and is it much more nutritious too.

A little chopped basil will give this soup its Provençal flavour.

Stephen Yeung

Chef de Cuisine/Proprietor
Henry Wong Restaurant
283 High Street
Harborne
Birmingham B17 9QH
Tel: (021) 427 9799

Stephen Yeung was born in Yungcow (Hunan Province), South West China. He moved to Britain, via Hong Kong, in 1966 and has gained valuable experience and acquired new skills in catering. He opened his present restaurant in Harborne in 1984 and within months his reputation spread near and far.

From a spring-fried roll to butterfly prawns, you can pick your choice of starters, including soups made with crab or chicken, and garnished with the Chinese kind of ravioli known as wonton. Crab claws are an ever-popular entrée as are Bamboo prawns, and then you move on to Spare ribs, Sweet and sour meat balls, Steamed pork dumplings, Chicken in sesame seeds, Honey roasted duck and Beggar's chicken baked in a clay dough of salt pastry. Even the beef dishes are gingered up with various spicy sauces.

Birmingham is a great industrial city, with an international population and a large Oriental community. Housed in what was once a branch of the Trustee Savings Bank this austere 120-seater restaurant is packed most evenings.

Barbecued Pork Spare Ribs

6 portions

1 kg (2 lb 3 oz) pork spare ribs
 (middle ribs too can be used)

Barbecue sauce
25 g (1 oz) honey
1 green chilli, sliced
60 ml (4 tbsp) vinegar
15 ml (1 tbsp) tomato purée
30 ml (2 tbsp) soya sauce
1.25 ml (¼ tsp) mixed spices
5 g (¼ oz) fresh ginger
2 cloves garlic
1.25 ml (¼ tsp) salt
150 ml (5 fl oz) sweet sherry or
 sake (rice wine)

Boil the spare ribs in water for 20 minutes. Keep simmering at a low heat.

Liquidize the sauce ingredients.

Drain the pork ribs and place them in a shallow dish. Cover with the barbecue sauce. Bake in a low oven at 180°C, 350°F, gas mark 4, for 1 hour. Baste frequently.

King Prawn Fritters

8 portions

450 g (1 lb) king prawns, raw
1 egg, beaten
30 ml (2 tbsp) cornflour or flour
Salt and pepper
1 hard-boiled egg, chopped
50 g (2 oz) diced ham
1 spring onion, chopped
4 toasted slices of bread, crusts
   removed and cut into 8
   oblongs
Oil for shallow frying

Shell the raw king prawns, leaving the tails intact. Remove the black intestinal veins from the tails, after cutting them in two without separating them completely. Flatten the tails by light pressure, in a fanwise fashion. Make a batter of the egg and flour. Reserve a little flour, coat the prawns in seasoned flour, then dip them into the batter and stick them on to the oblong pieces of bread. Sprinkle with chopped egg, onion, and ham mixture on top. Fry in deep fat for 2 minutes, keeping the upper parts on top where the garnish has been sprinkled. The batter will hold it together. Serve on Chinese lettuce leaves.

Fromage de Soy aux Champignons   Bean curd with mushrooms

4 portions

250 g (8 oz) tofu bean curd cut in
   2.5-cm (1-inch) cubes
3 sticks of celery, cut in thick
   slices
6 shallots, chopped
1 red pepper, deseeded and cut
   into small squares
150 g (5 oz) mushrooms, sliced
15 ml (1 tbsp) cornflour
75 ml (3 fl oz) water
30 ml (2 tbsp) tomato juice
15 ml (1 tbsp) soya sauce
15 ml (1 tbsp) sake wine or sherry
30 ml (2 tbsp) oil

Heat the oil in a wok and stir-fry the tofu cubes for 1 minute until golden brown. Remove from the wok and keep warm. In the same fat toss the celery, shallots and mushrooms for 4 minutes, keep on stirring. Add water, tomato juice, and soya sauce and boil for 3 minutes.

   Mix cornflour with 45 ml (3 tbsp) water and add this mixture to the main ingredients and toss again. Season to taste and lastly add the cooked tofu. Reheat for 30 seconds and serve with boiled rice.

Index

A Passion for
FOOD

Over 100 top international chefs have given recipes from
their own repertoires of highly personal but superlative
cuisine to create this unique eclectic cookbook.

As members of the prestigious Cercle Epicurien Mondial
(International Epicurian Circle) they have a common aim in
working together on this book: for every copy sold a
contribution will be made to the National Children's Home.

Readily available ingredients are magically woven by these
great food artists into delicious and versatile dishes. The
recipes are set in the context of the chefs' careers and the
establishments they now work in — be it a manor house in
the Cotswolds, a pub in Berkshire, a star-studded restaurant
in rural France, a cosy corner in Amsterdam, a romantic
Parisian cafe, British Rail 'Travellers' Fare', or a little
hideaway on a busy road through the centre of Manchester.

All food lovers will delight in the impressive flair and
creativity they can show by using these easy-to-follow
recipes.

Jean Conil is founder and President of the Cercle Epicurien
Mondial and Christopher, his son, is the Cercle's General
Secretary.

FOOD/COOKERY

UK £7.99

ISBN 1-85336-081-3

9 781853 360817